Engaging the Law in China

Engaging the Law in China

State, Society, and Possibilities for Justice

Edited by NEIL J. DIAMANT,
STANLEY B. LUBMAN,
and KEVIN J. O'BRIEN

Stanford University Press
Stanford, California

2005

Stanford University Press
Stanford, California
www.sup.org

© 2005 by the Board of Trustees of the Leland Stanford Junior University. All rights reserved.

No part of this book may be reproduced or transmitted in any form or by any means, electronic or mechanical, including photocopying and recording, or in any information storage or retrieval system without the prior written permission of Stanford University Press.

Library of Congress Cataloging-in-Publication Data

Engaging the law in China : state, society, and possibilities for justice / edited by Neil J. Diamant, Stanley B. Lubman, and Kevin J. O'Brien.
   p. cm.
Includes bibliographical references and index.
ISBN 978-0-8047-7180-1
   1. Justice, Administration of—China.   I. Diamant, Neil Jeffrey, 1964–   II. Lubman, Stanley B., 1934–   III. O'Brien, Kevin J.
KNQ1572.E54 2005
340'.115'0951—dc22   2004009113

Printed in the United States of America on acid-free, archival-quality paper.

Original Printing 2005

Last figure below indicates year of this printing:
14   13   12   11   10   09   08   07   06   05

Designed and typeset at Stanford University Press in 10.5 / 12 Bembo.

*NJD: For D.T., Lani, and Eli, and my parents,
Arline and Ralph Diamant*

*KOB: To my children: Molly O'Brien and
Spencer O'Brien (in memoriam)*

SBL: To Judith

Contents

List of Tables and Figures	ix
Acknowledgments	xi

Part I. Introduction

1. Law and Society in the People's Republic of China
   NEIL J. DIAMANT, STANLEY B. LUBMAN,
   AND KEVIN J. O'BRIEN ... 3

Part II. Legal Mobilization and Culture

2. Suing the Local State: Administrative Litigation in Rural China
   KEVIN J. O'BRIEN AND LIANJIANG LI ... 31

3. "Use the Law as Your Weapon!": Institutional Change and Legal Mobilization in China
   MARY E. GALLAGHER ... 54

4. One Law, Two Interpretations: Mobilizing the Labor Law in Arbitration Committees and in Letters and Visits Offices
   ISABELLE THIREAU AND HUA LINSHAN ... 84

5. What's in a Law?: China's Pension Reform and Its Discontents
   MARK W. FRAZIER ... 108

6. Hollow Glory: The Politics of Rights and Identity among PRC Veterans in the 1950s
   NEIL J. DIAMANT ... 131

Part III. Legal Institutions

7. Shifting Legal and Administrative Goalposts: Chinese Bureaucracies, Foreign Actors, and the Evolution of China's Anti-Counterfeiting Enforcement Regime
   ANDREW C. MERTHA — 161

8. Rethinking Law Enforcement and Society: Changing Police Analyses of Social Unrest
   MURRAY SCOT TANNER — 193

9. Punishing for Profit: Profitability and Rehabilitation in a *Laojiao* Institution
   H. L. FU — 213

   List of Contributors — 231
   Index — 233

Tables and Figures

Tables

2.1	First-Instance ALL Cases by Disposition, 1990–2001	32
3.1	Labor Disputes per 100,000 by Ownership Type, 1998–2001	59
4.1	Overall Comparison of Arbitration Committees with Letters and Office Visits	95
7.1	Judicial vs. Administrative Cases of Anti-Counterfeiting Enforcement	164
9.1	Budget and Actual Costs in the LB, 1999–2000	218
9.2	Production Items and Income Generated in the LB, 2000	219

Figures

1.1	The Disputing Pyramid	7
3.1	Labor Disputes at Arbitration, 1994-2002	55
3.2	Causes of Dispute by Ownership, 2000	64
3.3	Labor Disputes Settled by Mediation, 1987–2000	68
3.4	Number of Labor Disputes Mediated by Employer, 1996–2001	69
3.5	Labor Dispute Resolution, 1996–2001	70
3.6	Percent of Labor Disputes Resolved by Mediation, 1996–2001	71
3.7	Percent of Labor Disputes Resolved by Arbitration, 1996–2001	72
3.8	Percent of Labor Disputes Resolved by Other Means, 1996–2001	73

Acknowledgments

This book would have been impossible without the support and encouragement of a number of colleagues at the University of California at Berkeley. When the idea of holding a conference on Chinese law to highlight the research of young social scientists who had recently returned from the field was mentioned to him, Professor Robert Kagan of the Center for the Study of Law and Society immediately came forward with an offer of financial assistance. Professors T. J. Pempel, Chair of the Institute of East Asian Studies, and Liu Xin, Chair of the Center for Chinese Studies, were equally generous when we turned to them for aid. Shortly thereafter, John Dwyer, then Dean of the School of Law (Boalt Hall) offered us staff support and a venue that provided a pleasant setting for what turned out to be a very lively exchange of views. And, finally, the clocklike unfolding of events on that warm weekend in September 2002 hinged (as always) on the hard work and professionalism of the staff members who helped organize the conference, most notably, John Groschwitz (Institute of East Asian Studies), Joan Kask (Institute of East Asian Studies), Melissa Martin (Boalt Hall), and Rod Watanabe (Center for the Study of Law and Society).

We, and the chapter writers, also benefited immeasurably from the advice of the three discussants who joined us at the conference: William Alford, Stinson Professor of Law at the Harvard Law School; Marc Galanter, Professor of Law at the University of Wisconsin; and Robert Kagan, Professor of Political Science at the University of California. Each brought his own experiences, disciplinary knowledge, and practiced eye for cant and ambiguity to the task of reading and commenting on the papers.

Finally, we wish to thank Muriel Bell, acquisitions editor for Asian studies at Stanford University Press, for attending the Berkeley conference and for ushering our volume toward publication. Muriel has played a role second to none in making scholarship on Chinese law better known, and we are delighted to be the latest beneficiaries of her work.

NEIL J. DIAMANT, STANLEY B. LUBMAN, KEVIN J. O'BRIEN

PART I

Introduction

NEIL J. DIAMANT, STANLEY B. LUBMAN,
AND KEVIN J. O'BRIEN

1

*Law and Society in the People's
Republic of China*

In today's China, law matters more than it ever has. Twenty-five years of energetic legislating, both by the National People's Congress (NPC) and local congresses, has created new legal rights and institutions; the courts, the bar and legal education have been revived, and a framework for foreign investment has been fashioned. At the same time, the Chinese government has promoted a reform it often calls "legalization" (*fazhihua*). This initiative has brought legal institutions and discourses into countless areas of everyday life. Legalization, among other things, has provided the regime with a gloss of legitimacy and has enhanced predictability such that few believe China can once again be torn apart by the whims of a powerful ruler, as it was during the Cultural Revolution. Increased reliance on law has also affected how disputes are resolved. This is not unprecedented in Chinese history,[1] but as market reforms have deepened and social inequality has widened, legal forums—ranging from mediation and arbitration commissions to courts—have come to play an increasingly prominent role in politics and society. As an instrument of trade, legitimacy, and social control, there is little doubt that law matters.

Compared to its past, China has more laws, more people have at least rudimentary legal knowledge, and law is becoming increasingly accessible. This volume thus does not focus on whether law matters. Nor does it chart the course of legal reform or systematically describe how Chinese legal institutions operate, since this has been done elsewhere.[2] Instead, we concentrate on questions of how, when, and to whom law matters, and how we should go about studying the dynamic relationship between law and society.

These are questions of some import, not least because China is experiencing a market transition and an explosion in economic transactions. This transformation is affecting how people think about the law and is creating expectations and controversies that legal mechanisms can play a part in addressing. Yet, at the same time, for every Chinese businessperson who turns to a court or an arbitration commission to resolve a contract dispute, there are several other individuals who have been left behind. How will workers or villagers respond if growing inequality and corruption are not ameliorated by the legal system and cadres no longer fear Maoist-style campaigns?[3] Knowing that there are more rules that govern official conduct,[4] and that class background no longer impedes a person from gaining a hearing, does not mean that all Chinese have equal access to justice—something that even far more mature legal systems cannot boast. There may be hundreds of laws on the books, but many are not wholly or even partially enforced.[5] And, while it is true that more people are aware of laws that could benefit them, we cannot assume that such knowledge automatically translates into "rights consciousness" or an ability to seize on legal norms to defend one's "lawful rights and interests" (*hefa quanyi*).

If law matters, then for whom does it matter most, and for what purposes is it used? At a time when both Chinese law and society are becoming increasingly multidimensional and complex, these questions can be profitably explored by relying on a methodology that (1) seeks to capture interactions between the two, and (2) is sensitive to history. One such approach, often referred to as scholarship in the "law-and-society" tradition, is particularly well suited to study the extent to which law in China is becoming, in the words of Patricia Ewick and Susan Silbey, "a terrain for tactical encounters through which people marshal a variety of resources to achieve strategic goals."[6]

We thus believe that research on socio-legal affairs in China could profit by drawing on insights from disciplines which, to date, have been somewhat peripheral to Chinese legal studies. Over the last decade, historians—including Mark Allee, Kathryn Bernhardt, Philip Huang, Melissa Macauley, Bradly Reed, and Matthew Sommer—have skillfully mined Qing, Ming, and Republican era archives to question much of what we thought we knew about the role of law in China.[7] Whereas earlier scholarship emphasized the irrelevance of civil law to ordinary Chinese and the obstacles to deploying it, we now know that courts were affordable and frequently used in conjunction with community mediation. Litigation masters (*songgun*) often assisted peasants in filing plaints, much to the consternation of local magistrates who fretted about society becoming overly litigious. Almost without exception, however, these pathbreaking historical studies have not availed themselves of insights from work in comparative legal history and the social sciences (especially political science, legal anthropology, and the sociology of law). Nor has much of this research appeared in journals such as the *Law and Society Review*, *Journal of Legal Pluralism*, or *Law and Social Inquiry*. As a result, too many scholars of law and society remain unaware of the major changes that have occurred in our understanding of the role of law in Chinese society.

This lack of "importing" from other fields has also characterized the other main branch of Chinese legal studies. Most experts on Chinese law are themselves lawyers, teach in law schools, and/or have worked as intermediaries between Western and Chinese firms and governments. Both their training and professional role has inclined these scholars to focus more on law as centered in the state rather than law as practiced in society—the latter referring to law as an institution that draws in "numerous actors, involved in diverse projects, employing different legitimating discourses [and] material resources."[8] Like students of Chinese legal history, the next generation of researchers on contemporary Chinese law could benefit from deeper integration with the bread-and-butter issues of the law-and-society field, such as the debate between Michael McCann and Gerald Rosenberg on the role of courts in social change, Laura Nader's exploration of dispute resolution in non-Western societies, Charles Epp's comparative analysis of the conditions for "rights revolutions," Sally Engle Merry's ethnography of legal cultures in the United States, Patricia Ewick and Susan Silbey's study of law in everyday life, and Joel Migdal's "state-in-society" approach to the study of political and legal institutions. One of the main objectives of this volume, accordingly, is to begin spanning the gap between fields that have a lot to offer each other but have yet to really speak to one another.

Readers of this volume will perhaps notice that, with the exception of H. L. Fu, none of the authors has received formal legal training. Most are political scientists or sociologists, and their essays reflect the characteristic approaches (and perhaps blind spots) of those fields. Readers will also note that most of the chapters are the product of fieldwork in the PRC and have made extensive use of newly available sources, including archives (Diamant), transcribed letters to "Letters and Petitions Offices" (Thireau and Hua), police handbooks (Tanner), the popular legal press (O'Brien and Li), participant observation (Mertha), and interviews (Frazier, Gallagher, Mertha, Tanner). Using such sources to study legal practice has a history in the China field.[9] Understanding the relationship between law and society in contemporary China, we feel, will be well served by interdisciplinary research combined with fieldwork, just as the study of law in the West has benefited from such methods.[10] Adopting a worm's-eye perspective can enable us to enrich our understanding of how law actually works in Chinese society, and how members of various social groups think about and use law.

This prescription alone, however, is far too vague to guide scholars embarking on the study of law and society in China: "interdisciplinary" can mean just about anything and most China scholars today are frequent visitors to the PRC who recognize the limitations of working from legal texts.

What we will do in the remainder of this introduction, therefore, is underscore several perspectives that we think may be useful in illustrating how law and society interact, show how they were employed by various authors, and suggest how they might inform future projects. These approaches are by no means mutually exclusive, and we can foresee extending this list as more sources become available and legal scholarship on other parts of the world develops. For now, however, we simply highlight three broad concepts—mobilization of law, legal culture, and formal legal institutions—and suggest that these are likely to be fruitful starting points for the disciplinary cross-fertilization that we envision.

Mobilizing the Law

The Chinese government's view of law's role in society is highly instrumental, as a number of scholars have observed.[11] The present-day "legalization" program was not generated by a Chinese enlightenment based on a concept of natural, inalienable rights, nor was it the product of a compromise between central state and feudal or merchant elites, or the rise of a bourgeoisie. Rather, it echoes a long-standing tradition in late developers (Confucian and otherwise) which accorded the state a key, proactive role in political, economic, and social development (other examples include Meiji Japan, Bismarck's Germany, and Ataturk's Turkey). In China, this statist orientation was apparent throughout the dynastic era and only intensified when the Leninist conception of a vanguard party was grafted onto an already authoritarian political tradition. Even thinkers commonly understood to be liberal in the Chinese context, men such as Liang Qichao, were reluctant to suggest that law and rights should empower commoners vis-à-vis the state.[12]

Several generations later, in a vastly different political system, this approach to law is still evident. In a time of rapid change in the absence of institutionalized means to express political preferences, one of the key functions of law is to provide an outlet for expressing grievances; it is not, by and large, conceived of as a precursor to democracy or a sign of liberalization. Intentionally or not, China's leaders have been astute students of Samuel Huntington, who, in his book *Political Order in Changing Societies,* warned that social change without political institutionalization can easily lead to chaos (see Murray Scot Tanner's essay). As a conflict management tactic, the PRC's emphasis on law and legality has been fairly successful. Today, we are witnessing an outpouring of grievances from, among others, people who lost money in the stock market, pensioners, veterans, unemployed laborers, disgruntled peasants, and unhappy couples. Yet, only a small proportion of these complaints spread to other sectors, lead to violence, or threaten the existence of the regime. Institutions like courts, arbitration commissions, and media-

Figure 1.1. The Disputing Pyramid

tors have all played a notable role in channeling social discontent into moderated forums. In the view of most PRC elites, law thus is essential because it contributes to a more orderly society. For citizens, the mere fact that their complaints are heard, or should be heard, helps make the regime a bit more palatable.

But how exactly do perceptions of injustice turn into legal disputes? Sociologists of law have identified a "disputing pyramid" (see Figure 1.1), in which the majority of people who feel they have experienced an "injurious experience" do not seek outside assistance.[13] Instead, they tolerate it, particularly when the offender has higher social status than the aggrieved party or both have low status. According to Donald Black, toleration "is probably the most frequent response to conduct regarded as wrong, improper, injurious or otherwise deviant.... Most illegality is tolerated."[14] Some experiences, however, become "claims": people demand some form of remediation; they "name" and "blame" someone as responsible for their injurious experience. A "dispute" then arises when the parties cannot reach a settlement. Only at the top level of the pyramid do lawyers or other legal professionals become involved, and persons reaching this stage will always be far less numerous than those who have grievances and are actively involved in disputes.[15] Third parties, when they become involved, can transform the nature of a dispute by questioning the legitimacy of either claim or by supporting one party against the other.[16] In many societies, such intervention occurs in regular patterns, what socio-legal scholars call a "dispute trajectory"—the "progress of a particular dispute over time through particular combinations of disputing areas, processes and outsiders towards particular outcomes."[17] Still, the pyramid analogy emphasizes that most "action" in the legal realm occurs at the bottom rungs, well beyond the reach of formal legal institutions.

This perspective on how disputes are transformed—as beginning with often inchoate feelings of injustice that sometimes result in some form of third-party intervention—has implications for how we study law in China. Legal anthropologists such as Laura Nader have long attempted to plumb how the moral, ethical, and political universes of ordinary people produce predictable responses when legal norms and shared assumptions are violated.[18] Feelings of injury and injustice, after all, do not bubble up in a vacuum; they emerge and can only be observed in the context of expectations about what is ethical, fair, and just, and these, in turn, are often shaped by wider communities and individual experiences.[19] Studies of law and society in China, accordingly, might wish to pay more attention to the moral and ethical norms whose violation can lead to the emergence of disputes. Several papers in this volume suggest the payoffs of doing this. Neil Diamant's essay on veterans, for example, shows that demobilized soldiers initiated protests when local officials violated what they considered to be a sacrosanct moral and political "contract" made by the state when they joined the military: namely, that they would be taken care of after their service was over and treated with respect. Mark Frazier, Mary Gallagher, and Isabelle Thireau and Hua Linshan touch upon workers who invoke the state's moral obligation (sometimes couched in Confucian or Maoist language) to guarantee their livelihood in the event of retirement or factory layoffs. Since it is probable that more and more groups will join the ranks of the discontented in the coming years, more researchers might want to focus on the understandings, assumptions, and expectations of these groups prior to the appearance of a formal, observable, dispute.[20] Such studies would provide important, indeed essential, background for understanding which disputes emerge, their formal setting, and their eventual outcome.

In addition to highlighting preexisting norms and expectations, the notion of a disputing pyramid suggests other research topics. As Donald Black has argued, even though an individual or group might feel aggrieved and want to do something about it, few actually act upon these feelings. Between "naming and blaming" and actually "claiming" something in a legal form, many things can intervene. In China, there are untold numbers of disgruntled workers and peasants but only a limited number of protests, petitions, and lawsuits (see Gallagher's essay). We should ask, therefore, how and why some grievances were transformed into claims and others were not? How do groups mobilize to take advantage of certain laws and institutions? Collective mobilization is, of course, not new to China studies (although the extent of group petitioning might surprise those more familiar with Western cases). Still, studies of law in China have yet to integrate one of the more promising approaches to how law works in practice. This approach focuses less on legal substance and procedure—as pivotal as these are[21]—than on the ability of aggrieved parties to forge a group identity and engage in law-based contention. Law, in this perspective, is both a critical resource in collective action and the final destination in a dispute's trajectory.

By shifting the focus from law as text to issues surrounding legal mobilization, we can broaden our horizons and speak in a vocabulary common to scholars in a number of fields. For instance, the collective-action literature highlights the role played by "political entrepreneurs" in overcoming people's natural tendency to free-ride on the efforts of others.[22] Often, these individuals are, for whatever reason, particularly feisty and relatively immune to risk. In Diamant's essay, veterans were sometimes troublesome to the authorities because, having served in the military, they were often physically tough, more difficult to intimidate, and willing to bear the start-up costs of organizing to defend their benefits. Risk-takers, often with atypically forceful personalities, also play a role in the essay on the Administrative Litigation Law (ALL) by O'Brien and Li, as well as other articles they have authored on popular resistance in rural China.[23] While the source of individual assertiveness is often obscure, the role of such individuals in spearheading legal action needs to receive more attention, perhaps through a biographical approach to the study of legal contention, much as students of social movements have explored recruitment to high-risk activism, leadership dynamics, and the effects protest can have on a person's life course.[24] While this research strategy poses obvious challenges in China, it is worth considering since it has the potential to help us understand how and why only some feelings of injustice end up becoming formal claims. This approach has already been used to good effect by Ewick and Silbey in their *The Common Place of Law: Stories from Everyday Life*, which assesses Americans' understanding of law and legality (shared schemas and interpretative frames for understanding law) by focusing on the experiences of several individuals.

Highlighting how people take advantage of the law is important not only because it calls attention to individuals who are willing to initiate petitions, lawsuits, and protests, but also because it emphasizes the role of resources—social as well as financial—in legal mobilization. For some aggrieved parties, the law may not provide an effective tool to redress wrongs, insofar as they lack leaders (e.g., the "peasant heroes" in O'Brien and Li's account) willing to incur significant risks or because they cannot mobilize sufficient resources to exploit existing laws. An example of a study that explores this issue is Charles Epp's award-winning *The Rights Revolution: Lawyers, Activists, and Supreme Courts in Comparative Perspective*. Epp examined the growth of individual rights in four countries (the United States, Canada, Great Britain, and India) and found that, given equally liberal laws and activist judiciaries, countries with a variety of interest groups, lobbies, foundations, and rights advocacy groups ready to provide financial resources to poor litigants experienced the greatest expansion of rights. "Successful rights litigation," he argues,

> usually consumes resources beyond the reach of individual plaintiffs—resources that can be provided only by an ongoing support structure. . . . Ordinary individuals typically do not have the time, money, or experience necessary to support a long-running lawsuit through several levels of the judicial system. . . . A support structure can provide the consistent support that is needed to move case after case through the courts.[25]

Thus, India, despite a well-respected Supreme Court and new laws expanding individual rights, experienced relatively little rights-based litigation. This arose because "the Indian interest group system is fragmented, the legal profession consists primarily of lawyers working individually, not collectively, and the availability of resources for non-economic appellate litigation is limited."[26]

The concept of "support structure," we believe, merits attention in studies of Chinese legal contention. Support can, for instance, come in the form of community solidarity.[27] Collective petitions (by groups of workers, peasant men, women, veterans, etc.) to township, city, or national authorities are a common feature of law in today's China but were not unknown even during the more restrictive Maoist era.[28] Building coalitions and creating solidarity is never an easy feat and typically depends on the ability of leaders to recast grievances into a public discourse in a way that persuades audiences, reassures those who might be alarmed by collective action, and generates a critical mass of followers.[29] The essays in this volume by Thireau and Hua, Frazier, Gallagher, and Diamant all detail such efforts by a variety of social groups. In contemporary China, support can also appear in the form of media attention (radio, television, legal magazines, newspapers, letters to the editor, and so on). While press outlets remain subject to state control, increased editorial freedom and competitive pressures have given rise to a more market-oriented media in which muckraking reporters and daring magazines can draw huge audiences and high-level attention by exposing official wrongdoing. Petitioners know this and sometimes try to gain public and official sympathy for upholding existing laws and regulations by seeking media exposure. The media are thus a key legal actor in the contemporary scene, and individuals and groups that can locate champions for their appeals (see the essays by Frazier, and O'Brien and Li, for examples) have a greater chance of elevating their feelings of injustice to the status of "claim."[30] Those groups that have difficulty ferreting out media allies, on the other hand, can find their entry to remedial institutions impeded. Diamant's veterans, for example, have long had direct access to the state through veterans' committees as well as high-level representation, but because their plight is underreported (for security reasons), their efforts to gain redress are hampered by a weak support structure. Most ordinary people assume, absent contrary information, that the state implements its own laws and is taking care of them.

Whether China will develop support structures for rights-based litigation is still an open question. But there are signs of change. Although Ethan Michelson has shown that urban lawyers do not take part in as much collective action as might be expected,[31] legal-aid offices have sprung up in many villages, townships, and counties, and foreign legal-aid schemes have supported domestic lawmaking and efforts to enhance legal knowledge among the populace (*pufa*). There is, however, still too little research on how aggrieved parties work to generate solidarity and a critical mass of supporters, a topic that will only grow in importance as social inequalities deepen.

Access to justice in China is thus likely to vary widely, often depending on people's willingness to take risks, generate solidarity, raise money, and create alliances with the media or intrepid lawyers. Yet, even if such efforts are successful, they do not guarantee entry to legal forums. First, in asserting claims (for unenforced rights or benefits) both individuals and groups have to learn how to couch their grievances in terms that will garner public and official support. This might be in the form of what Kevin O'Brien has termed "rightful resistance" (citing laws, policies, and other leadership commitments to combat local officials who are not implementing those laws, policies, and commitments),[32] or in evoking broader moral themes, such as "fairness" in tax policy, or "humanity" in supporting unemployed workers or retirees, that resonate with agreed-upon norms for behavior.

A number of the essays in this volume offer examples of legal and moral claims-making at work. Thireau and Hua pay especially close attention to the role of legal norms and legally valid claims in mobilization, insofar as they become resources people use to pursue or defend their interests, not only within courts but outside of them as well. Whether out of cleverness, naiveté, optimism, wishful thinking, or a "majestic" conception of law that places it outside of everyday life,[33] many people take the state at its word and profess little more than a desire to make the system live up to what it's supposed to be. Specific legal clauses are central in O'Brien and Li's account of the ALL, Gallagher's workers using the labor law, Thireau and Hua's workers using the Letters and Visits Office, and Diamant's veterans. At the same time, however, we also need to investigate how legal norms are supplemented by larger, morally based appeals for justice (see Gallagher's essay), many of which do not explicitly emphasize individual rights but rather assert claims that are more palatable to key state officials. Such appeals might be thought of as "counter-hegemonic," in the Gramscian sense, since they attempt to rework some elements of the prevailing hegemony (arguing, for instance, that "workers are the masters of state") without trying to subvert them completely. This perspective recognizes that "all struggles commence on old grounds"[34] and that today's legal claims share important similarities with a rules consciousness and sensitivity to government discourse that has been present in China for centuries.[35] Members of the popular classes, in other words, have long been adept at taking advantage of state commitments, professed ideals, and legitimating myths, while seizing on official rhetoric (whether framed in terms of Confucianism, class struggle, or legal rights) to press their demands. How contemporary legal, often proactive, claims differ from appeals based on equity and fairness directed at dynastic officials who, for example, neglected proper tax collection procedures or employed biased conversion ratios deserves further research.

Second, and perhaps more important in an authoritarian state such as China, mobilization, whether by individuals or by groups, and with or without a support structure, is likely to produce counter-mobilization from the state's coercive organs. The plaintiff-oriented dispute pyramid might thus be laid next to a parallel "defendant pyramid" in which agencies of the state take steps, sometimes of increasing harshness, to crush legal mobilization at its point of greatest vulnerability.[36] The authorities can (and often do) detain risk-taking legal entrepreneurs; they attempt to suppress information about relevant laws, such as handbooks intended for plaintiffs; they refuse to confirm the existence of new rights, benefits, or regulations; and they limit access to or arrest enterprising lawyers and journalists. O'Brien and Li's essay on the ALL provides us with a blow-by-blow account of how the authorities can impede legal activism, and demonstrates that even when plaintiffs overcome the many hurdles to mobilization they may still encounter formidable obstacles. Similarly, Diamant's essay on veterans reveals how factory union officials and management launched counteroffensives against veterans who complained to higher levels about illegal, corrupt, or wasteful practices. Gallagher also finds that in state-owned enterprises the presence of a trade union has a demobilizing effect on workers, reflected in the relatively low rate of labor disputes lodged by workers. Likewise, Frazier's account of pensions examines how local governments push for more comprehensive and binding pension legislation in order to give them greater clout vis-à-vis enterprises that sometimes fail to fork over contractually agreed-upon pension contributions to retired or laid-off workers. In short, to the extent that individuals and groups manage to overcome internal obstacles to legal action, they still face antagonists within the state apparatus who can respond with coercion and, in many cases, their own rhetorical and legal arsenal. On the trajectory from "injurious experience" to third-party intervention a great deal can happen, and once intervention occurs, even the most resourceful plaintiffs can find themselves right back where they started.

Or so it may seem. Michael McCann, in his *Rights at Work: Pay Equity Reform and the Politics of Legal Mobilization*, argues persuasively that even though courts in the United States became increasingly reluctant to address pay-equity complaints and employers developed successful countertactics, one by-product of legal mobilization was an enhanced sense of collective identity among activists and greater understanding of law and the political process. He writes:

> My primary finding was that the political advances in many contexts matched or exceeded wage gains. One important advance was at the level of rights consciousness. Interviews revealed that activists were deeply engaged with the basic terms of antidiscrimination law, which at once shaped their general understandings of social relations and in turn were refashioned into sophisticated instruments of reform action. Legal rights thus became increasingly meaningful both as a general moral discourse and as a strategic resource for ongoing challenges to status quo power relations. . . . This newly developed solidaristic strength in many contexts quickly facilitated a variety of other successful struggles for new workplace rights and reforms.[37]

McCann's analysis lends support to the tried-and-true observation that in assessing how and when legal institutions are meaningful in China, it is best to take the long view. It also suggests how to go about understanding some of the forces that researchers witness at work. The very process of engaging the state's legal system, reaching out to different media, and acquiring and studying legal texts may or may not produce a favorable settlement. But, whatever the result, creative engagement with official "rights talk" can still be a transformative event for those involved. Legal entrepreneurs may peddle their expertise elsewhere; legal documents can be passed on to others; *guanxi* (connections) established with other legal actors may be called upon in future battles; and, most important, popular identities and aspirations may be altered as organizers, in particular, undergo a learning experience, become aware of new possibilities, and often end up more inclined to participate in larger struggles (on this last point, see the essays by Gallagher, Thireau and Hua, Diamant, and O'Brien and Li). All of this can happen in an authoritarian state that has an instrumentalist view of law because every political or legal act, irrespective of regime type, has both intended and unintended consequences, and one of the latter might well be the emergence of enterprising, assertive, litigation-hardened individuals who are willing to take a chance on inserting their grievances into the legal arena.

To be sure, McCann's notion of litigation-induced identity change is difficult to measure, but there is an emerging body of evidence suggesting that political and legal engagement can result in a notable thickening of skins.

Some of O'Brien and Li's litigants under the ALL experienced these transformations and became important players in other lawsuits. In the 1950s and 1960s, Diamant argues, veterans who felt empowered owing to their military background also displayed a readiness to articulate legal claims in villages and factories. Efforts to discredit and disrupt their actions scarred many litigants, but also led some to take their cases all the way to Beijing. In short, there was a feedback loop in the dispute trajectory in which third-party intervention demobilized some claimants but also strengthened the resolve of others. Finding the sources to trace disputes from their origins to intervention and back again will not be easy, but the potential payoffs could be large. In-depth interviews, participant observation, semi-structured biographies, ethnographies, and unpublished government and legal documents will probably yield far more of the data needed to do this than purely text-based accounts.

Law and Legal Culture

Much like the legal-mobilization literature, the second way in which this volume aims to build a bridge between studies of Chinese law and legal history and the social sciences also emerges from the law-and-society field, and focuses on the issue of rights. To understand how law affects social practice in China, it helps to use the prism of rights, insomuch as laws matter mainly when people see themselves as empowered by them. Changes in China over the last two decades have certainly provided enough grounds for debate. Scholars have asked whether Chinese are becoming more aware of their rights (often termed "rights consciousness") or simply more knowledgeable about laws, rules, and regulations promulgated by the government.[38] This exchange has been fueled both by findings that ordinary Chinese nowadays frequently cite rules, laws, and regulations when dealing with the state, as well as by a sense, among some, that enhanced rights consciousness may foreshadow the spread of citizenship practices, if not the appearance of citizenship as a secure, universally recognized status.[39]

While certainly thought-provoking, this debate is problematic for several reasons. First, the Anglo-American conception of "rights" (derived from Locke and Mill) is popularly associated with individuals and is often linked with defying state or community authority. In China, however, rights are more commonly associated with collectivities and claims made to community membership rather than negative freedoms vis-à-vis the state.[40] Interviewees who are asked about "rights" might thus be thinking about something quite different.[41] Second, it is necessary to consider the effect of rights consciousness, rules awareness, or simply enhanced legal knowledge on how people interact with state institutions and how the latter respond to law-based claims. There is evidence that even in the Qing, Republican, and

Maoist eras citizens filed lawsuits and had some awareness of their rights, while judges often rendered verdicts much as their modern counterparts do—although their rulings had little impact on the overall nature of the regime.[42] Finally, as in any society, in China, it is probable that however one wants to label the practice of using state law to exploit the gap between rights promised and rights delivered, the skills and knowledge to do this will not be shared equally by all.

To capture the uneven distribution of legal consciousness, it is worthwhile to consider how researchers working in the law-and-society tradition have addressed the spread of legal knowledge. Although some legal scholars have considered Chinese legal culture,[43] law-and-society scholars have adopted a perspective on law and rights that is broader and more inclusive than most treatments of law in China. For instance, in his article "The Radiating Effects of Courts," Marc Galanter argues, following Clifford Geertz,[44] that law should be seen not only as a set of "operative controls," but "as a system of cultural and symbolic meanings. . . . It affects us primarily through communication of symbols—by providing threats, promises, models, persuasion, legitimacy, stigma and so on."[45] In the Chinese case, it might seem that threats and persuasion overwhelm the other functions of law. However, what this scholarship emphasizes is that legal discourses do not exist above society or simply to control citizens, but instead are embedded in how people interact as legal conventions or cultures. According to Michael McCann, "Legal knowledge . . . *prefigures* social activity; inherited legal conventions shape the very terms of citizen understanding, aspiration, and interaction with others."[46] These legal conventions or cultures (e.g., placing a chair where one has just shoveled snow to assert property rights), furthermore, are not shared by all members of a given society: different groups—be they social classes, ethnicities, or occupational groups—are likely to have inherited different legal cultures, and these are likely to change over time. In *Getting Justice and Getting Even: Legal Consciousness Among Working-Class Americans*, legal anthropologist Sally Engle Merry writes that law "consists of a complex repertoire of meanings and categories understood differently by people depending on their experience with and knowledge of the law. The law looks different, for example, to law professors, tax evaders, welfare recipients, blue-collar homeowners and burglars."[47]

As Chinese society becomes more diverse and stratified, and legal discourses multiply, it strikes us that future research on law and society in China should reflect the mélange of legal cultures that is coming into being. Fortunately, we already have strong historical foundations to build upon. Studies of law in the Ming and Qing have demonstrated that elite Confucian discourse was largely normative, but that it was also deployed in practice by ordinary people seeking justice in county *yamens* or from village elites.[48]

Joseph Esherick and Mary Rankin's volume, *Chinese Local Elites and Patterns of Dominance*, includes several essays that show considerable regional disparity in the penetration of Confucian norms in core and peripheral areas, and differences in how Northern, Southern, Southwestern, Lower Yangzi, and other elites exercised domination.[49] For the Maoist period, Diamant's *Revolutionizing the Family* has argued that peasants and "rural educated" workers had a far more vibrant legal culture than urban educated elites.

These accounts of diversity and pluralism, however, have yet to be replicated in the study of contemporary Chinese law. There is nothing comparable yet to Merry's study of working-class legal cultures, or to Tom Tyler's *Why People Obey the Law*, a survey-based study of the importance of procedural versus distributive justice in the United States.[50] Of course, until recently researchers have been hobbled by limited access to much of the Chinese urban and rural population. Now, however, with improved field-research opportunities, we are better placed to explore the many legal cultures extant in today's China. In this volume, for example, Thireau and Hua's analysis of migrant workers' letters reveals a legal culture formed by the workers' experiences as outsiders in a city, along with Confucian norms and an updated version of Maoist ideology. Diamant's veterans developed a highly adversarial legal culture in factories and villages, shaped by their military experiences, the cold reception they often received upon demobilization, and the violence that was nearly endemic in the North China villages from which they came. Gallagher likewise explores the extent to which disgruntled Chinese workers have become increasingly litigious and willing to demand rights enshrined in the 1995 Labor Law (especially provisions on safety, contracts, unemployment benefits, and settling disputes). Mertha shows that foreign actors are a new force to be dealt with in intellectual property disputes. All these efforts to mobilize rights claims have produced mixed results, but they do point to a certain irony: in China, workers and peasants are often surprisingly at the forefront of battles to realize "bourgeois rights."[51] This can be seen both historically—in the 1950s, few intellectuals were enthusiastic about the eminently bourgeois Marriage Law—and in the contemporary period, as a great deal of middle- and upper-class wealth has arisen from cozy, corporatist arrangements with the state. In other words, the well-off and powerful may be well placed to make use of legal institutions, but they may also choose to strengthen their privileged position at the expense of legality. Many entrepreneurs, for example, prefer to evade laws rather than fight for their enforcement, and not a few intellectuals have distinctly elitist attitudes toward the popular classes.[52]

All of the essays in this volume share an important assumption. To understand how law matters in China, we have to unpack society and discover how different political, cultural, economic, and personal experiences shape attitudes toward the law and lead to different forms of legal and political action (see Thireau and Hua, and Mertha, on this). Older workers in the Northeast, facing unemployment, for instance, will inevitably see the Labor Law differently than workers in more vibrant private enterprises; veterans who were discharged at the rank of colonel experienced the state differently than those of lower rank; rural and urban women may come to different conclusions about the importance of the 1980 Marriage Law. Given China's diversity and a varied repertoire of popular contention (including litigation, petitions, strikes, parades, demonstrations, blocking roads, protests, riots, and so on) honed over centuries, a disaggregated, bottom-up perspective on legal culture, along with a similar approach to legal mobilization and countermobilization, is warranted. This implies the use of more anthropological, contextualized, and thickly descriptive methods to capture the many ways the popular classes deploy the regime's laws as a weapon when combining legal tactics with collective action (or the threat of it) to defend their "lawful rights and interests."

Disaggregating the State

The passage of hundreds of laws and the expansion of judicial institutions since the late 1970s has not only provided ordinary citizens with more outlets for expressing their grievances; it has also increased the predictability of economic, political, and social life, much as Max Weber predicted when contemplating the legal consequences of capitalism.[53] Mertha's essay on the enforcement of intellectual property laws, Frazier's on the drive for comprehensive pension legislation, and Gallagher's and Thireau and Hua's essays on the Labor Law can all be viewed as efforts to gauge the effect of various laws on predictability in the economy and society. It is too early to assess whether such legislation signals convergence between China and more mature capitalist economies (as Doug Guthrie and Edward Steinfeld have argued),[54] but even at this stage it is clear that a great deal has changed in how law and legal organizations (such as courts, the bar, arbitration commissions, and mediation committees) operate.

At the same time, few would claim that the growth of the state's legal apparatus stems from liberal impulses, or has resulted in a significant weakening of the discretion enjoyed by the state's coercive organs or the political character of many legal forums. Indeed, the essays by Tanner and Fu show how the state's disciplinary apparatus has grown (and profited) in tandem with heightened concerns about social unrest. Even as the private sector expands, formal legal institutions have yet to gain significant autonomy from the Communist Party. Judges are still on the payroll of local governments, their professionalism is limited, and the influence of "local protectionism" on courts is strong (as noted in Mertha's essay).[55] In these circumstances it is not surprising that invoking the ALL to sue cadres (see O'Brien and Li's essay) remains a daunting undertaking. The embeddedness of law in politics suggests that even as we advocate greater attention to social pluralism in China and a range of legal forums, we still have to keep in mind that the party-state remains a strong presence in Chinese society, and that its officials work hard to create the impression that what it legislates, decides, and claims truly makes a difference.

The growth of legal institutions, police forces, and reform-through-labor camps, combined with the ritualistic excitement that accompanies new policies or legislation (in China one can walk into a bookstore and immediately be confronted with a rack of pamphlets on recent laws passed by the National People's Congress) can easily lead to several assumptions about the role of the state, law, and society in China. It is often tempting to assume that if the central party-state decides on a course of action, its agencies act in a concerted fashion to carry it out. The roundup of Tiananmen protesters after 1989 and the "Strike Hard" campaigns against crime and the Falun Gong could be cited as evidence of precisely this. Such campaigns, coupled as they often are with gruesome testimony about what happens inside labor camps and prisons, can easily lead to skepticism about citizens' ability to "fight the power." "The very idea of granting citizens standing to pursue their self-interest in opposition to the state's interest," according to Damaška, "runs counter to fundamental premises of activist government."[56] Or, to use language from the literature on contentious politics, in powerful, one-party states such as China, it would appear that the political and discursive opportunity structures for contesting state power are quite narrow.

The existence of a powerful coercive apparatus and this state-cultivated image of "invincibility,"[57] however, need to be reconciled with findings that show many laws and policies are only partially or selectively implemented,[58] that state agencies often work at cross-purposes, that citizens are becoming increasingly adept at engaging the state at multiple levels, and that the "state" is often difficult to differentiate from "society." In this volume, Fu shows that guards in labor-reform camps and inmates often collude to advance their interests, and guards' salaries even depend on how hard inmates work. Meanwhile, Tanner discusses conflicts within the Public Security Bureau about how to deal with social unrest. Some police officers, he notes, have relatives and friends among the unemployed and are unsympathetic to factory owners who have amassed great wealth at workers' expense. In Frazier's essay, Labor and Social Security officials often lambaste factory managers for not turning over revenue earmarked for the social security system and are seeking national legislation to help them ensure that mandated pension funds are deposited. In Diamant's essay on veterans, central authorities were often stymied by factory Party secretaries, who would turn to the courts to illegally prosecute "bothersome" veterans. Such conflicts between the central and local states can also be seen in the discussions of intellectual property, the labor law, and the ALL. These intrastate tussles are not particularly surprising to political scientists studying the Chinese scene, and they have been discussed elsewhere by Diamant, Perry, and O'Brien.[59] But, much like the law-and-society literature on legal mobilization and legal culture, such a perspective on state power could be more fully incorporated in studies of Chinese law and legal history.[60]

The third opportunity for bridge-building between studies of Chinese law and the social sciences comes, thus, not from the law-and-society field but from political science. Reacting against scholarship which often reified and anthropomorphized the state ("Washington decided to adopt this policy"), scholars such as Joel Migdal have proposed an understanding of state power that emphasizes not internal cohesiveness but fragmentation and the inability to speak in a single voice. This approach entails disaggregating the state by looking both at interactions between governmental authorities at multiple levels and at how they interact with assorted social groups. This "anthropology of the state" would have us pay as much attention to lower-level officials and field offices (regional and local bodies such as courts and military and police units) as the pinnacle of leadership in the capital. Agents of the state who work "in the trenches" and field offices, he suggests, may or may not share common ground, interests, and worldviews with those at the top. Methodologically, Migdal stresses the importance of fieldwork and participant observation, since government documents often try to create the impression that the state is a coherent organization that always succeeds in achieving its goals.[61] In short, the disaggregation of society in the study of legal cultures should be supplemented by an equally disaggregated approach to state and legal institutions, even in a one-party state such as China's.

Unpacking law and political power might be particularly useful in China inasmuch as it could help us reconcile the often looming presence of the state with evidence that laws and policies are only partially enforced and social forces are adept at exploiting the many cracks in the façade of elite unity. It also suggests that the "opportunity structure" for legal challenges (both individual and collective) may be more open than previously thought. For people disgruntled with employers, officials, and husbands or wives, the sheer variety of state and legal institutions authorized to deal with disputes offers at least statistical hope that one of them will lend a hand. Aggrieved individuals and groups are aware of this and search for effective ways to "frame" their demands while actively "venue shopping."[62] They typically press their claims wherever they have the best chance of success: in one place this might be a civil affairs bureau; in another it might be a people's congress;

in a third it could be a discipline inspection committee, a higher court, or a procurator's anti-corruption office. O'Brien and Li's plaintiffs, for instance, frequently find it advisable to bypass their local adversaries while searching for points of vulnerability and a sympathetic ear. Diamant's veterans often appealed to Beijing or municipal people's congresses for justice. Thireau and Hua's workers write letters to arbitration committees and "Letters and Visits Bureaus." Frazier's retirees, even without a pension law, sometimes find advocates on labor arbitration committees. And Mertha's foreign actors fan the flames of bureaucratic competition while searching for "white knights" willing to enforce anti-counterfeiting statutes. The proliferation of formal state institutions does not, of course, guarantee anyone justice: bureaucracies are often shielded from legal challenges under a sea of "protective umbrellas" (*baohu san*), and personal relations among judges, local officials, and enterprise managers can prevent even the most egregious injustices from receiving a fair hearing. This reminds us that we should not exaggerate the likelihood of Chinese citizens "getting justice and getting even" (but, then again, not a few students of U.S. law have similar concerns).[63] The point we are making is less about outcomes than about *possibilities* for justice and methods. Law-and-society research on China can benefit from peering into institutions that groups appeal to and exploring what strategies complainants use. One recurring pattern in China, for instance, entails seeking redress at high levels for abuses of power committed by local officials.[64] That this is so common suggests that many Chinese have a very different attitude toward central authorities than Americans, for whom "Washington" can often do no right and "local authorities"—being more in tune with local circumstances—are more legitimate.[65] There is also evidence that local, provincial, and the National People's congresses are also becoming more willing to investigate appeals from the citizenry, though again with mixed results.[66] Such patterns of state–society interaction, we suggest, can best be explained if we stress diversity in both Chinese society and the state. While the former will help us account for different support structures and legal cultures, the latter will help uncover opportunity structures that both constrain legal action and enable it to proceed.

Conclusion

When we thought about organizing the Berkeley conference on Law and Society in China, we hoped to provide a forum for relatively young scholars who had recently conducted fieldwork on law-related topics but whose disciplines and methodological eclecticism did not make for an easy fit within existing scholarship. As noted earlier, most of the conference participants were not trained in law schools but more often arrived via a circuitous route to use law to study politics, political economy, and social change. Our primary aim was to explore ways to open up the study of Chinese law, and we knew that our conclusions about law's role in society would inevitably be tentative. At the same time, we sought to draw on insights from the law-and-society literature and were pleased that several leading figures in this field (Robert Kagan, Marc Galanter, and Philip Selznick) were able to participate in the conference. On the other hand, two longtime students of Chinese law, Stanley Lubman and William Alford, made sure we did not stray too far off course. This volume, therefore, is as much about themes, concepts, methodologies, and possibilities for law-and-society research in China as it is about any particular substantive issue. Consistent with this intent, neither we nor the authors of the chapters that follow have reached an overall assessment concerning how Chinese citizens "engage the law." So long as Chinese society and institutions of governance, legal and otherwise, are undergoing such profound changes, it is simply too early to foresee the trajectory along which legal institutions will evolve and the effect future developments will have on interactions between law and society.

Still, it is our hope that law-and-society scholars who have little familiarity with Chinese law will find chapters from this book grist for their comparative mill, and that students of Chinese law will read this volume not only to learn about the Labor Law, or the ALL, or intellectual property, or veterans, but also to see how questions and approaches drawn from political science and the law-and-society field can inform research on Chinese law.

Bringing together scholars from several disciplines inevitably has some disadvantages. Those interested primarily in the details of particular laws or in the legislative process will probably be disappointed. However, by refracting the study of Chinese law through themes, concepts, and studies emphasized in the law-and-society literature—such as the disputing pyramid, disputing trajectories, legal mobilization, and legal culture—as well as underscoring an approach to the state borrowed from political science, we are hopeful that the advantages of this enterprise will outweigh the disadvantages. Still, what we have presented here is only the tip of the iceberg. There remains much to be done to span the gap between Chinese legal studies as practiced by historians and scholars at law schools and their counterparts in the social sciences and the law-and-society community. It is our hope that some of the readers of this volume will take up this challenge.

Notes

1. Kathryn Bernhardt and Philip C. C. Huang, *Civil Law in Qing and Republican China* (Stanford, Calif.: Stanford University Press, 1994); Neil J. Diamant, "Conflict and Conflict Resolution in China: Beyond Mediation Centered Approaches," *Journal of Conflict Resolution* 44, no. 4 (August 2000): 523–51.

2. Stanley Lubman, *Bird in a Cage: Chinese Legal Reform in China After Mao* (Stanford, Calif.: Stanford University Press, 1999); J. Chen, *Chinese Law: Toward an Understanding of Chinese Law, Its Nature and Development* (The Hague: Kluwer Law International, 1999); Pitman B. Potter, *The Chinese Legal System: Globalization and Local Legal Culture* (London: Routledge, 2001); Randall Peerenboom, *China's Long March Toward Rule of Law* (Cambridge: Cambridge University Press, 2002).

3. Unchecked corruption has led to some nostalgia for campaigns in the countryside. See Kevin J. O'Brien and Lianjiang Li, "Campaign Nostalgia in the Chinese Countryside," *Asian Survey* 39, no. 3 (1999): 375–93.

4. This is not altogether surprising since liberalizing an economy often brings forth more state intervention. See Steven K. Vogel, *Freer Markets, More Rules: Regulatory Reform in Advanced Industrial Democracies* (Ithaca, N.Y.: Cornell University Press, 1996).

5. See Donald C. Clarke, "The Execution of Civil Judgments in China," *China Quarterly*, no. 141 (March 1995): 65–81; Chen, *Chinese Law*, 119; Peerenboom, *China's Long March*, 488.

6. Patricia Ewick and Susan Silbey, *The Common Place of Law: Stories from Everyday Life* (Chicago: University of Chicago Press, 1998), 28.

7. See, e.g., Matthew H. Sommer, *Sex, Law, and Society in Late Imperial China* (Stanford, Calif.: Stanford University Press, 2000); Bradly Reed, *Talons and Teeth: Clerks and Runners in the Qing Dynasty* (Stanford, Calif.: Stanford University Press, 2000); Melissa Macauley, *Social Power and Legal Culture: Litigation Masters in Late Imperial China* (Stanford, Calif.: Stanford University Press, 1998).

8. Ewick and Silbey, *The Common Place of Law*, 19.

9. In the 1960s, when foreign scholars could not travel to China, they relied, out of necessity, on émigré interviews to supplement more conventional academic research. See, e.g., Jerome A. Cohen, *The Criminal Process in the People's Republic of China* (Cambridge, Mass.: Harvard University Press, 1968); Stanley Lubman, "Mao and Mediation: Politics and Dispute Resolution in Communist China," *California Law Review* 55, no. 5 (1967): 1284–1359. More recently, Pitman Potter has been one of the few law-trained students of Chinese law to conduct survey research. See, e.g., his "Civil Obligations in Shanghai: A Survey of the Getihu," *Canadian Journal of Law and Society* 9, no. 2 (Fall 1994): 41–72.

10. We note also that the essays in this volume were written by members of two growing groups of scholars who are increasingly influential in contemporary Chinese studies: younger Western academics who have spent considerable time studying and doing research in China and Western-trained Chinese researchers. See, generally, Andrew G. Walder, "The Transformation of Contemporary China Studies, 1977–2002," UCIAS [University of California International and Areas Studies Digital Collection], http://repositories.cdlib.org/uciaspubs/edited volumes/3/8.

11. See Lubman, *Bird in a Cage*, 130–35; Potter, *The Chinese Legal System*, 10–12.

12. See Andrew Nathan, *Chinese Democracy* (Berkeley: University of California Press, 1986), ch. 3.

13. Richard L. Abel, "A Comparative Theory of Dispute Institutions in Society," *Law and Society Review*, Vol. 8, No. 2 (Winter 1973), 228.

14. Donald Black, *Sociological Justice* (New York: Oxford University Press, 1989), 76.

15. William Felstiner, Richard Abel, and Austin Sarat, "The Emergence and Transformation of Disputes: Naming, Blaming, Claiming . . . ," *Law and Society Review* 15, nos. 3–4 (1980–81): 631–54. It is also possible that by the time a dispute is aired, the original grievance might no longer be the object of the dispute. On this point, see Lynn Mather and Barbara Yngvesson, "Language, Audience, and the Transformation of Disputes," *Law and Society Review* 15, nos. 3–4 (1980–81): 776.

16. During the Qing dynasty, for instance, magistrates' comments on a plaint were sometimes enough to persuade a plaintiff to give up a claim or settle through village mediation. See Philip C. C. Huang, *Civil Justice in China: Representation and Practice in the Qing* (Stanford, Calif.: Stanford University Press, 1996), 119.

17. Jeffrey Fitzgerald and Richard Dickins, "Disputing in Legal and Nonlegal Contexts: Some Questions for Sociologists of Law," *Law and Society Review*, 15, nos. 3–4 (1980–81), 691.

18. Laura Nader, *Law in Culture and Society* (Chicago: Aldine, 1969); Laura Nader and Harry F. Todd, eds., *The Disputing Process: Law in Ten Societies* (New York: Columbia University Press, 1978); Laura Nader, "Up the Anthropologist: Perspectives Gained by Studying Up," in *Reinventing Anthropology*, ed. Dell Hymes, 284–311 (New York: Vintage Books, 1974).

19. Laura Stoker, "Interest and Ethics in Politics," *American Political Science Review* 86, no. 2 (June 1992): 369–80.

20. For examples of such work on one aggrieved population, see Ching Kwan Lee, "The 'Revenge of History': Collective Memories and Labor Protests in Northeastern China," *Ethnography* 1, no. 2 (2000): 217–37; Ching Kwan Lee, "From the Specter of Mao to the Spirit of the Law: Labor Insurgency in China," *Theory and Society* 31, no. 2 (April 2002): 189–228; Marc J. Blecher, "Hegemony and Workers' Politics in China," *China Quarterly*, no. 170 (June 2002): 283–303; William Hurst and Kevin J. O'Brien, "China's Contentious Pensioners," *China Quarterly*, no. 170 (June 2002), 345–60; Dorothy J. Solinger, "The Potential for Urban Unrest: Will the Fencers Stay on the Piste?" in *Is China Unstable?* ed. David Shambaugh, 79–94 (Armonk, N.Y.: M. E. Sharpe, 2000).

21. As, e.g., in class actions (Benjamin L. Liebman, "Note: Class Action Litigation in China," *Harvard Law Review* 111, no. 6 [1998]: 1523–41).

22. In the Asian studies field this view is often associated with Samuel Popkin (*The Rational Peasant: The Political Economy of Rural Society in Vietnam* [Berkeley: University of California Press, 1979], especially ch. 6).

23. Kevin J. O'Brien and Lianjiang Li, "The Politics of Lodging Complaints in Rural China," *China Quarterly*, no. 143 (September 1995): 756–83; Lianjiang Li and Kevin J. O'Brien, "Villagers and Popular Resistance in Contemporary China," *Modern China* 22, no. 1 (January 1996): 28–61.

24. See Doug McAdam, "Recruitment to High-Risk Activism: The Case of the Freedom Summer," *American Journal of Sociology* 92, no. 1 (1986): 64–90; Ron Aminzade, Jack A. Goldstone, and Elizabeth J. Perry, "Leadership Dynamics and Dynamics of Contention," in *Silence and Voice in the Study of Contentious Politics*, ed. Ronald

R. Aminzade et al., 126–54 (New York: Cambridge University Press, 2001); Doug McAdam, "The Biographical Impact of Activism," in *How Social Movements Matter*, ed. Marco Guigni, Doug McAdam, and Charles Tilly, 119–46 (Minneapolis: University of Minnesota Press, 1999).

25. Charles Epp, *The Rights Revolution: Lawyers, Activists, and Supreme Courts in Comparative Perspective* (Chicago: University of Chicago Press, 1998), 95.

26. Ibid., 18–19.

27. On winning community support for popular action, see Yongshun Cai, "The Resistance of Chinese Laid-off Workers in the Reform Period," *China Quarterly*, no. 170 (June 2002): 327–44; Xiaolin Guo, "Land Expropriation and Rural Conflicts in China," *China Quarterly*, no. 166 (June 2001): 431–35; and O'Brien and Li, "The Politics of Lodging Complaints," 771–75.

28. John P. Burns, *Political Participation in Rural China* (Berkeley: University of California Press, 1988); Victor C. Falkenheim, "Political Participation in China," *Problems of Communism* 27, no. 3 (May–June 1978): 18–32. For groups of women petitioning for divorce in the Maoist period, see Neil J. Diamant, *Revolutionizing the Family: Politics, Love and Divorce in Urban and Rural China, 1949–1968* (Berkeley: University of California Press, 2000), chs. 3, 4, and 6.

29. Mather and Yngvesson, "Language, Audience, and the Transformation of Disputes," 777; Pamela Oliver, Gerald Marwell, and Ruy Teixeira, "A Theory of the Critical Mass I: Interdependence, Group Heterogeneity, and the Production of Collective Action," *American Journal of Sociology* 91, no. 3 (November 1995), 522–56; Gerald Marwell, Pamela Oliver, and Ralph Prahl, "Social Networks and Collective Action: A Theory of the Critical Mass III," *American Journal of Sociology* 94, no. 3 (November 1988): 502–34.

30. For an analysis of stories covered by China's most popular television program devoted to investigative journalism, see Alex Chan, "From Propaganda to Hegemony: *Jiaodian Fangtan* and China's Media Policy," *Journal of Contemporary China* 11, no. 30 (February 2002): 35–51.

31. Ethan Michelson, "They Talk the Talk, But Can They Walk the Walk? Obstacles to Collective Action Among Chinese Lawyers," paper presented at the Conference on Law and Society in China, University of California, Berkeley, September 20–21, 2002.

32. Kevin J. O'Brien, "Rightful Resistance," *World Politics* 49, no. 1 (October 1996): 31–55.

33. Ewick and Silbey, *The Common Place of Law*, 28.

34. Alan Hunt, "Rights and Social Movements: Counter-Hegemonic Strategies," *Journal of Law and Society* 17, no. 3 (Fall 1990): 313, 324.

35. On rules consciousness in dynastic China, see R. Bin Wong, *China Transformed* (Ithaca, N.Y.: Cornell University Press, 1997), 235–37; Lubman, *Bird in a Cage*, 236–37, 307; and various selections in Merle Goldman and Elizabeth J. Perry, eds., *Changing Meanings of Citizenship in Modern China* (Cambridge, Mass.: Harvard University Press, 2002). On competitive, reactive, and proactive claims in contemporary China, see Kevin J. O'Brien, "Collective Action in the Chinese Countryside," *China Journal*, no. 48 (July 2002): 142–46.

36. We thank Marc Galanter for raising this issue.

37. Michael W. McCann, *Rights at Work: Pay Equity Reform and the Politics of Legal Mobilization* (Chicago: University of Chicago Press, 1994), 281.

38. On the case for growing rights consciousness, see Liebman, "Note: Class Action Litigation"; Kevin J. O'Brien, "Villagers, Elections, and Citizenship in Contemporary China," *Modern China* 27, no. 4 (October 2001): 407–35; David Zweig, "The 'Externalities' of Development: Can New Political Institutions Manage Rural Conflict?" in *Chinese Society*, ed. Elizabeth J. Perry and Mark Selden, 120–42 (New York: Routledge, 2000).

39. O'Brien, "Villagers, Elections, and Citizenship," 425–26.

40. Wang Gungwu, *The Chineseness of China* (Hong Kong: Oxford University Press, 1991); Randle R. Edwards, Louis Henkin, and Andrew J. Nathan, *Human Rights in Contemporary China* (New York: Columbia University Press, 1986). According to Mirjan Damaška, in countries with legal systems such as China's, "claims flowing from state decrees, even though routinely designated 'rights,'" should "not be equated with personal entitlements.... The citizen of the activist state possesses no rights accorded by virtue of his being an end in himself.... All rights are at least potentially subject to qualification or denial" (see his *The Faces of Justice and State Authority: A Comparative Approach to the Legal Process* [New Haven, Ct.: Yale University Press, 1986], 83).

41. Randall Peerenboom, "Rights, Interests, and the Interest of Rights in China," *Stanford Journal of International Law* 31, no. 2 (Summer 1995): 359–86.

42. Huang, *Civil Justice in China*; Diamant, *Revolutionizing the Family*. Although rights discourses were not in vogue during the Maoist era, borrowing slogans from the government arsenal to express heterodox views was a common tactic during both the Cultural Revolution and the Hundred Flowers Movement (see Elizabeth J. Perry, "'To Rebel Is Justified': Cultural Revolution Influences on Contemporary Chinese Protest," in *The Chinese Cultural Revolution Reconsidered: Beyond Purge and Holocaust*, ed. Kam-Yee Law, 262–81 [New York: Palgrave, 2003]; Sebastian Heilmann, "Turning Away from the Cultural Revolution," Occasional Paper 28, Center for Pacific Area Studies, Stockholm University, 1996).

43. See Lubman, "Bird in a Cage," 37–38, 230–32, 305–6; Potter, *The Chinese Legal System*, 12–13, 30–33, 52–55; Pitman B. Potter, "Guanxi and the PRC Legal System: From Contradiction to Complementarity," in *Social Connections in China: Institutions, Culture, and the Changing Nature of Guanxi*, ed. Thomas Gold, Doug Guthrie, and David Wank (Cambridge: Cambridge University Press, 2002).

44. See his *Local Knowledge: Further Essays in Interpretative Anthropology* (New York: Basic Books, 1983).

45. Marc Galanter, "The Radiating Effects of Courts," in *Empirical Theories About Courts*, ed. Keith Boyum and Lynn Mather (New York: Longman, 1983), 127.

46. McCann, *Rights at Work*, 6 (emphasis added).

47. Sally Engle Merry, *Getting Justice and Getting Even: Legal Consciousness Among Working Class Americans* (Chicago: University of Chicago Press, 1990), 5.

48. Huang, *Civil Justice in China*, 1–20.

49. See Joseph Esherick and Mary Rankin, eds., *Chinese Local Elites and Patterns*

of Dominance (Berkeley: University of California Press, 1990); essays by Edward McCord and Rubie Watson provide contrasting perspectives.

50. Tom Tyler, *Why People Obey the Law* (New Haven, Ct.: Yale University Press, 1990).

51. See Lee, "From the Specter of Mao," 220; Minxin Pei, "Citizens v. Mandarins: Administrative Litigation in China," *China Quarterly*, no. 152 (December 1997): 832–62; Diamant, *Revolutionizing the Family*, ch. 8; Elizabeth J. Perry, "Casting a Chinese 'Democracy' Movement: The Roles of Students, Workers, and Entrepreneurs," in *Popular Protest and Political Culture in Modern China*, ed. Elizabeth J. Perry and Jeffrey Wasserstrom (Boulder, Colo.: Westview, 1994); O'Brien, "Rightful Resistance."

52. In the context of the 1989 protest movement, see Perry, "Casting a Chinese 'Democracy' Movement"; Daniel J. Kelliher, "Keeping Democracy Safe from the Masses: Intellectuals and Elitism in the Chinese Protest Movement," *Comparative Politics* 25, no. 4 (July 1993): 379–96. But also cf. Teresa Wright, "State Repression and Student Protest in Contemporary China," *China Quarterly*, no. 157 (March 1999): 142–72.

53. This is a bit of a simplification. According to Weber, the formal-rational legal system emerged while capitalist transformation was taking place; it was not a preceding condition or its direct consequence. For Weber's views, see David Trubek, "Max Weber on Law and the Rise of Capitalism," *Wisconsin Law Review* 3 (1972): 720–53.

54. Doug Guthrie, *Dragon in a Three-Piece Suit: The Emergence of Capitalism in China* (Princeton, N.J.: Princeton University Press, 1999); Edward S. Steinfeld, "Moving Beyond Transition in China: Financial Reform and the Political Economy of Declining Growth," *Comparative Politics* 34, no. 4 (July 2002): 379–98.

55. See Peerenboom, *China's Long March*, 310–12; Lubman, *Bird in a Cage*, 263–69, ch. 9; Chen, *Chinese Law*, 162.

56. Damaška, *The Faces of State Power*, 86.

57. Joel S. Migdal, "The State in Society: An Approach to Struggles for Domination," in *State Power and Social Forces: Domination and Transformation in the Third World*, ed. Joel Migdal, Atul Kohli, and Vivienne Shue (Cambridge: Cambridge University Press, 1994), 14.

58. Kevin J. O'Brien and Lianjiang Li, "Selective Policy Implementation in Rural China," *Comparative Politics* 31, no. 2 (January 1999): 167–86; Thomas P. Bernstein and Xiaobo Lü, *Taxation Without Representation in Contemporary Rural China* (New York: Cambridge University Press, 2003). But cf. Maria Edin, "State Capacity and Local Agent Control in China: CCP Cadre Management from a Township Perspective," *China Quarterly*, no. 173 (March 2003): 35–52.

59. Elizabeth J. Perry, "Trends in the Study of Chinese Politics: State-Society Relations," *China Quarterly*, no. 139 (September 1994): 704–13; Neil Diamant, "Making Love 'Legible' in China: Politics and Society During the Enforcement of Civil Marriage Registration, 1950–66," *Politics and Society* 29, no. 3 (2001): 447–89; Kevin J. O'Brien, "Neither Transgressive Nor Contained: Boundary-Spanning Contention in China," *Mobilization* 8, no. 1 (February 2003): 51–64. These conflicts are also reflected in treatments of "local protectionism." On problems faced by Chinese courts

in complying with obligations agreed to when China joined the World Trade Organization, see Donald C. Clarke, "China's Legal System and the WTO: Prospects for Compliance," *Washington University Global Studies Law Review* 2, no. 1 (2003): 97–118.

60. At the same time, judging by the contents of the *Law and Society Review* in recent years, the law and society literature, for its part, has become increasingly focused on legal norms and discourses and much less concerned with close analyses of state institutions and structures.

61. Migdal, "The State in Society," 15–16.

62. On "venue shopping," see Thomas R. Rochon, *Culture Moves* (Princeton, N.J.: Princeton University Press, 1998), 237. For a review of social-movement research on "framing," see Sidney Tarrow, *Power in Movement*, 2nd ed. (New York: Cambridge University Press, 1998), ch. 7.

63. Marc Galanter, "Why the Haves Come Out Ahead: Speculations on the Limits of Legal Change," *Law and Society Review* 9, no. 1 (Fall 1974): 95–160. Galanter distinguishes between litigants who are "one-shotters" and "repeat players." One-shotters are inexperienced with the legal system and focus primarily on short-term gain. Repeat players participate actively in the legal system, have many resources at their disposal (including organization, knowledge, and money), and focus on long-term interests. One-shotters, he argues, are often at a disadvantage when litigating against repeat players. This article inspired a great deal of research on why repeat players enjoy advantages, whether such standing is different than simply having wealth or power, and the extent to which Galanter's findings can be replicated elsewhere. See the special issue of the *Law and Society Review* (vol. 33, no. 4 [1999]) for articles that evaluate Galanter's original paper. Although there are few "repeat players" currently in China, as the legal system develops and people gain greater access to courts, Galanter's analysis may prove useful.

64. This has a long history in China. See Jonathan K. Ocko, "I'll Take It All the Way to Beijing: Capital Appeals in the Qing," *Journal of Asian Studies* 47, no. 2 (May 1988): 291–315; Lee, "From the Specter of Mao," 215; O'Brien, "Rightful Resistance"; Diamant, *Revolutionizing the Family*, ch. 8.

65. On faith in higher levels and disdain for local authorities, see Lianjiang Li, "Political Trust in the Chinese Countryside," *Modern China* 30, no. 2 (2004): 228–58.

66. Young Nam Cho, "From 'Rubber Stamps' to 'Iron Stamps': The Emergence of Chinese Local People's Congresses as Supervisory Powerhouses," *China Quarterly*, no. 171 (September 2002): 724–40; Kevin J. O'Brien, "Agents and Remonstrators: Role Accumulation by Chinese People's Congress Deputies," *China Quarterly*, no. 138 (June 1994): 368–77.

PART II

Legal Mobilization and Culture

KEVIN J. O'BRIEN AND LIANJIANG LI 2

Suing the Local State: Administrative Litigation in Rural China

---

The promulgation of the Administrative Litigation Law (ALL) in 1989 was hailed in China as a "milestone of democratic and legal construction."[1] Hopeful observers anticipated that the law, by empowering citizens to dispute unlawful administrative acts, would curb official misconduct. However, more than a decade after the ALL came into force, the best evidence suggests that its deterrent effect has been modest. While the number of cases has grown (see Table 1.1) and about two-fifths of them reportedly result in some form of relief,[2] the law's implementation has been hounded by interference and feigned compliance.[3] To this day, the law is widely regarded to be a "frail weapon" that has not greatly reduced administrative arbitrariness.[4]

The ALL's effect has been especially problematic in the countryside, where many local officials continue to mistreat villagers in egregiously illegal ways. Litigating is expensive, getting a case accepted is difficult, and long delays are common. Even when rural complainants manage to win a lawsuit, they often face uncertain enforcement or retaliation. Many villagers have understandably concluded that it is futile or even dangerous to contest unfair administrative decisions or unjust sanctions.[5] In a 1999–2001 survey in Fujian, Jiangsu, and Jiangxi, for instance, only 9 percent of 1,368 respondents said they would consider filing an administrative lawsuit if they discovered that their township government had made a decision that did not accord with central policies and regulations.[6]

Still, despite a widespread belief that suing the powerful is like "throwing an egg against a stone,"[7] hundreds of thousands of rural people have used the ALL to challenge acts by county and township governments, public security bureaus, industrial and commercial departments, cultural, environmental, and public hygiene agencies, and civil affairs bureaus. Charges commonly involve actions taken against individual villagers (such as detention, land confisca-

TABLE 2.1
First-Instance ALL Cases by Disposition, 1990–2001

	Accepted	Concluded	Upheld	Rescinded	Modified	Refused	Withdrawn	Other	Administrative compensation only
1990	13,006	12,040	4,337	2,012	398		4,346	947	
1991	25,667	25,202	7,969	4,762	592		9,317	2,562	
1992	27,125	27,116	7,628	5,780	480	2,116	10,261	851	
1993	27,911	27,958	6,587	5,270	430		11,550	4,121	
1994	35,083	34,567	7,128	6,547	369		15,317	5,206	
1995	52,596	51,370	8,903	7,733	395		25,990	8,349	
1996	79,996	79,537	11,549	11,831	1,214		42,915	12,028	
1997	90,557	88,542	11,230	12,279	717	7,501	50,735	6,080	
1998	98,350	98,390	13,036	15,214		10,570	47,817	9,376	2,377
1999	97,569	98,759	14,672	15,251		11,837	44,395	9,491	3,113
2000	85,760	86,614	13,431	13,635		11,146	31,822	14,078	2,502
2001	100,921	95,984	15,941	12,943		11,516	31,083	21,736	2,765

SOURCES: Stanley B. Lubman, *Bird in a Cage* (Stanford, Calif.: Stanford University Press, 1999), 208; *Zhongguo falü nianjian* [Law yearbook of China] (Beijing: Zhongguo Falü Nianjian She,1999–2002), 1023 (for 1999), 1211 (for 2000); 1258 (for 2001); 1240 (for 2002).

tion, or home demolition), as well as decisions that affect many people (such as increasing fees, closing village clinics, selling fake seed, or disposing of village land). Some suits are filed by individuals; others are organized efforts that involve hundreds, thousands, or even over ten thousand plaintiffs.[8] These suits, particularly collective ones, are often preceded, accompanied, or followed by non-judicial popular action, such as joint letter-writing, sending delegations to government compounds or media outlets, and group appeals to Party authorities or people's congresses.[9]

That some villagers find the ALL to be a useful, if imperfect tool to combat official malfeasance suggests that state–society relations in rural China can be fruitfully explored by examining the dynamics of administrative litigation. The cases recounted below cannot be said to be representative but are instead illustrative of certain problems that many plaintiffs encounter. They were chosen mainly to shed light on such questions as: What tactics do litigants and their targets employ both in and out of court? How have villagers fared in their struggles with local officials? What can the emerging set of practices surrounding the ALL tell us about the relationship between law and politics in contemporary China?

Dynamics of Administrative Litigation: Gaining Access to Court

Although there is evidence that Chinese officials have become somewhat more accepting of being sued,[10] local officials generally do not welcome legal challenges and often do everything possible to preempt, derail, or undermine administrative litigation. They sometimes even block the local populace's access to official documents and regulations. When a county government, for instance, began a book distribution program, township leaders ordered that no materials related to legal education be made available because "as soon as ordinary people learn anything about the law then they become impossible to govern."[11] In Dangshan County, Anhui Province, when villagers went to a township to request central and provincial circulars regarding the tax-for-fee reform, township officials said that they had received no such documents and had only been notified orally. Actually, the Anhui Party committee had instructed that all relevant materials, including "A Letter to Farmers" from the provincial government, a provincial circular, and a tax card, be hand-delivered to every household.[12]

Local officials may even use the police to limit popular knowledge of laws and regulations that they deem "inflammatory." In Henan, for example, the Qixian County public security bureau detained a man for fourteen days in 1998 for "distorting facts, spreading rumors, and instigating disturbances," simply because he publicized a central decision concerning rural tax and fee burdens that he had read about in the *Henan Daily*.[13] Sometimes more extreme measures are employed to keep villagers in the dark. In 2000, a journal editor in Jiangxi compiled a small book of laws, regulations, and central policies regarding the countryside and agriculture. Fearing that publication of the book might spur resistance to illegal fees, Jiangxi's leaders ordered that every copy be confiscated and pulped. County and township officials, village cadres, and the police were mobilized to carry out this directive. Among other acts, the police raided the home of one villager and detained another for fifteen days for making the collection available to his neighbors.[14]

Partly owing to such strong-arm tactics, many villagers remain unaware of laws and policies that can work to their benefit, despite the nationwide campaign to increase popular legal awareness (*pufa*) that has been underway since the 1980s. A 1997–98 survey that we conducted in seven provinces (Anhui, Beijing, Fujian, Hebei, Jiangsu, Jiangxi, and Shandong) showed that only a quarter of the 9,843 respondents knew that township and village fees must not exceed 5 percent of the average village income. When asked about a ten-year-old law that enables villagers to elect grassroots cadres, only 3 percent of the respondents said they understood it fairly well, while 28 percent said they knew something about it and 70 percent said they knew nothing at all about it.[15]

Aggrieved villagers have developed a number of techniques to circumvent information blockades. Some try to acquire legal texts and regulations through relatives who work in the government; others buy legal compendia in bookstores. Others may even hire lawyers. Local officials can do little to head off the first two tactics, but they sometimes try to stop lawyers from helping villagers file a lawsuit. They may warn local attorneys not to aid potential litigants and they may work to discredit outsiders. In December 2000, because no local lawyer would assist them, villagers in Longnan County, Jiangxi Province, hired two attorneys from a neighboring county to prepare a suit against the county for increasing rural taxes and fees. The Longnan leadership responded by having the local TV station repeatedly broadcast a speech by a county leader, who labeled the two outsiders "illegal lawyers" (*bufa lüshi*), accused them of "coming to Longnan to disrupt social order and public security," and threatened to "subject them to severe legal punishment." To defend themselves, the two lawyers finally felt they had no choice but to sue the county for slander.[16]

Despite such pressure, lawyers and legally savvy officials often play a critical role in the early stages of litigation.[17] In Anhui Province, for instance, an elderly villager was so panicked after county police and township officials rushed into his home looking for his son that he committed suicide. The son went to the provincial Legal Aid Center, where he found a lawyer who volunteered his time to sue the county public security bureau for conducting a search without a warrant and also paid the man's court fees.[18] Similarly, the director of a county agricultural station played a crucial part in a large lawsuit in Lezhi County, Sichuan. He informed a villager who complained to him of excessive fees about the 5 percent limit set by a 1991 State Council Regulation, gave him a copy of Sichuan's *Regulations Concerning Farmers' Burdens*, and advised him that the fees were legally actionable. The villager then returned home and began organizing a collective lawsuit.[19]

The toughest battle most litigants face is persuading a court to accept a case.[20] To start with, there are a number of restrictions on whom villagers can sue. They cannot sue any Party committee or secretary, because the Party is not subject to administrative litigation—even though the Party and government are often difficult to disentangle. Local authorities sometimes try to use this overlap and the Party's immunity to deflect lawsuits. As one Chinese scholar explained: "In some places administrative departments employ illegitimate (*bu zhengdang*) means to preclude litigation. Whenever an action is subject to the ALL, they will have the Party committee or the Party secretary be the entity that officially performs it, so that the administrative department can avoid any potential suits."[21] Moreover, villagers can sue only for specific misdeeds, not "abstract" decisions. According to a Chinese researcher: "Courts can only maneuver around a handful of so-called 'concrete administrative acts,' and dare not undertake big moves on the numerous general actions based on 'policies' (*zhengce*). Taking into account the large number of illegal actions, lawsuits filed and accepted amount to one cup of water when a whole cart of hay is on fire."[22]

Yet another factor limits the scope of administrative litigation: Party committees may issue internal orders forbidding courts to accept suits on sensitive matters. As a result, in some locations, "the people's court simply doesn't have the nerve to accept cases related to 'hot issues' such as excessive financial burdens, violations of enterprise autonomy, unlawful birth control enforcement, land expropriation, and illegal demolition of homes."[23] Even when such prohibitions do not exist, a local court will often consult the Party committee and government at the same level before it accepts litigation on a hot-button issue.[24] One 1994 study showed that one-third of judges who presided over administrative lawsuits thought that "it is inappropriate for the court to offend administrative departments."[25] This tactfulness is hardly surprising, insofar as the appointment and promotion of judges as well as the court's budget are controlled by the local Party committee and government.[26] As a deputy chair of the Hainan provincial people's congress concluded: "Although courts have the authority to work independently, in reality appointment and promotion of major court leaders is controlled by the number one Party and government officials in a locality. If a court offends them by ruling according to law and the government loses, the consequences are obvious."[27]

To generate pressure to accept a lawsuit, villagers sometimes turn to dramatic acts. In Lezhi County, Sichuan Province, for instance, dozens of villagers knelt before a county judge when they submitted their complaint concerning financial burdens. The strategy worked. The court's judiciary committee held an emergency meeting, at which it was decided to place the case on the docket.[28] But getting a case into court typically remains a high hurdle. Suits often are summarily rejected. In Shanxi, for instance, when villagers sued a township in 1993 for imposing illegal fees, the county court refused to accept the case and refused to give any explanation.[29]

Officials under threat of prosecution (or their protectors) may even question whether the complainants have a right to sue. This is particularly common when a group of plaintiffs files a collective lawsuit concerning the sale of village land. One routine tactic is to insist that the litigants do not constitute a legal person and thus cannot act on behalf of a village. In Hainan, for instance, over two thousand villagers sued Lin'gao County in 1996 for illegally selling collective property to a real estate company. Over the next five years, a series of elected villagers' small-group leaders (who were representing the village) were either detained or not granted legal standing, on grounds that their election had not been authorized.[30] The litigation was finally accepted only after the Hainan Provincial People's Congress intervened.[31]

After a Suit Is Filed

Sometimes, acceptance of a suit induces the defendants to pursue a settlement out of court.[32] In many cases, however, the struggle between villagers and local authorities only intensifies after a suit is filed. Some officials go so far as to employ unlawful means to encourage complainants to drop an action.[33] In Gongyi County, Henan Province, a villager was detained in 1997 after a dispute with a township policeman. He was confined in a guesthouse run by two relatives of a county police officer and was grossly overcharged for substandard food and lodging. Upon his release, he sued the county public security bureau for illegal detention. The following day, the county police jailed him again and charged him with raping his former girlfriend. This time, he was denied food and sleep for forty-eight hours while the police tried to extract a confession. His onetime girlfriend later told a journalist that the police took her to the public security bureau, made her kneel on the floor, and threatened to imprison her for three years unless she accused her former boyfriend of rape. The beleaguered villager was finally released after two weeks, "at the urging of relevant departments at higher levels," which stepped in after his relatives made repeated visits to plead his case.[34]

If local officials cannot persuade a complainant to drop a suit, they sometimes intervene directly in the legal proceedings. One practice is simply to dictate a verdict, usually on grounds that cadres in judicial departments must obey Party leadership and support the government's work.[35] Local officials can also apply pressure on the judges who preside over administrative litigation. When 1,770 households sued a township in 1996 for selling phony rice seed, the county judge had to resist "all sorts of pressure" from the county Party committee and government. He rejected an unreasonably low estimate of the losses and spent over a year collecting evidence from the affected families. He ultimately withstood the pressure largely because he had managed to obtain support from the city Party committee and People's Congress. Eventually, he ruled that the township had to pay the plaintiffs 510,000 yuan in compensation.[36]

Such conscientious and determined judges are not the rule, however. Judges often find it difficult to resist a Party committee or government department that decides to intervene—not least because courts and their personnel are ranked lower in the local bureaucratic hierarchy than many other administrative officials at the same level.[37] This interference may come in the form of an "inquiry" about a case or an "exchange of views" on a legal interpretation. It may be a direct approach to a judge or be done through a court's top leadership. It may even arrive unobtrusively as a higher court tells a lower court to "pay more attention to a case."[38] As one observer explained, most judges wish to be impartial but many eventually cave in to outside forces. They may be embarrassed when this happens but also know that they might otherwise pay career consequences and even "cause the court itself to lose its supply of food and drink."[39]

Nonetheless, local officials by no means always dictate verdicts, particularly when the evidence is strong and it is widely known which party is in the right. But this does not mean that all interference stops. Instead, outside parties (e.g., Party secretaries, government heads[40]) often press a court to procrastinate, hoping that endless delays will induce the plaintiffs to drop their suit. One time-tested strategy is to fail to appear in court. According to one Chinese researcher: "It is not rare that administrative departments refuse to show up in court, refuse to answer questions, refuse to pay litigation fees, and reject court rulings."[41] In over two hundred first-instance ALL cases handled by a municipal court in Jiangxi from 1989 to 2000, 95 percent of the time the defendant agency failed to appear on occasions when it was required to be present.[42] According to a 1997 investigation in Hunan, when public security bureaus "meddled in" economic disputes, the court had to proceed without the defendant in up to 90 percent of the cases.[43] (Unfortunately, our sources do not report the final outcome of these cases, though presumably the plaintiff often still did not win.)

When representatives of a concerned department do show up,[44] they sometimes perjure themselves or challenge the court to reject testimony that is widely held to be false. In Henan in 2001, when township authorities tried to confiscate the TV of a village woman who refused to pay a fine for having a second child, the villager asked for a receipt but the officials refused. A brawl broke out and a township staff member wrestled her to the ground, injuring her. During the ensuing trial, however, the officials who had been at the scene all testified that the woman had fallen herself, although a number of villagers who had witnessed the incident all disagreed.[45] In a similar case, when a Hebei villager sued a county public security bureau for illegal detention, a township policeman was instructed to give false testimony and the county court readily accepted this. The plaintiff had to appeal to the Shijiazhuang city court, which overruled the county verdict.[46]

Mobilizing Support

Many villagers understand how the legal system works, so they refuse to give up when a verdict goes against them. They know, in other words, that ultimate authority does not rest with local courts. This encourages them to do two things. First, they frequently appeal to a higher court, hoping that the higher they go, the better the chance of locating a judge who can ignore the pleas of their local adversaries.[47] This strategy sometimes works. Higher courts are more likely to render favorable verdicts, not least because the effects of local protectionism are less pronounced at higher levels.[48] After a search without a warrant led to the Anhui suicide mentioned above, the Huangshan municipal court ruled that the county police were "undertaking a criminal investigation" and were not subject to litigation. It also determined that the township was not liable because it was simply fulfilling its duty of dispatching representatives to assist in an investigation. The plaintiff appealed. The Anhui provincial court then ruled that the police had not been engaged in a criminal investigation but rather in a "concrete administrative action"[49] liable to litigation.

The second strategy is to seek a helping hand from sympathetic leaders— sometimes through personal connections or through bureaucratic allies who have a stake in upholding a given policy, as stressed in Neil Diamant's chapter. Largely based on faith in the good intentions of Beijing,[50] some rural residents believe that highly placed backers can be found somewhere. Since they are often not precisely sure where such allies might be, villagers typically cast their net wide by appealing to all departments they can think of, including Party committees, disciplinary inspection commissions, anti-corruption bureaus, letters and visits offices, and people's congresses. They also seek to expose official malfeasance through media outlets such as TV stations, magazines, and newspapers, hoping that such attention will draw in higher-level authorities.[51]

Over the last decade, as Frazier and Thireau and Hua detail in their chapters, letters and visits offices and the media have shown an increased willingness to respond to popular appeals.[52] What is more notable, however, is that people's congresses have also become more assertive in overseeing the disposition of administrative litigation. In an effort to control judicial corruption, in the late 1990s a number of provincial people's congresses (e.g., Sichuan, Yunnan) issued regulations that boosted their role in supervising specific court cases. The involvement of congresses in reopening misjudged ALL cases has commonly taken three forms. Sometimes a case attracts the attention of public-spirited legislators. In Yi'an County, Heilongjiang Province, for instance, thirty-three villagers filed suit on behalf of two thousand people against a neighboring county for refusing to pay them for tree-planting after a large fire in 1987.[53] Both the prefectural court and the provincial court ruled against the county government. Instead of remitting the overdue wages, however, the county placed the two principal organizers of the lawsuit under detention on a trumped-up charge of fraud. After angry villagers mobilized a large collective complaint, a provincial congress deputy agreed to take it to his congress, so long as the villagers postponed their plans to go to Harbin, the provincial capital. The deputy chair of the Heilongjiang congress then promptly called on the provincial public security bureau to conduct an investigation.[54]

Media reports have also prodded people's congresses to intervene directly in litigation. In Henan, three villagers who organized a collective complaint against a corrupt village Party secretary were jailed by the Wuzhi county court in 1998 for disrupting the work of the county government, and their appeal was rejected by the Jiazuo city court. Just when their situation looked hopeless, *Legal World*, a magazine affiliated with Henan's judicial bureau, objected. The magazine's official commentator pointed out that allowing complaints to be lodged had always been a means by which the Party maintained close contact with the masses and that judicial authorities had to distinguish between minor violations of the regulations on letters and visits and "disrupting social order."[55] The commentator warned that if the letters and visits channel was blocked, a temporary peace might be achieved by scaring off potential complainants, but that the long-term consequences were "inconceivable." This analysis attracted the attention of the Henan People's Congress, which urged the provincial court to reopen the case. In October 1999 the high court overruled the original verdict and freed the three villagers. The village Party secretary was also removed.[56]

Villagers also find their own ways to draw in people's congresses. In May 1999 a group of complainants went to the Haikou City Congress after the city court handed down a verdict they felt was unjust. Six months later, the congress's standing committee reviewed the case and unanimously decided to issue a "supervision letter" (*jiandu han*) that requested that the Haikou court handle the litigation through an open trial,[57] make a judgment according to law, and be impartial. In an unusual step, the congress even invited several of the complainants to attend the standing-committee meeting at which their appeal was discussed.[58]

Complainants may also contact people's congresses through written petitions, much as the veterans discussed in Neil Diamant's chapter did in the 1950s. In the Hainan land sale case discussed earlier, villagers appealed to various government departments without success. In 2000 they finally wrote to the deputy chair of the provincial people's congress. The congress agreed to intercede, and at its urging, the Hainan court accepted the suit but then handed down a strangely mixed verdict. On the one hand, it ruled against the villagers, but nonetheless it ordered the county to pay them compensation of 170,000 yuan. The villagers rejected the verdict and appealed to the provincial congress. Finally, in 2001, the congress stepped in yet again and the Hainan court ruled unambiguously in their favor.[59]

Largely because officials at higher levels tend to be less susceptible to pressure, access to them has become a source of friction between villagers and local leaders. Efforts by litigants to find a sympathetic ear at higher levels are often obstructed in the local power structure. In the last few years, officials in many places have, among other tactics, used a selective reading of the 1995 Regulation on Letters and Visits Work to prohibit collective complaints and bypassing levels.[60] In Dangshan County, Anhui Province, for instance, grassroots leaders plastered their village's walls with posters announcing "It is illegal to send more than five people to lodge a complaint" and "It is illegal to instigate the masses to lodge a complaint."[61] Villagers then sought counsel from a magazine affiliated with the newspaper *Legal Daily*, which clarified that the 1995 regulations prescribed procedures for but did not outlaw collective complaints.[62] Local officials in Henan similarly put up big-character posters that declared: "Bypassing levels when lodging complaints is to be severely punished." Villagers in this case sought clarification from the State Council's Bureau of Letters and Visits, which instructed the poster-writers to take down their misinterpretation of the regulation.[63]

We must not, of course, overestimate the effect of intercession by officials at higher levels. The fate of the two organizers of the collective lawsuit in the Heilongjiang tree-planting case is instructive. The provincial public security bureau, at the urging of the provincial people's congress, examined the files submitted by the prefectural and county public security bureaus, concluded that the charges against the two villagers were groundless, and ordered their immediate release. Most likely because the directive did not come from a superior who directly controlled their careers, the county leadership feigned compliance. Immediately after the public security bureau released the two men, the county procurator charged them with bribery and detained them again. When the prefectural procurator intervened in response to complaints from other villagers, the county procurator dropped its charges. But instead of freeing the men, it handed them back to the county public security bureau, which again charged them with fraud and again asked the county procurator to approve their arrest. As the case dragged on, the provincial deputy who initially reported the case became increasingly frustrated and remarked that in this county "laws are treated with disrespect."[64]

Even when villagers emerge victorious from the courtroom, it does not mean that their grievances will be redressed; in many cases a favorable verdict is just the beginning of another round of struggle. Rulings for plaintiffs sometimes go unexecuted when local governments either ignore them or subvert them.[65] In rural Henan, several township leaders engineered the dismissal of a director of a letters and visits office because they suspected he had exposed their corruption to the county discipline inspection commission and anti-corruption bureau. They accused the director of using the township's seal without authorization and instructed a staff member to testify against him. Although the director ultimately won a lawsuit against the corrupt officials, the township simply refused to accept the court's order to rehire him.

Finally, in some cases where villagers prevail and the verdict is duly executed, their gains are soon lost when the officials they bested retaliate. Although two studies by Chinese researchers have quoted rates of retaliation, respectively, of one-tenth of 1 percent and 5 percent, we find these figures to be improbably low.[66] In our experience, local cadres typically make little attempt to hide their contempt for the villagers who sue them, and they often strike back when the attention of higher levels moves on to other matters.[67] In one such case, a villager won a suit against a township which had illegally fined him. The township Party secretary then openly announced: "If we are required to carry out the court's ruling, we are going to teach the villager a lesson. We will never permit him to obtain any compensation." The villager was terrified and dared not pursue enforcement of the court's decision.[68] Likewise, in Hengyang County, Hunan, a hotbed of rural activism, a number of "peasant leaders" (*nongmin lingxiu*) told us in early 2003 that they had won lawsuits concerning unlawful fees, illegal detention, and the use of excessive force by township officials, but few if any of the rulings had been enforced. As one Chinese researcher concluded: "Even when a few peasants who know how to use laws file suits or lodge complaints to protect their legal rights and interests, only a few get results, and this often starts a long journey in which they face retaliation, suffer much hardship, and ultimately lose everything they have."[69]

Outcomes

The fact that in many cases justice is either denied or delayed can, of course, be demoralizing. Long waits, in particular, drain a complainant's money, energy, and time.[70] A Yunnan villager who sued a township for confiscating his television set ended up spending well over ten thousand yuan to win his suit, with which he could have bought ten color TVs. As a legal analyst in Henan put it, "Endless delay is a kind of 'judicial corruption'; it seriously undermines people's trust and confidence in the legal system."[71]

Yet the victories that plaintiffs have won are equally significant. Successful litigation sometimes results in compensation for miscarriages of justice and relief (though often temporary) from excessive fees, while also restoring a litigant's sense of self-respect. Involvement in a legal case also teaches villagers how to use the law, as they work their way through a complex and hitherto unfamiliar legal and political thicket.[72] The Yunnan villager who lost his TV learned so much about legal affairs that he was able to act as his own lawyer, and at various points in his trial he came up with arguments that the counsel for the township could not counter. Furthermore, successful suits can enhance a villager's sense of efficacy, as litigants who win one case feel able to go after bigger fish the next time.[73] Lastly, victorious plaintiffs may also gain stature in the community. The Yunnan man who took the township to task won so much respect from his fellow villagers that they now come to consult him whenever they have legal questions.[74] The organizer of the collective suit against excessive fees in Lezhi County, Sichuan, was later elected a small-group leader.[75]

Administrative litigation is often a learning experience for both parties. Local officials also learn lessons, particularly if they lose. Some cadres have realized that suits can bring them not only "embarrassment and insult,"[76] but threats to their career. In response, some of them undoubtedly ratchet up efforts to prevent villagers from filing or winning their cases. But others may draw a different conclusion and take more care not to break the law. In fact, in one recent survey in Jiangsu, 73 percent of officials said that the ALL had led them to be more attentive to their duties and had increased their awareness of rule by law.[77]

Finally, administrative litigation may play a part in enlarging the still small bundle of rights villagers possess. Legal knowledge and assertiveness is growing in the countryside, and in our 1997–98 survey 14 percent of the villagers queried in Anhui, Beijing, Hebei, Fujian, Jiangsu, Jiangxi, and Shandong judged the ALL to be "very useful." In a Sichuan case that may portend things to come, a villager sued the township police for failing to take action against a mentally unstable man who was harassing him. The stalker repeatedly demanded money from the villager and eventually drove him to leap from the second floor of his home, thereby injuring himself. When the case was turned over to the city court, it halted the proceedings because there was no regulation that stipulated a public security bureau could be required to pay compensation for its inaction. After receiving an account of the case from the municipal court, Sichuan's provincial court reported it to the Supreme Court and asked for an interpretation. The Supreme Court ruled that public security bureaus should bear responsibility for compensation if, owing to a failure to fulfill their duties, citizens, legal persons, or other organizations' legal rights are violated. On July 17, 2001, the Supreme Court issued this decision to the nation as a legal interpretation (No. 23).[78] This ruling has already paved the way for other plaintiffs to file similar suits. When Jiangxi villagers filed two lawsuits in 2002 against a county public security bureau for inaction, they no longer had to appeal all the way to the Supreme Court to establish their claim to compensation.[79]

Some Implications

China's judicial system remains deeply embedded in politics. For rural litigants, a strong legal argument is indispensable, but even compelling evidence can fail to produce a favorable verdict. Just as important as a legal case per se are the political resources villagers mobilize in the course of filing suits and navigating their way through the courts. To offset the many advantages defendants enjoy, including the propensity of judges and other officials to protect one another,[80] plaintiffs often need to secure support from advocates within officialdom or in the media. Collective action, or the threat of it, can also increase the likelihood of winning, so long as litigants frame their demands and act in a way that does not alienate potential allies. Consequently, in many cases, pursuing a complaint does not entail seeking redress through the courts *or* through other institutions (e.g., people's congresses, letters and visits offices, high-ranking officials, the media), but both—used together or in sequence (defendants also, of course, rally whatever extrajudicial support they can muster throughout the process). In administrative litigation at least, mobilization seldom involves a choice between recourse to the law *or* to other strategies, but recourse to the law *and* to other strategies.[81]

The evidence presented in this chapter also provides a window on state–society relations in China. In particular, focusing on the interplay of plaintiffs, defendants, and third parties puts courts in a broad, political context and draws attention to the inner workings of a far-flung, many-layered state. That complainants can sometimes locate backers among the authorities encourages us to abandon dichotomies such as state-versus-society and us-against-them and to examine how specific parts of the state interact with (and provide opportunities for) particular social forces. What emerges when we undertake an "anthropology of the state"[82] is less a monolith than a hodgepodge of disparate actors, some of whom have multiple identities and conflicting interests.[83] Disaggregating the Chinese state, much as it does in Diamant and Tanner's chapters, reveals institutions that sometimes work at cross-purposes. Unpacking political power also highlights the state's segmented, layered structure, helps us understand how litigants work the terrain between courts and people's congresses, or lower courts and higher courts, and enables us to see how villagers' strategies adapt to the contours of a reforming regime as they discover which openings can be exploited and where their best opportunities lie.[84]

Peering under the hood of the state also clarifies some of the reasons why officials at the Center continue to promote the ALL. It supports the idea, for example, that the current legal revival has as much to do with bureaucratic regularization as with any abiding commitment to individual rights or the rule of law,[85] and suggests that empowering ordinary people to serve as watchdogs can make sense even to dyed-in-the-wool Leninists, who, like trucking companies that print 800 numbers on the back of their rigs, need on-the-ground sources of information if they are to uncover and stop misconduct by their local agents. Seen in this light, the ALL is first and foremost a solution to a principal-agent problem: it has less to do with liberal ideology or any newfound affection for citizens' rights and more to do with cadre monitoring.

It is still far too early to gauge the long-term impact of the ALL in rural China. Many villagers undoubtedly continue to associate "law" with a duty to obey rather than rights against the state. For such people, laws exist to punish, not to protect;[86] they are instruments of domination, not weapons to be deployed in disputes with local officials. Even so, some villagers, particularly the better-educated and better-off,[87] have adopted a view that laws can be used to "name, blame, and claim"[88] and that they provide a means to check improper official conduct. As time passes, the ALL may take on a life of its own as rural people with deep grievances, a little legal knowledge, and outside support persist in litigating. These individuals, like the workers described in Mary Gallagher's chapter, may choose to ignore the defects of existing legal institutions and to use the laws they find at hand to press for their legal rights and interests. About 100,000 administrative suits have been filed annually in recent years, and there are signs that rights consciousness is on the rise.[89] Should confidence in the ALL spread, a reform designed to extend the life of an authoritarian regime may play a part in nudging China a step closer to the rule of law.

Notes

For helpful comments, we would like to thank Anita Chan, Donald Clarke, Neil Diamant, Marc Galanter, Stanley Lubman, Randall Peerenboom, and Jonathan Unger. Generous financial support was provided by the Asia Foundation, the Henry Luce Foundation, the Research and Writing Program of the John D. and Catherine T. MacArthur Foundation, the Research Grants Council of Hong Kong, the Institute of East Asian Studies at the University of California at Berkeley, and Hong Kong Baptist University.

1. *Renmin ribao*, 10 April 1989, 1; also Yang Haikun, "Baituo xingzheng susong zhidu kunjing de chulu" [The way out of the difficult situation in the administrative litigation system], *Zhongguo faxue* [Chinese Legal Science], no. 3 (June 1994): 51; Minxin Pei, "Citizens v. Mandarins: Administrative Litigation in China," *China Quarterly*, no. 152 (December 1997): 835.

2. Randall Peerenboom, "Globalization, Path Dependency, and the Limits of Law: Administrative Law Reform and Rule of Law in the People's Republic of China," *Berkeley Journal of International Law* 19, no. 2 (2001): 217; Pei, "Citizens v. Mandarins," 843–44. On doubts about the representativeness of Pei's sample, however, see Stanley B. Lubman, *Bird in a Cage: Legal Reform in China after Mao* (Stanford, Calif.: Stanford University Press, 1999), 210. Statistics concerning redress hinge on the interpretation of withdrawn cases, some of which undoubtedly arise due to intimidation rather than negotiation. That said, the likelihood of plaintiffs prevailing, even if considerably lower than 40 percent, compares favorably with rates in the United States (12 percent) and Taiwan and Japan (4–8 percent) (Randall Peerenboom, *China's Long March Toward Rule of Law* [Cambridge: Cambridge University Press, 2002], 400).

3. On obstacles to implementation, see Veron Mei-Ying Hung, "Administrative Litigation and Court Reform in the People's Republic of China," Ph.D. diss., Stanford Law School, June 2001; and Jianfu Chen, *Chinese Law: Towards an Understanding of Chinese Law, Its Nature and Development* (The Hague: Kluwer Law International, 1999), 155–56.

4. For the quoted text, see Lubman, *Bird in a Cage*, 209. See also Hung, "Administrative Litigation," 273–74, 329; and Robyn Marshall, "Administrative Law in the People's Republic of China: A Process of Justice," Ph.D. diss., Australian National University, 2003, 253, 259. Assessments that highlight achievements include Peerenboom, "Globalization, Path Dependency," 161–264; and Pei, "Citizens v. Mandarins," 832–62.

5. On people who dare not sue, are not willing to sue, or don't know how to sue, see Hung, "Administrative Litigation," 129–59.

6. For more on the sampling in this survey, see Lianjiang Li, "Political Trust in Rural China," *Modern China* 30, no. 2 (2004): 228–58. A survey of 745 villagers in Shanxi also showed that about 10 percent of the respondents would consider "seek-

ing assistance from a lawyer or the court" if they had a conflict with a government agency (Shi Qinghua and Chen Kai, "Xian jieduan nongmin falü yishi fenxi" [An analysis of legal consciousness of today's farmers], *Zhongguo nongcun guancha* [Rural China Survey], no. 2 [March 2002]: 73).

7. Susan Finder, "Like Throwing an Egg Against a Stone? Administrative Litigation in the People's Republic of China," *Journal of Chinese Law* 3, no. 1 (Summer 1989): 10, 28.

8. On 12,688 out of 18,841 villagers in a Shaanxi township joining an administrative suit concerning excessive fees, see Thomas P. Bernstein and Xiaobo Lü, *Taxation Without Representation in Contemporary Rural China* (New York: Cambridge University Press, 2003), 193–95. Benjamin Liebman mainly discusses multiparty suits filed under the Civil Procedure Law, though he notes that rural plaintiffs have also filed similar suits under the ALL (see Liebman, "Class Action Litigation in China," *Harvard Law Review* 111, no. 6 [April 1998]: 1523–41, 1530–31).

9. On lawsuits being a last resort, see Hung, "Administrative Litigation," 132–33. On a long-simmering water dispute in which non-judicial forms of pressure set the stage for a collective suit, see Zhang Heping and Zong Xuan, "Wenzhou nongmin gao dao buzuowei de xian zhengfu" [Farmers in Wenzhou win a lawsuit against county government inaction], *Minzhu yu fazhi* [Democracy and Legality], no. 7 (6 April 2001): 11–13.

10. Forty-six percent of the officials who responded to a Hunan survey of agencies involved with public security, commerce, hygiene, construction, and government (*zhengfu*) recalled that they believed the law would decrease administrative efficiency shortly after it was enacted. By 1996, only 5 percent expressed this concern (see Jiang Ming'an, *Zhongguo xingzheng fazhi fazhan jincheng diaocha baogao* [An investigative report of the course of China's administrative legal development] [Beijing: Falü Chubanshe, 1998], 348). Of course, this reduction may have occurred partly because officials concluded that the law did not have teeth and was unlikely to affect them. The survey also assumed that respondents had been officials since the early 1990s and could accurately remember what they thought then. On "amazingly few [ALL] cases relative to the total number of specific administrative acts," see Peerenboom, *China's Long March*, 404; also, Hung, "Administrative Litigation," 129–89.

11. Chen Lumin, "Dou shi pufa re de huo" [The disaster is all due to the legal education drive], *Minzhu yu fazhi*, no. 11 (6 June 2001): 31–32.

12. Zhang Cuiling, "Zenyang duidai zheli de nongmin shangfang—Anhui Chengzhuang shijian diaocha baogao" [How to deal with farmers lodging complaints? An investigative report on Anhui's Chengzhuang incident], *Fazhi yu xinwen* [Legality and News], no. 1 (January 2002): 6.

13. Ma Zhongdong, "Huan gei wo, yige gong min de quanli" [Return me my citizenship rights], *Fazhi shijie* [Legal World], no. 1 (January 2000): 36–37.

14. See Wang Zhiquan, "WTO neng gei nongmin dailai shenmo?" [What can WTO bring farmers?], *Fazhi shijie* [Legal World], no. 4 (April 2002): 6; Yang Xuewu, "Ling ren tongxin de zaoyu" [Deplorable mistreatment], *Nan feng chuang* [Window on the South Wind], no. 4 (April 2001): 39.

15. On the extent to which the *pufa* campaign has aided villagers in learning about laws, the results were: 23 percent, "very helpful"; 53 percent, "a little helpful"; 7 percent, "not helpful"; 17 percent, "there is no such campaign in my village."

16. Wang Zhiquan, "WTO neng gei nongmin dailai shenmo," 6. On lawyers who have been detained for helping villagers lodge complaints, see Hung, "Administrative Litigation," 158–59.

17. In one survey, having a good lawyer was rated a very important determinant of success by 83 percent of ALL plaintiffs (Jiang Ming'an, *Zhongguo xingzheng fazhi*, 430). It is sometimes difficult, however, to obtain legal representation because there is limited monetary reward in handling most ALL cases (Marshall, "Administrative Law," 212).

18. Zhu Xiaokai and Chu Jie, "Nongjia han zhuanggao gonganju" [A farmer sues the public security bureau], *Fazhi daokan* [Legal Guide], no. 11 (November 2000): 4–6.

19. Peng Fangzhi, "Anningcun diaocha" [Investigation of Anning Village], in "Nongcun nongmin" [The countryside and farmers], ed. Zhao Shukai (mimeo), 57–61. On successful collective suits against unlawful local taxes in rural Sichuan, see Pei, "Citizens v. Mandarins," 851.

20. On Party and government interference being most common before a case is accepted, see Hung, "Administrative Litigation," 160; and Marshall, "Administrative Law," 259. Unlike courts in some countries, Chinese courts can reject litigation. The decision is supposed to be based on the merits of the case, but the rules that govern this are not always clear or consistent (Donald Clarke, Professor of Law, University of Washington, personal communication, September 2002).

21. Yang Haikun, "Baituo xingzheng susong," 54. On avoiding litigation by issuing decisions in the Party's name, see also Jiang Ming'an, *Zhongguo xingzheng fazhi*, 351; and Peerenboom, "Globalization, Path Dependency," 223. But since Party officials must formally act through government organs, for instance, when they detain a person, this loophole may not be as large as it appears (Donald Clarke, Professor of Law, University of Washington, personal communication, September 2002).

22. Yang Haikun, "Baituo xingzheng susong," 52. On the narrow scope of the ALL, see Chen, *Chinese Law*, 156–58; and Lubman, *Bird in a Cage*, 206–7. Peerenboom ("Globalization, Path Dependency," 212) notes that China is not the only nation that prohibits review of abstract acts, but that such countries are in the minority. Marshall ("Administrative Law," 190) finds the distinction between abstract and specific acts to be a gray area amenable to abuse by officials who wish to shield their decision making from popular scrutiny.

23. Yang Haikun, "Baituo xingzheng susong," 52; also, interview with a researcher at the Development Research Center of the State Council, Beijing, 1999. According to an assistant judge in the administrative department of the Supreme Court, in some places courts are particularly hesitant to accept cases involving (1) birth control, owing to their sensitivity and resistance from township governments and public security bureaus, and (2) rural taxes and fees, because they often involve large numbers of plaintiffs and judicial officials fear that accepting these cases will produce a flood of similar suits (Gan Wen, "Woguo xingzheng susong zhidu fazhan jincheng

diaocha baogao" [Investigative report on the development course of our country's administrative litigation system], in *Zouxiang fazhi zhengfu* [Toward government by laws], ed. Ying Songnian and Yuan Shuhong [Beijing: Falü Chubanshe, 2001], 466).

24. On locations in which all suits related to birth control and fees are considered "high voltage lines" and are rejected in the name of defending national policy and facilitating government work, or where courts must have the approval of the Party committee, government and people's congress to accept such cases, see Jiang Ming'an, *Zhongguo xingzheng fazhi*, 351–52.

25. Yang Haikun, "Baituo xingzheng susong," 55.

26. Fan Jinxue, "Lun falü xinyang weiji yu Zhongguo fazhihua" [On the crisis of faith in law and China's effort to build the rule of law], *Shandong shehui kexue* [Shandong Social Sciences], no. 6 (November 1997): 49. See also Wang Binglu, "Yingxiang xiangzhen ganbu falü yishi xingcheng de zhuyao yinsu" [Primary factors that affect the formation of township officials' legal consciousness], *Zhongguo nongcun guancha* [Rural China Survey], no. 1 (January 1999): 63. Hung ("Administrative Litigation," 179) argues that the "heavy reliance on local funds exerts tremendous pressure on judges."

27. Li Chao, "Min gao guan, kanke qi zai liu shen, guan baisu, yuan yu renda jiandu" [An administrative lawsuit lasts seven years and has six trials, the government loses due to the supervision of a people's congress], *Minzhu yu fazhi*, no. 5A (6 March 2002): 41. On judges feeling beholden to local governments that provide courts salaries, housing, and benefits, see Peerenboom, "Globalization, Path Dependency," 214–15.

28. Zhao Changfan, "Jianqing nongmin fudan yao kao falü" [Reducing farmers' burdens must rely on the law], *Minzhu yu fazhi*, no. 2 (February 1993): 28–29.

29. *Fazhi ribao* [Legal Daily], 16 March 1993.

30. On construing legal standing narrowly, see Peerenboom, "Globalization, Path Dependency," 235.

31. Li Chao, "Min gao guan," 40–41. Support within the village and the threat of collective action can also be critical. On representatives from 134 households signing or thumb-printing a petition that denounced a township decision to close a village clinic (and the village leadership endorsing it), see Li Jihong, "Xiangzhengfu weifa xiao nüzi buqu shanggao" [A township broke the law and a young woman refused to give in and sued], *Fazhi yuekan* [Legality Monthly], no. 1 (January 2002): 34–36.

32. On such settlements, see Pei, "Citizens v. Mandarins," 839, 843. On resolving cases through disguised forms of mediation (e.g., *xietiao*), see Hung, "Administrative Litigation," 260–65. Marshall ("Administrative Law," 211) prefers the term "pre-end-of-trial settlement" because judges are often intimately involved in the process.

33. In each of the years from 1997 to 2001, between 31 percent and 56 percent of suits filed under the ALL were withdrawn (see Table 2.1). On withdrawn cases often representing out-of-court settlements (rather than official pressure), see Pei, "Citizens v. Mandarins," 843–44. Reasons for withdrawal include "an administrative organ realizes it is in the wrong and alters its act"; "plaintiffs come to realize a suit is groundless"; or "the parties settle out of court" (see Hung, "Administrative Litigation," 258–59). Although some of the judges Hung interviewed said that pressure to

drop a suit was not a problem or a problem of the past, other interviewees and an internal investigation conducted in Guangdong found that many plaintiffs were pressured to withdraw their cases by administrative organs. For analysis of the many reasons behind withdrawal, see Marshall, "Administrative Law," 233–38; and Jiang Ming'an, *Zhongguo xingzheng fazhi*, 336–37.

34. Hu Zhenjie, "Gongyi: nongmin gaodao gonganju" [A farmer from Gongyi wins a lawsuit against the public security bureau], *Fazhi yu xinwen*, no. 12 (December 1998): 8–10.

35. Peerenboom ("Globalization, Path Dependency," 195, 215, 224) argues that direct intervention by the Party in specific cases is the exception and is declining. Others have detailed substantial interference (see Hung, "Administrative Litigation").

36. Jin Kunping, Hu Jie, and Liang Jian, "Fayuan wei 7000 nongmin chengqi baohusan" [The court raises a protective umbrella for 7,000 rural people], *Zhengfu fazhi* [Government and Legality], no. 11 (November 1998): 39–41. On defendants' wining and dining judicial personnel and seeking out leaders at higher levels to apply pressure on courts, see Jiang Ming'an, *Zhongguo xingzheng fazhi*, 352.

37. The president of a provincial high court, for instance, has the same rank as a deputy provincial governor rather than a governor (Marshall, "Administrative Law," 206).

38. Hung, "Administrative Litigation," 162–63. She concludes (274) that judges remain susceptible to bribery and interference, and despite recent improvements, many local officials still lack a thorough understanding and respect for laws.

39. Yang Haikun, "Baituo xingzheng susong," 51; see also Wang Binglu, "Yingxiang xiangzhen ganbu," 63. On threats to impartiality arising from outside control of funds and material resources, see Finder, "Like Throwing an Egg Against a Stone," 23; and Marshall, "Administrative Law," 198–99. On county leaders retaliating against a county court by withholding judges' salaries, and on people's congress deputies being mobilized to vote against court heads who ruled against the government, see Jiang Ming'an, *Zhongguo xingzheng fazhi*, 344–45.

40. In a survey of Anhui judges, respondents noted that interference in ALL cases, when it appeared, came mainly from administrative organs (72 percent), Party organs (52 percent), people's congresses (23 percent), and unspecified outside parties (38 percent) (Jiang Ming'an, *Zhongguo xingzheng fazhi*, 444). To be fair, when local protectionism, judicial corruption, or intra-agency disputes appear, Party organs may intervene to ensure that a final outcome is in accord with the law (Randall Peerenboom, Professor of Law, University of California at Los Angeles, personal communication, August 2003).

41. Yang Haikun, "Baituo xingzheng susong," 52. Also see Li Chao, "Min gao guan," 41; and Wang Zhiquan, "Daguansi nan zai nali?" [Why is suing difficult?], *Fazhi shijie*, no. 10 (October 2000): 10. On officials who prefer not to "condescend" to go to court with ordinary citizens, see Finder, "Like Throwing an Egg Against a Stone," 18. Although courts are free to proceed without the defendant, courts nonetheless sometimes allow defendants to frustrate proceedings in this way.

42. Yang Bingsheng, Luo Laidong, and Lu Chunlai, "Xingzheng lingdao chuting weihe shanshan laichi?" [Why are administrative leaders so slow in coming to

court?], *Fazhi ribao*, 24 October 2000, cited in Hung, "Administrative Litigation," 161–62.

43. Jiang Ming'an, *Zhongguo xingzheng fazhi*, 352.

44. This may become more common. A July 24, 2002, Supreme Court interpretation requires a court to invalidate all evidence provided by defendants who fail to respond to a subpoena "without a legitimate [*zhengdang*] reason" (see "Zuigao renmin fayuan guanyu xingzheng susong zhengju ruogan wenti de guiding" [A Supreme Court measure concerning certain questions on evidence in administrative litigation], http://www.court.gov.cn/lawdata/explain/executivecation/200303200028.htm [accessed 3 June 2004]).

45. Luo Shui, "Qiang zheng fakuan shangren, xiangzhengfu baisu peiqian" [A township government loses a lawsuit and pays compensation for extorting fines by force and injuring a villager], *Fazhi shijie*, no. 4 (April 2002): 17–18.

46. Xiao Ming, "Nongmin gao dao gonganju" [A farmer wins a lawsuit against the public security bureau], *Minzhu yu fazhi*, no. 3 (6 February 2001): 50–51.

47. Peerenboom (*China's Long March*, 399) notes that lower courts may even encourage such actions by ruling for an agency but then telling the plaintiff to appeal to a higher court that is less subject to local protectionism.

48. Pei ("Citizens v. Mandarins," 847) argues: "Given the higher professional qualifications of judges and legal staff in the appellate courts and their relative insulation from local government agencies involved in the lawsuits, it is reasonable to assume that Chinese appellate courts exercise a higher level of impartiality and autonomy in judicial review." The Hunan High Court, for one, has noted that as many as 80 percent of initial rulings by some lower courts are reversed because the law was not enforced impartially (Gan Wen, "Woguo xingzheng susong," 468).

49. Zhu Xiaokai and Chu Jie, "Nongjia han zhuanggao gonganju," 4–6.

50. See Li, "Political Trust"; Kevin J. O'Brien, "Neither Transgressive Nor Contained: Boundary-Spanning Contention in China," *Mobilization* 8, no. 1 (February 2003): 51–64; and Kevin J. O'Brien, "Rightful Resistance," *World Politics* 49, no. 1 (October 1996): 31–55.

51. See Bernstein and Lü, *Taxation Without Representation*, ch. 6; and Kevin J. O'Brien, "Collective Action in the Chinese Countryside," *China Journal*, no. 48 (July 2002): 151–53.

52. On the muckraking television show "Focus," see Alex Chan, "From Propaganda to Hegemony: *Jiaodian Fangtan* and China's Media Policy," *Journal of Contemporary China* 11, no. 30 (February 2002): 35–51. But it is also common for local authorities to delay, censor, or block media coverage of ALL cases (see Hung, "Administrative Litigation," 115–23). On "letters and visits," see Laura M. Luehrmann, "Facing Citizen Complaints in China," *Asian Survey* 43, no. 5 (September–October 2003): 845–66.

53. For a journalist's account of this fire, see Harrison E. Salisbury, *The Great Black Dragon Fire: A Chinese Inferno* (Boston: Little Brown, 1989).

54. Peng Fei, "Shi nongmin zhapian, haishi zhengfu keng nong?" [Do farmers cheat the government, or does the government frame farmers?], *Fazhi yu xinwen*, no. 12 (December 2000): 4–7.

55. On these regulations, see Luehrmann, "Facing Citizen Complaints."

56. Wang Zhiquan, "Shangfang nongmin bei cuopan, rujin wuzui fan jiayuan" [Rural complainants are wrongfully convicted, now they return home acquitted], *Fazhi shijie*, no. 2 (February 2000): 33.

57. On the wide discretion courts enjoy under the ALL to justify nonpublic hearings, see Pitman B. Potter, "The Administrative Litigation Law of the PRC: Judicial Review and Bureaucratic Reform," in *Domestic Law Reforms in Post-Mao China*, ed. Pitman B. Potter (Armonk, N.Y.: M. E. Sharpe, 1994), 286; and Hung, "Administrative Litigation," 114–15.

58. Lian Jimin, "Min gao guan renda jiandu zuo houdun" [People's congress supervision supports ordinary people suing officials], *Minzhu yu fazhi*, no. 7 (6 April 2000): 28–30. On chairs of local people's congress standing committees using their institutional power to obstruct administrative litigation, however, see Marshall, "Administrative Law," 250.

59. Li Chao, "Min gao guan," 40–41.

60. On "skipping levels" (*yueji*), see Kevin J. O'Brien and Lianjiang Li, "The Politics of Lodging Complaints in Rural China," *China Quarterly*, no. 143 (September 1995): 778; and Lianjiang Li and Kevin J. O'Brien, "Villagers and Popular Resistance in Contemporary China," *Modern China* 22, no. 1 (January 1996): 43. On this practice in earlier times, see Jonathan K. Ocko, "I'll Take It All the Way to Beijing: Capital Appeals in the Qing," *Journal of Asian Studies* 47, no. 2 (May 1988): 291–315.

61. Zhang Cuiling, "Zenyang duidai," 4–8.

62. Liu Wujun, "Shandai shumin de shangfang" [Treat villagers who lodge complaints well], *Fazhi yu xinwen*, no. 1 (January 2002): 9.

63. Wang Zirui and Wang Songmiao, "Yueji shangfang qineng yancheng?" [How can the government severely punish those who bypass levels when lodging complaints?], *Renmin xinfang* [People's Visits and Letters], no. 12 (December 2001): 31.

64. Peng Fei, "Shi nongmin zhapian," 4–7.

65. For typical enforcement problems, see Hung, "Administrative Litigation," 270–72; and Yang Haikun, "Baituo xingzheng susong," 52.

66. Cited in Peerenboom, *China's Long March*, 442.

67. Hao Fu, "Xinfangban zhuren biancheng shangfang ren" [A director of the letters and visits office becomes a complainant], *Fazhi shijie*, no. 4 (April 2002): 12–15.

68. Jiang Ming'an, *Zhongguo xingzheng fazhi*, 353.

69. You Zhanhong, "Nongmin wenti heshi jie?" [When will the peasant problem be resolved?], *Zhengfu fazhi*, no. 3 (March 1999), 11.

70. A villager in Jiangxi stressed that most rural people were in no position to engage in protracted legal struggles. He compared the law to a knife and insisted that officials held its entire handle, so that people like himself would have to grab it by its blade if they wished to sue (interview, Jiangxi, 1999).

71. Wang Zhiquan, "Daguansi nan zai nali?" 10.

72. See also Thireau and Hua's essay, this volume; O'Brien, "Rightful Resistance," 52–55; and Michael W. McCann, *Rights at Work* (Chicago: University of Chicago Press, 1994).

73. Peng Fangzhi, "Anningcun diaocha," 57–61.

74. Zhang Jinming, "Nongmin Chen Haiquan de jiannan kangzheng, zhi ma?" [Is Chen Haiquan's difficult battle worthwhile?], *Ren yu fa* [Man and Law], no. 8 (August 1999): 18–21.

75. Peng Fangzhi, "Anningcun diaocha," 57–61.

76. Wang Binglu, "Yingxiang xiangzhen ganbu," 62.

77. Reported in Peerenboom, *China's Long March*, 404. A 1992 poll also found that 74 percent of government officials said that they had begun to exercise greater caution in their work owing to the ALL (reported in Pei, "Citizens v. Mandarins," 860).

78. Xiao Wanging, "Bashu nongmin 'min gao guan'" [A Sichuan farmer sued the government], *Lüshi yu fazhi* [Lawyers and Legality], no. 3 (March 2002): 16–20.

79. Lu Chengjian, "Xiean diechu shouhairen jiashu zhuanggao Tongguxian gonganju buzuowei" [Families of murder victims sue the Tonggu County public security bureau for inaction], *Minzhu yu fazhi*, no. 2A (6 February 2002): 37–39.

80. For many villagers a court is just another government department and judges are just another group of officials. "In the understanding of many rural people, judges (*fa guan*) are nonetheless officials (*guan*)" (Tian Chengyou and Li Yixiong, "Xiangtu shehui minjian fa yu jiceng faguan jiejue jiufen de celue" [Customs in rural communities and strategies of conflict resolution adopted by grassroots judges], *Xiandai faxue* [Modern Law Science] 24, no. 1 [February 2002]: 121; also Jiang Ming'an, *Zhongguo xingzheng fazhi*, 336). On the perception that officials protect each other, see Gan Wen, "Woguo xingzheng susong," 468. In a survey of 5,673 respondents from eleven cities, 40 percent deemed judges incompetent, unfair, or controlled by administrative agencies and the Party (see Hung, "Administrative Litigation," 138).

81. This is not unique to China. See, e.g., McCann, *Rights at Work*.

82. For this term, see Joel S. Migdal, *State in Society* (New York: Cambridge University Press, 2001), ch. 4.

83. Key organizers of a collective lawsuit that involved two-thirds of the villagers in a Shaanxi town ran the gamut from retired county and township officials, to former and sitting village cadres, to incumbent deputies in the county people's congress (Wang Haian, "Shang wan nongmin weihe shang fating?" [Why did over ten thousand rural people go to court?], *Zhengfu fazhi*, no. 11 [November 1998]: pp. 15–17).

84. On disaggregating the Chinese state, see Elizabeth J. Perry, "Trends in the Study of Chinese Politics: State-Society Relations," *China Quarterly*, no. 139 (September 1994): 704–13; O'Brien, "Rightful Resistance," 31–33; and Neil J. Diamant, "Making Love 'Legible' in China: Politics and Society during the Enforcement of Civil Marriage Registration, 1950–66," *Politics and Society* 29, no. 3 (September 2001): 453, 473.

85. Lubman, *Bird in a Cage*; Kevin J. O'Brien, *Reform Without Liberalization: China's National People's Congress and the Politics of Institutional Change* (New York: Cambridge University Press, 1990).

86. See Fan Jinxue, "Lun falü xinyang weiji," 49; and Li Changqi, "Nongcun fazhi jianshe ruogan jiben wenti de sikao" [Reflections on some basic questions regarding building rule of law in the countryside], *Xiandai faxue* 23, no. 2 (April 2001): 34. According to a Chinese analyst, "For a long time, many Chinese have not distinguished

between 'laws' and 'penalties'; they one-sidedly think that only criminal law is law" (Wang Junying, "Qian xi chuantong falü wenhua yu fazhi xiandaihua de chongtu" [A preliminary analysis of the conflict between traditional legal culture and legal modernization], *Zhongzhou xuekan* [Academic Journal of Zhongzhou], no. 1 [January 1998]: 61). Hung ("Administrative Litigation," 130–31) cites long-standing fears of encountering the legal system, embodied in such proverbs as "Don't go to courts when alive, don't go to hell after death."

87. Our 1997–98 survey showed that such people were more likely to rate the ALL "very useful" or "somewhat useful," and our 1999–2001 survey showed that they were also more likely to file suits under the ALL.

88. William Felstiner, Richard Abel, and Austin Sarat, "The Emergence and Transformation of Disputes: Naming, Blaming, and Claiming," *Law and Society Review* 15 (1980–81): 631–55.

89. On growing rights consciousness in the countryside, see David Zweig, "The Externalities of Development: Can New Political Institutions Manage Rural Conflict?" in *Chinese Society*, ed. Elizabeth J. Perry and Mark Selden (New York: Routledge, 2000), 120–42; Bernstein and Lü, *Taxation Without Representation*; Kevin J. O'Brien, "Villagers, Elections and Citizenship in Contemporary China," *Modern China* 27, no. 4 (October 2001): 407–35; O'Brien, "Rightful Resistance"; and Liebman, "Class Action Litigation." On rules consciousness prior to 1949, however, see R. Bin Wong, *China Transformed* (Ithaca, N.Y.: Cornell University Press, 1997), 235–37.

MARY E. GALLAGHER 3

"Use the Law as Your Weapon!"
Institutional Change and Legal Mobilization in China

"The Labor Law is a weapon to protect the rights of workers" reads an excerpt from a page in the official workers' newspaper heralding the second year of the law's implementation. The page details new regulations, shows pictures of child workers in a Yunnan mine, and has a write-in advice column for disgruntled workers as well as information about a legal-aid center for workers. Exhorting workers to "use the law as a weapon" is an apt and ironic phrase for this new emphasis on legal institutions. It reflects both the new importance that the state places on law as well as the state of labor politics, that is increasingly contentious and even violent (hence the need for a weapon).[1]

In the past several years labor disputes in China have risen at an exponential rate (see Figure 3.1). In 1994, 19,098 disputes occurred. The year-on-year rate jumped by 73 percent in 1995, 46 percent in 1996, 49 percent in 1997, and 31 percent in 1998. In 2002 labor disputes reached an all-time high of over 180,000.[2] This increase took place in tandem with rapid changes in industrial relations, a boom in foreign direct investment, important legal reforms, and a renewed commitment to state-enterprise reform/privatization by the central leadership. In this context, increasing contentiousness is perhaps not a complete surprise, though contentiousness that emerges as legal mobilization is intriguing in a regime characterized by underdeveloped legal institutions and an incomplete commitment to the rule of law. Such a growth in legal mobilization also seems at odds with much current analysis of the Chinese legal system, which depicts it as weak, easily corrupted, and subservient to the Chinese Communist Party (CCP).

This chapter argues that varying rates of legal mobilization across different types of firms are partly explained by patterns of legal and institutional change, and in particular by how new labor laws have been written. That is,

"Use the Law as Your Weapon!"   55

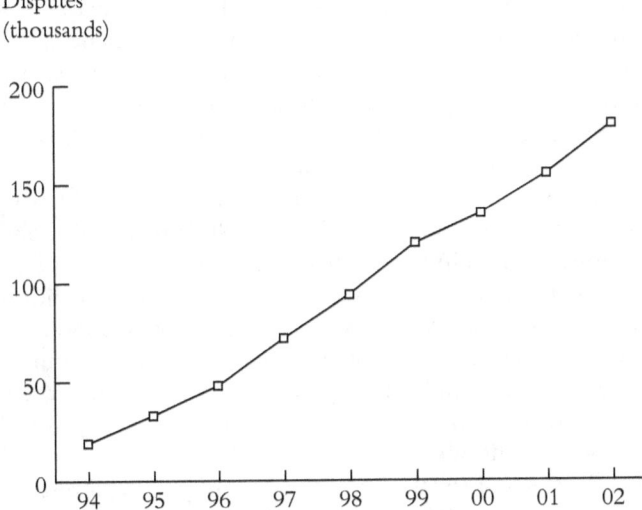

FIGURE 3.1. Labor Disputes at Arbitration, 1994–2002
SOURCE: *Labor Statistical Yearbook* [Laodong tongji nianjian] (Beijing: State Statistical Publishing House), various years.

despite widespread pessimism about the enforcement of Chinese laws, laws matter greatly for how disputes arise and how disputes are resolved. We must thus pay attention to how China's burgeoning labor legislation has shaped the individual and collective action of workers while serving to mobilize or restrict their mobilization. For some types of disputes and some types of workers, wider legal channels and greater recourse to legal institutions have resulted. Yet, at the same time, the transition to a "rule of law" and contract labor relations has delegitimized the moral grievances of a large majority of the Chinese workforce, in particular those of state-owned enterprise (SOE) workers.

Changes in the legal realm have also interacted with broader institutional changes to impact legal mobilization. The latter half of the paper focuses on these effects, including the decline of enterprise-level institutions that mediate labor conflict and the opening up of new channels beyond the enterprise, especially local-level arbitration and litigation in civil courts.

This paper focuses on labor disputes (*laodong zhengyi*). To qualify as a labor dispute under Chinese law, a dispute must meet certain conditions; it must, for example, occur between two parties who have established labor relations. Labor disputes as measured and presented in Chinese statistical information are recordings of formal filings of a labor conflict and, as such, do not include many kinds of labor conflict, such as informally resolved disputes. In addition, it is often reported that the government takes over the handling of large collective disputes in order to mitigate the social and political consequences of large-scale demonstrations and strikes.[3] Thus, there are many instances of labor conflict that are not recorded as "labor disputes" and therefore are not included in this analysis.

Data on labor disputes and on the institutional causes of differing rates of legal mobilization also cannot be used to conclude that labor conditions in China are better in one kind of enterprise than in another. In fact, the rate of disputes may not be correlated with the state of labor conditions in particular types of enterprises. When we examine national rates across ownership types we see increasing convergence across all non-state urban firms.[4] These firms all have rates of labor disputes four to seven times the rates seen in SOEs. We also see a low rate of disputes in rural enterprises. Most research on labor conditions in China, however, finds severe problems in working conditions and treatment of workers in private, foreign, and rural firms.[5] Some research has found this in SOEs as well.[6] Moreover, given the large number of layoffs and firm bankruptcies in the SOE sector since the mid-1990s, we would also expect that disputes in SOEs would have risen quickly even if labor conditions otherwise were relatively good.[7]

The rate of labor disputes is also not an accurate indicator of generalized labor conflict. The lower rates of legal mobilization in the state and rural enterprise sectors do not necessarily imply that workers in those firms are quiescent. The information provided on labor disputes simply cannot tell us which other types of mobilization are being used in place of or in tandem with legal mobilization, including demonstrations, protests, visits to letter and visits offices, or simply seeking out a friend or patron at higher levels.

Labor Law Legislation in China

Since the advent of economic reform in 1978, one of the Chinese government's main tasks has been to liberalize and invigorate its labor and employment system. This includes the creation of labor markets and the dismantling of a state labor-allocation system, the introduction of a labor-contract system that ends lifetime employment, and laws and regulations that recognize diverse types of employers, including foreign investors, private entrepreneurs and publicly held conglomerates. The Chinese leadership has also had to respond to China's increasing integration into the global economy. Integration brought greater competition for foreign investment and for export markets, making reform of the inflexible labor allocation system a necessity. Global economic integration has also drawn increased attention to China's domestic working conditions and labor relations.

The reform and overhaul of China's labor and employment system coincided with a more general effort to rely on laws and regulations as a primary mode of governance. This building of "rule of law" in China is a state-led project that has proceeded in fits and starts. Rule of law is intended to substitute for more radical political change, and to bring with it increased channels for citizens to seek redress for their grievances and to protect their legal rights. It is also designed to legitimate the rule of the CCP as an institution that can not only bring rapid economic growth but also ensure social stability through the use of laws and courts. The ability of an authoritarian ruling party to institutionalize China's new legal infrastructure is constantly questioned, not least because of the continuing position of the Party itself outside the law's parameters. That said, many government organizations, including the National People's Congress, bureaucratic agencies, local governments, and the State Council have all taken an active role in building the rule of law.

THE NATIONAL LABOR LAW OF 1995

Chinese labor legislation consists of laws that regulate and mediate labor relations, as well as laws and regulations that regulate labor disputes and contracts and supervise labor standards. The National Labor Law of 1995 is the foundation of these other laws and the starting point for all analysis of Chinese labor legislation. The drafting of this law began in the early 1980s as China's leadership experimented with liberalizing economic reforms. It took nearly fifteen years to build the necessary consensus within the leadership, the ministries, and the All-China Federation of Trade Unions (ACFTU) for its passage by the Standing Committee of the National People's Congress in July 1994.

The 1995 National Labor Law is the first comprehensive labor law in PRC history. Its far-reaching nature is important for two reasons. First, it enshrines the basic rights of all Chinese workers, erasing some of the legal differences between permanent, contract, seasonal, and migrant workers—differences that had long existed and had shaped enterprise treatment of workers.[8] Second, the law was comprehensive. It did not discriminate between types of enterprises based on ownership (public or private) or nationality (Chinese or foreign). It instead set a basic standard for all enterprises and granted them significant autonomy in deciding personnel and labor matters.[9] By recognizing these rights, the state has signaled its abdication as the administrator of employment, much as it has withdrawn from formerly key duties in favor of legislation and markets in other areas of China's economy and society.

LABOR DISPUTE SETTLEMENT

China's regulations on labor disputes have proceeded in tandem with the general development of labor law. The 1993 Regulations for the Settlement of Labor Disputes are the primary guide here as well as certain clauses in the 1995 Labor Law. There are also many supplementary guidelines and clarifications that have been issued by the Ministry of Labor, the State Council, and the Supreme Court. Labor disputes are defined as disputes between the employer and the employee regarding their mutual legal obligations and responsibilities as dictated by Chinese law or by the contents of the employment contract. Disputes can be individual or collective. Collective disputes must include three or more workers.

The settlement process has three stages. The first stage is non-compulsory and consists of a mediation process directed by the enterprise mediation committee, which is chaired by a trade union leader with participation by management and the employee(s). The mediation committee attempts to find a mutually acceptable solution to the dispute. As discussed below, this mode of resolution has declined swiftly over the past fifteen years.

The second stage is arbitration, which is an administrative process conducted by the local-level Labor Arbitration Committee (LAC) under the jurisdiction of the local Labor Bureau. Theoretically, the local LAC consists of a representative of enterprise management, a representative from the local trade union, and Labor Bureau administrators. In practice, it is more common for the committee to be made up entirely of Labor Bureau employees who specialize in the settlement of labor disputes. In complex or large disputes, the trade union may be asked to participate, but this is rare. In fact, many labor lawyers and arbitrators find that there is a large disparity between the trade union's role as set out in legislation and regulations and actual practice.

The LAC has two main modes of settlement: arbitrated mediation (*zhongcai tiaojie*) or arbitral judgment (*zhongcai caijue*).[10] Arbitrated mediation is a form of mediation, but unlike enterprise-level mediation, it includes active participation of the LAC. Mediation is almost always attempted first before proceeding to the more formal arbitral judgment. Arbitral judgments must decide who is at fault and then issue any required compensation. Arbitral judgments in China are not binding. Either side has the right to appeal the judgment in civil court. The court may uphold or overturn the arbitration decision. The civil court process also involves the right to appeal. In the past, few arbitration cases went to court and in most cases the court upheld the arbitration decision. In the past few years, however, the number of labor disputes adjudicated in courts has risen sharply. In 2001 Chinese courts heard over 100,000 labor disputes, a 33 percent increase from the year before and a marked increase from the mid-1990s.[11]

TABLE 3.1
Labor Disputes per 100,000 Employees by Ownership Type, 1998–2001

Type of Firm	1998	1999	2000	2001
State-owned enterprises	24.5	31.2	40.4	56.1
Urban collectives	69.2	106.2	154.6	197.0
Foreign-invested enterprises	384.0	456.0	327.0	300.6
Private enterprises	110.0	132.0	159.0	156.6
Rural collectives	9.6	7.9	3.1	1.8
Joint-owned and stock-holding	81.0	66.5	108.0	199.0
Individually owned (*geti*)	7.0	10.2	19.1	30.1

The cost of arbitration in China is fairly low but not inconsequential for a low-paid worker. For example, in Shanghai the arbitration fee is 300 yuan, which is 20 percent of the average monthly salary in the city. The cost of court appeals is 50 RMB for each appeal. These costs do not include the costs of legal representation, which is increasingly common for both sides in labor disputes.[12]

Legal Mobilization and Labor Contracts

One of the striking features of Chinese labor disputes is the variation between types of firms, in particular the low rate of disputes in SOEs compared to other types of urban firms, with the exception of small, individually owned businesses (see Table 3.1). The dispute rate of SOEs is consistently below that of foreign-invested enterprises, private companies, urban collectives, and shareholding and limited liability companies. Only the rates in rural collectives and individually owned urban businesses are lower.

SOEs have undergone several years of major restructuring, accompanied by massive layoffs. From 1998 to 2001, 25 million SOE workers were laid off. The official unemployment rate stands at just below 4 percent.[13] External organizations, however, place the true rate of unemployment at closer to 23 percent of the entire labor force.[14] State-enterprise workers have protested en masse in large demonstrations in Sichuan and Liaoning. In most large Chinese cities, reports of state-enterprise workers sitting in front of government and enterprise offices waiting for their grievances to be heard are commonplace.[15] Yet during this period, the rate of labor disputes in SOEs has remained far below that of other urban firms. This is true even when we take into account disputes mediated by other means. This includes disputes mediated at the firm level by the trade union and the mediation committee, as well as some of the disputes mediated directly by government intervention.[16] When we include these other disputes, the SOE rate in 2000 increases to 87 disputes per 100,000 workers. This remains one-third to one-fifth the rate of disputes in foreign companies (492 disputes per 100,000 workers), private companies (239), and urban collectives (296).[17]

Labor disputes in SOEs are low in part because the switch to an emphasis on legal labor relations has narrowed and redefined the obligations and responsibilities of state firms. New labor laws and the labor-contract system have also restricted SOE workers' claims by making it difficult, if not impossible, for workers to contest the loss of their old benefits and security through legal channels. Much of the previous "social contract," which characterized the state–worker relationship in many state socialist societies, is simply not included in the contractually based laws and regulations that guide labor relations today.

The "social contract" that existed between the Party and urban state-enterprise workers in China was especially strong. SOE workers enjoyed what is commonly known as the "iron rice bowl"—a system of lifetime employment and welfare entitlements that were directly tied to their enterprise. As a relatively small labor aristocracy in a mostly peasant country, these workers made up the vast majority of the urban working class—the bulwark of Communist power.[18] Heralded as "masters of the country," these workers enjoyed an exalted position in society. Materially, they enjoyed a standard of living and economic stability that rural Chinese could only dream about.[19]

This social contract and the entitlements it brought state workers had a strong moral dimension. Party ideology reminded these workers that, as participants in the revolution, they were using their labor not to earn their enterprises profit or market share but rather to contribute to the nation's well-being and build socialism. While wages remained low throughout the pre-reform period, the system of work-unit employment entitled state workers to an array of social welfare benefits, including retirement, medical care, education, daycare, housing, and consumer and shortage goods. These goods and the security they guaranteed were bequeathed to workers by the state. This state–worker tie was, of course, mediated by the enterprise, and workers were subject to the vagaries of enterprise managers and party leaders. Cultivating clientelistic ties to Party authorities therefore was a critical aspect of getting by and improving one's own position within the factory.[20] However, under normal circumstances (in the absence of criminal behavior or grave political mistakes), the enterprise could not lay off or fire workers. Wages, benefits, and lifetime security were guaranteed by the state in recognition of the workers' moral and material contributions to the socialist project.

This morally based social contract has been gradually but radically transformed in the reform period. This transformation has occurred largely through the implementation of the labor-contract system, which now structures the vast majority of Chinese workers' relationship to their employers. The emphasis on labor contracts has had a great impact on the way in which SOE workers relate to their enterprises.[21] The implementation of the labor-contract system (LCS) has shifted the employment relationship away from a long-term, morally infused social contract between the state and the class in whose name it ruled. Labor contracts, which are by nature both temporary and legalistic, not only clarify and attenuate ties between the worker and his enterprise; they also reduce the state to a regulatory and supervisory role.

The principles of the labor-contract system include:

1. A contract detailing terms of employment that is signed by the employee and employer and is approved by the local labor bureau. The contract details the length of employment, workday and vacation length, welfare benefits, wages, insurance, punishments for disciplinary infractions, and terms for change, renewal, and cancellation of the contract.

2. The contract is voluntary and renewal of the contract is dependent on the agreement of both parties.[22]

3. The contract can be broken. An employee may terminate the contract with thirty days' written notice. The enterprise may abrogate the contract if the company is experiencing severe production difficulties as stipulated by Article 27 of the National Labor Law.[23]

Supplementary regulations and circulars issued by the Ministry of Labor and other bureaucratic organs have further clarified the implementation of the labor-contract system. These regulations were intended to extend the system to all workers and all types of enterprises. They also specify procedures for the termination of labor relations and for payment of compensation to redundant workers. These regulations make clear the ways in which labor relationships can be severed in the event of firm ownership change, management change, merger or acquisition, or economic difficulty.[24]

The labor-contract system was implemented gradually in the 1980s and early 1990s. In 1992 in Shanghai only 12.3 percent of the workforce had signed labor contracts.[25] When the State Statistical Bureau stopped publishing data on the number of contract workers in 1996, the national average still hovered at around 50 percent of the workforce. By the turn of the century, however, virtually all formerly permanent workers in the state sector had signed labor contracts.[26] Shanghai's figures, 80 percent by 1997, 98 percent by 2002, mirror national reports that show rapid implementation of a policy that had previously been approached in a cautious fashion. This acceleration was accompanied by renewed emphasis on restructuring of SOEs, in particular, on large-scale layoffs of redundant employees.

With the rapid extension of the LCS and the acceleration of SOE reforms and layoffs in 1997, SOE workers became eminently easier to lay off, fire, and "send to society." Through application of the LCS, as dictated by the National Labor Law and its supplementary regulations, SOE workers' relationship to their work-unit and their claims on that work-unit were reduced to wages and benefits (in the event that they continued to work) and legally sanctioned compensation (in the event that they were laid off or fired). This reduction of the worker–enterprise relationship to a contractual relationship had consequences for legal mobilization by SOE workers. For example, the Ministry of Labor has ruled that disputes involving work-unit housing sales are not within their jurisdiction. For SOE workers, low-cost housing supplied by their workplace was one of the major perquisites of state employment, making up in part for low wages. Worker resistance to changes in their housing benefits cannot be channeled into labor disputes.[27] In addition, many LACs and courts will not accept cases that deal with issues related to *xiagang*,[28] on the grounds that this is also not within their jurisdiction. *Xiagang* is a government policy that has been implemented through administrative channels, not the courts or LACs. While there are many regulations and administrative instructions concerning *xiagang*, the word itself is not mentioned in the National Labor Law, which lays the basis for its exclusion from labor disputes unless there is also a solid contractual basis for the dispute. For example, if a permanent worker has signed a labor contract and has then been let go due to firm restructuring or privatization, the case will qualify as a labor dispute. This focus on the labor contract as the foundation of the employment relationship tends to restrict rather than expand the legal options of SOE workers.

This may seem at odds with what is commonly believed about contracts. In the Chinese labor context, the implementation of the labor-contract system was touted as a more efficient and modern way to administer labor relations. Contracts would allow firms to have greater autonomy in choosing employees and setting the terms of employment. Workers would be guaranteed some minimum terms of employment. Both sides would enter into employment relations more or less freely, without intervention from the state. The labor-contract system was thus intended to serve two somewhat conflicting interests—enhancing labor efficiency and flexibility, while also protecting workers' rights and interests.[29] How labor contracts affect the employment relations of Chinese workers, however, varies considerably across types of firms. For SOE workers, in particular, it is important to put the transition to contract labor in a historical and social context. State-enterprise workers experience labor contracts as a loss of rights and entitlements and as a diminution of their social and political position. The "social contract" of communism has been replaced with the legal contracts of a market economy.

Despite all the restructuring and reform of the past five to ten years, SOE workers are still less likely to file disputes against their employers. Through the use of contracts and legal regulations which allow for the termination of contracts and their nonrenewal, SOEs can shake off some of the moral expectations that SOE workers have of their firms. The labor contract specifies the firm's legal obligations and leaves the moral expectations of workers mostly aside. Because labor disputes are confined to the parameters of the legal labor relationship, moral claims cannot be addressed through these new legal institutions.

I have focused so far on how laws have been written and implemented, especially the restrictive content of labor contracts and the government's reliance on contractual language when defining disputes, as explanations for the lower rate of disputes among SOE workers. There are, however, other factors that may help explain why SOEs have lower rates. Authority relations in Chinese SOEs, as shown by Andrew Walder, are highly clientelistic. Workers often use personal connections to patrons to gain benefits and preferential treatment. This "communist neo-traditionalism," may be more long-lived than some have thought. Rather than lodging an official dispute, workers in state firms may still be inclined to work through informal networks. In interviews with labor lawyers, state-enterprise managers, and other experts on labor disputes, a common belief about state-enterprise workers, particularly older workers, is that they tend to rely on leaders and relationships (*zhao lingdao*) to resolve disputes related to employment.

In comparison to SOEs, private firms, urban collectives, and even restructured SOEs all have high rates of labor disputes. A low level of legal mobilization seems to be a characteristic of state firms but not a defining characteristic of other types of Chinese domestic firms. This finding adds some weight to Walder's claim that communist neotraditionalism is a variant of communist authority relations more generally and as such has no specific culturally Chinese component. Although the aggregate data used here is not helpful in probing the importance of clientelism in state firms, it remains an issue for future research.[30]

There is further evidence of the importance of the labor contract in shaping the legal mobilization of SOE workers. Even while the overall rate of disputes in SOEs is low, SOE workers are increasingly using the labor law to resist the state's recourse to contracts, with contractual disputes easily outnumbering all other types of disputes.[31] (See Figure 3.2.) That is, while workers in private firms and rural collectives are most concerned with salaries and benefits, SOE workers remain focused on the contract itself and the terms it sets for their employment and unemployment.[32] SOE workers

64 MARY E. GALLAGHER

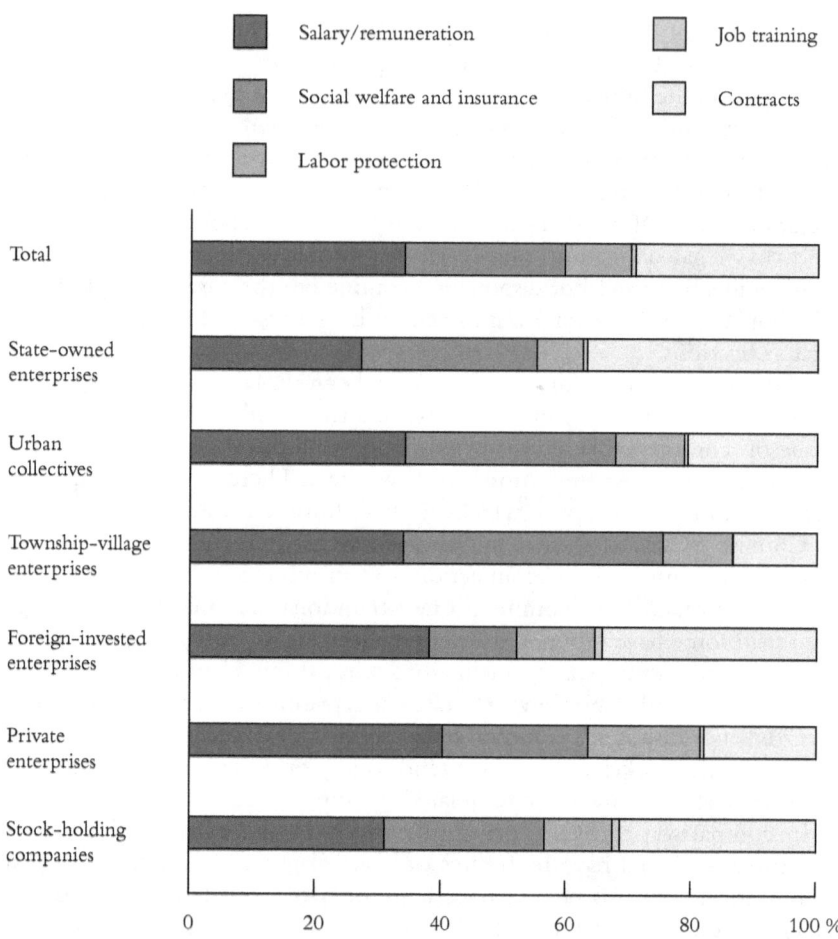

FIGURE 3.2. Causes of Disputes by Ownership, 2000
SOURCE: *Labor Statistical Yearbook* [Laodong tongji nianjian] (Beijing: State Statistical Publishing House), various years.

are clearly resisting their reduction in status from "masters of the nation" to mere commodities in China's new labor markets.

SOE workers' recourse to the labor law to contest contractual agreements is interesting when set against conclusions reached by other researchers. For example, Hurst and O'Brien find that among the worker demonstrations and sit-ins that take place in Chinese inland cities (where the unemployment rate is high and new employment opportunities scarce), issues of pensions and pension arrears are paramount.[33] They argue that pensions tend to arouse SOE workers to take the risk of demonstrating because "they are a symbolic recognition by the state and firm of an employee's years of devoted service."[34] Contestation over the labor contract, on the other hand, seems to impel workers to mimic the state's own recourse to legality and to draw the aggrieved toward court (or at least to the local arbitration committee.)[35]

Differences in types of protest (legal disputes vs. semi-legal or illegal demonstrations) might also be related to the fact that certain types of grievances are simply beyond the employment relationship defined by the labor contract. As stated earlier, LACs do not accept cases unless they are clearly within their jurisdiction. Embezzlement or mismanagement of pension funds (common reasons for the protests cited by Hurst and O'Brien) are not considered labor disputes, forcing the retirees to find other venues in which to lodge their complaints. The formalistic application of the labor law in LACs and their focus on existing labor relations is further evidence of the restriction of the employment relationship by the labor-contract system.[36] Contestation over the moral issues of past debts and future obligations to former permanent workers is pushed to the street.

Other evidence that state workers contest contracts can be seen in their resistance to the termination of the labor relationship. Previously, under the socialist system, this relationship was for life, cradle to grave, and extremely difficult to sever from either side. Under the labor-contract system, this relationship is temporary. Its ending through a negotiated agreement, a one-time payment of compensation, or through the expiration of the labor contract shuts off the worker's claim on that enterprise. Unlike a moral claim, with its emphasis on work completed, contributions given, and sacrifices made, the legal responsibility of the firm ends once the worker accepts the terms of the labor contract or the terms of the buyout (a practice common during this period of restructuring).[37] Many workers understand this and therefore try to delay the legal termination of labor relations for as long as possible.[38] Laid-off workers often choose to languish at home, "waiting for work" (*daiye*), rather than break off the labor contract entirely and enter the ranks of the unemployed. A recent survey of nearly 10,000 laid-off workers found that 91.5 percent did not wish to end labor relations with their former employers, despite the fact that many of their firms were near bankruptcy.[39] While the official media often charges these individuals with laziness and a weak mentality, in reality they wait in the hope that the continuing existence of the labor contract will result in compensation that takes their previous identity as permanent workers into account.[40]

In a recent news article, interviews with laid-off workers in China's Northeast demonstrate this desire to retain a labor relationship. Most of the interviewees had chosen to remain laid-off rather than to receive a one-time payment and to "enter society." Rather than indicating their passivity, the workers' decision to remain attached to their work-unit demonstrated their struggle to be compensated for their past moral relationship with the state firm. As one worker explained it: "I'd have to see the conditions, they could buy out my contract, (but) every year for RMB300? I worked there for 20 years, RMB6,000 is not acceptable, it's too little! If they gave me RMB20,000, then I'd think about it."[41] A fifty-three-year-old male worker in Nanning City, Guangxi, similarly felt that the new system was unjust for those who had worked for many years in the old:

> In three years, I will have to sever relations with my factory, I worked for the company for 29 years, I made a contribution to the company and to society, could you be shoved out like this? . . . Undertaking reform, in studying the market economy of other countries, there remains the problem of national character. Workers in other countries have worked for years and have some accumulation; while we have worked for years and years, made contributions to the company and to the nation, but we ourselves have no money. How can we be pushed to the market?[42]

These attitudes toward payment of compensation as mandated under the new contract-labor system suggest the level of conflict between the state and former permanent SOE workers. Chinese labor regulations now specify guidelines for economic compensation for termination or expiration of the labor contract. They do not, however, grant former permanent workers any special privileges.[43] They may be compensated for ending their contract and their years of employment, but not for their low wages or for "their contributions to socialism and the nation." In these conflicts the state and enterprise management often take a distinctly legalistic interpretation of their obligation, while the worker is left to emphasize his now discounted moral contributions.

SOE workers now frame their many grievances using both legal and extralegal claims, and in particular focus on the moral claim that they are owed something for their past contributions to the enterprise and the nation. In today's China, we see many protests that are distinctly moralistic, such as waiting in front of government or enterprise offices for handouts, remonstration via street protests, and even threats to commit suicide unless one's moral claims are addressed.

Modes of mobilization within the state sector thus remain largely traditionalistic, with legal mobilization trailing behind rates of mobilization in other types of firms. In part, this is a consequence of the state's own recourse to labor contracts, which has reshaped relations between employees and their firms. There may also be cultural and institutional legacies of socialist authority relations, which further incline workers toward modes of resolution that rely on vertical ties within the enterprise and beyond.

CHOICE AND PROCESS IN DISPUTE RESOLUTION

One of the most significant aspects of the National Labor Law and the regulations for the resolution of labor disputes (1993) is the range of options available to workers who wish to lodge a suit against their employer. The 1993 PRC regulations, in particular, allow either party to bypass enterprise-level mediation and proceed directly to local-level arbitration. Since the passage of these regulations, dispute resolution methods have shifted toward higher levels of arbitration and litigation. Enterprise mediation has suffered across the board and is no longer the principal method to resolve labor conflicts.

These changes in dispute resolution are closely tied to China's economic reforms, which have relied on creating a dynamic, non-state sector through liberalization of foreign direct investment (FDI) and, more recently, on nurturing domestic private industry. By the mid-1990s, the non-state sector had become a sizable presence in Chinese coastal cities and development zones. Large-scale strikes and well-publicized abuse of workers had already occurred in many foreign and private factories.[44] Leaving labor relations to the firm was clearly untenable. The Chinese government needed to restrain the ability of non-state owners and managers to dictate labor relations. Labor arbitration at the local level opened up new channels for dispute resolution.

The trends discussed in this section are relevant to our understanding of law and social change for several reasons. First, rising levels of arbitration and litigation have come at the expense of mediation, which is a method often associated with Chinese cultural sensibilities and the Communist past.[45] Various forms of mediation indeed continue to be promoted by arbitration committees and the courts, which makes its decline even more striking. This decline may indicate that the earlier popularity of mediation was closely tied to the lack of alternatives. Second, a higher level of legal mobilization is an indication that societal actors are increasingly using the law strategically. Chinese workers are becoming adept at pursuing methods of resolution that promise favorable outcomes. On the other hand, this mobilization, in particular the rising level of litigation, is also a reminder of the state's inability to find a workable resolution system between firms and the courts.

FIRM-LEVEL MEDIATION AND ITS DECLINE

Direct access to local-level arbitration has resulted in a steep decline in the use of firm-level mediation to resolve labor disputes (see Figure 3.3).[46] This decline has been most apparent in the foreign-invested sector, but even in other sectors the enterprise mediation rate has at best remained steady while disputes at the local arbitration level across all sectors and ownership have risen markedly (see Figure 3.4). In SOEs, for example, which are likely

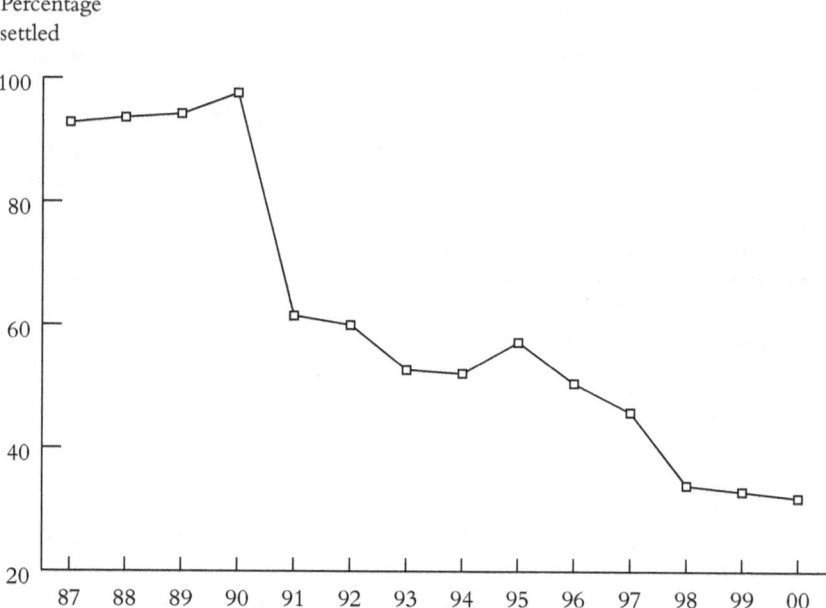

FIGURE 3.3. Labor Disputes Settled by Mediation, 1987–2000

to have the strongest capacity to engage in mediation, the proportion of mediated disputes has fallen to 39 percent of total disputes. Surveys in Shanghai show that while 73 percent of labor disputes were resolved by firm mediation in 1997, by 2002, nearly 40 percent of all cases did not even attempt mediation and instead proceeded directly to arbitration.[47] The rapid decline in mediation as a mode of dispute resolution provides more evidence to support Diamant's argument that mediation's role in China has been overestimated.[48] As Diamant points out, mediation is often the method most preferred by the state but it is often not the sole or even the most important method of resolving disputes. At varying times since 1949, the state has had the capacity and will to dictate or at least strongly encourage mediation for nearly every type of dispute.[49] In the reform era, however, with the explosion of new types of ownership and newly empowered economic actors, the state has not attempted to force mediation. When mediation is voluntary, and other methods are available, its role has declined sharply.

Foreign-invested and private enterprises have the highest rate of arbitration for labor disputes. They also have low (and declining) rates of mediation at the enterprise level. For example, in 2000, SOEs accepted over 21,000 labor disputes for enterprise-level mediation, while foreign-invested enter-

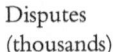

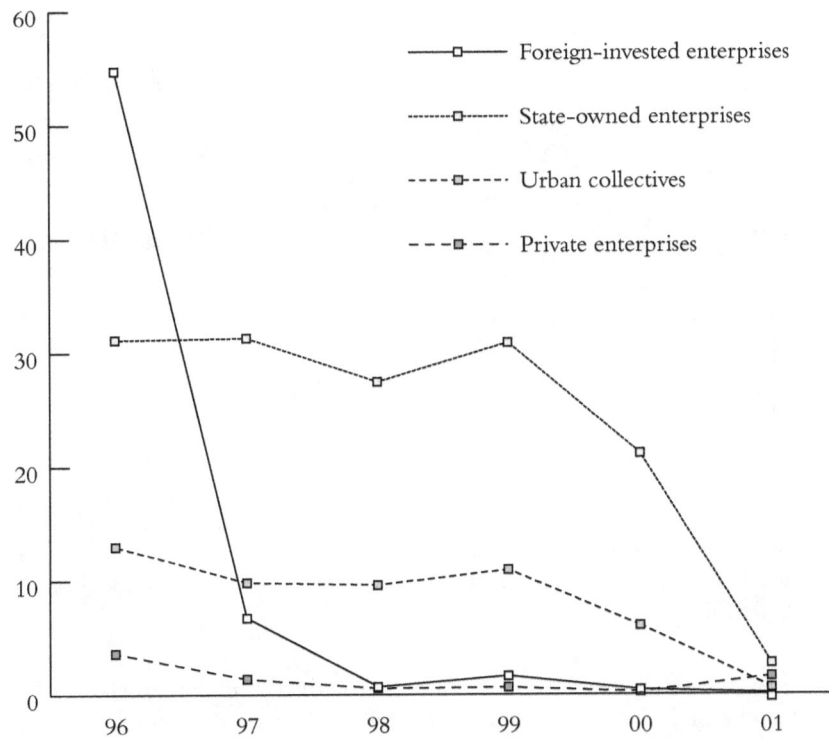

FIGURE 3.4. Number of Labor Disputes Mediated by Employer, 1996–2001
SOURCE: *Labor Statistical Yearbook* [Laodong tongji nianjian] (Beijing: State Statistical Publishing House), various years.

prises accepted only 447 and private enterprises accepted 251. The ability of SOEs to mediate disputes is directly related to the greater presence of enterprise-level trade unions, worker representative councils, and labor mediation committees.[50] On the other hand, the low level of unionization in private and foreign firms and the complete lack of other labor-related organizations lead to very high rates of arbitrated disputes.[51]

This finding, however, is not necessarily an indicator of workers' lack of power in non-state firms and their power in state firms. Chinese trade unions, which are directly under the control of the Communist Party, do not function as strong advocates of workers' rights and interests. Enterprise trade-union branches also lack legitimacy and respect in the eyes of most

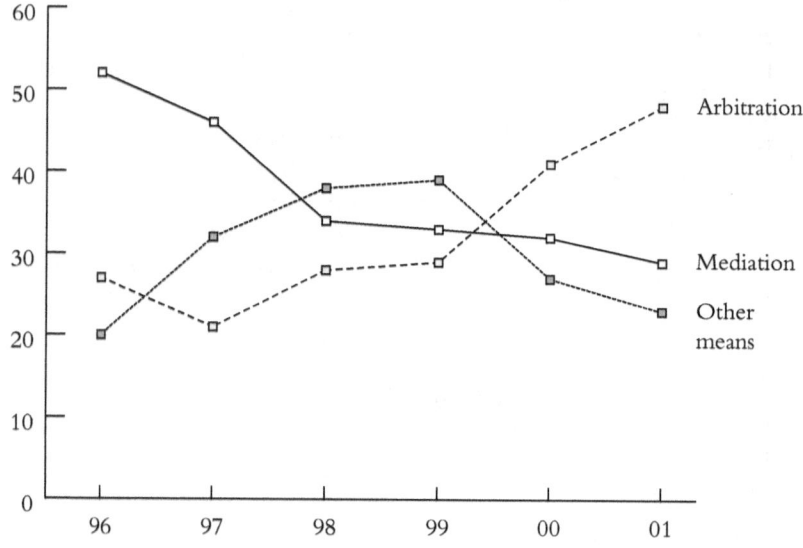

FIGURE 3.5. Labor Dispute Resolution, 1996–2001
SOURCE: *Labor Statistical Yearbook* [Laodong tongji nianjian] (Beijing: State Statistical Publishing House), various years.

workers.[52] The ability to proceed directly to arbitration may in fact indicate wider channels for legal mobilization by workers in the non-state sector. State-enterprise workers may be restricted by the presence of these "worker organizations" at the firm level and coerced into more informal, enterprise-controlled mediation.

Institutional differences between the state and non-state sectors are, however, beginning to wane. As privatization and restructuring continue, organizations such as the trade union are increasingly marginalized, eliminated, or merged with general administrative offices. Vertical ties that may have previously linked workers with cadres and managers have also been attenuated or erased. The ability of all firms to mediate labor relations under the current system is in doubt. An ironic result of marketization and firm autonomy is the increased need for the local state, especially the labor bureau, to become involved in firm-level disputes.

LOCAL LEVEL ARBITRATION AND SETTLEMENT

As mentioned above, local-level arbitration cases can be resolved through mediation, which is a negotiated settlement or an arbitration lawsuit that

"Use the Law as Your Weapon!" 71

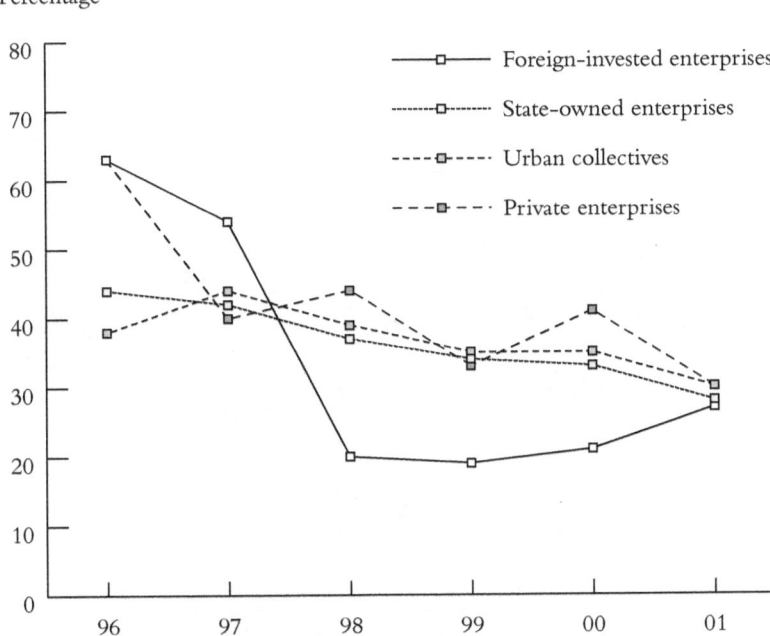

FIGURE 3.6. Percent of Labor Disputes Resolved by Mediation, 1996–2001
SOURCE: *Labor Statistical Yearbook* [Laodong tongji nianjian] (Beijing: State Statistical Publishing House), various years.

ends in an arbitral judgment. Mediation is often encouraged by LACs, which are always looking for ways to cut their caseloads. A large number of the cases are resolved "through other means." This category "through other means" includes three different outcomes. The most common, accounting on average for about 60 percent of arbitrated cases, is settlement. Settlement is distinct from mediation because it occurs privately between two parties. Another 20 percent of the cases are simply abandoned by the worker due to the time and money required to pursue the suit through the arbitration process. Finally, another 20 percent of cases are rejected by the LAC after it has already accepted the suit for hearing.[53] These cases are counted among the yearly disputes, but a ruling is not made.[54]

In examining arbitration at the local level, trends include a greater reliance on arbitration lawsuits and "other means" as avenues of dispute resolution. This is at the expense of local-level mediation (see Figures 3.5 and 3.6).[55] These trends suggest growing complexity in labor relations and also increasing litigiousness by Chinese workers (workers lodge well over 90 percent of labor disputes). These workers avoid resolution processes that en-

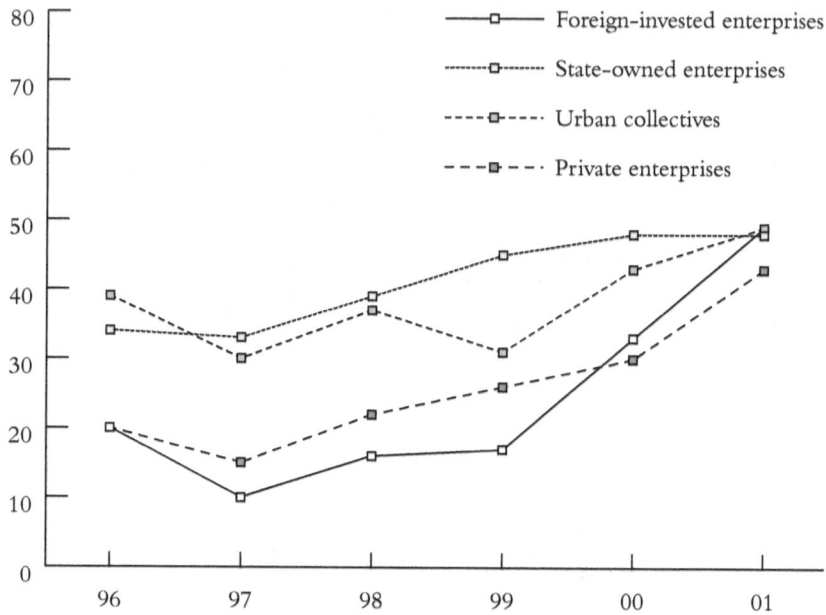

FIGURE 3.7. Percent of Labor Disputes Resolved by Arbitration, 1996–2001
SOURCE: *Labor Statistical Yearbook* [Laodong tongji nianjian] (Beijing: State Statistical Publishing House), various years.

hance managerial power and influence on the arbitration decision, preferring dispute-resolution processes that are more formal and actively involve the government.

The high rate of disputes now settled "by other means" is especially apparent in the foreign-invested sector but is also growing in private enterprises. These enterprises are often inclined to offer a settlement once the threat of a lawsuit becomes real (see Figures 3.7 and 3.8). Foreign managers often fear bad publicity that can be portrayed in the domestic media as foreign exploitation of Chinese workers.[56] Private and foreign firms also may have greater ability to pay settlements and thus avoid bad publicity, investigative attention from the local labor bureau, and high legal costs.

THE INCREASING IMPORTANCE OF THE COURTS

There has also been a marked increase in labor litigation since the late 1990s. In 2001, Chinese courts handled 100,440 labor disputes.[57] Labor

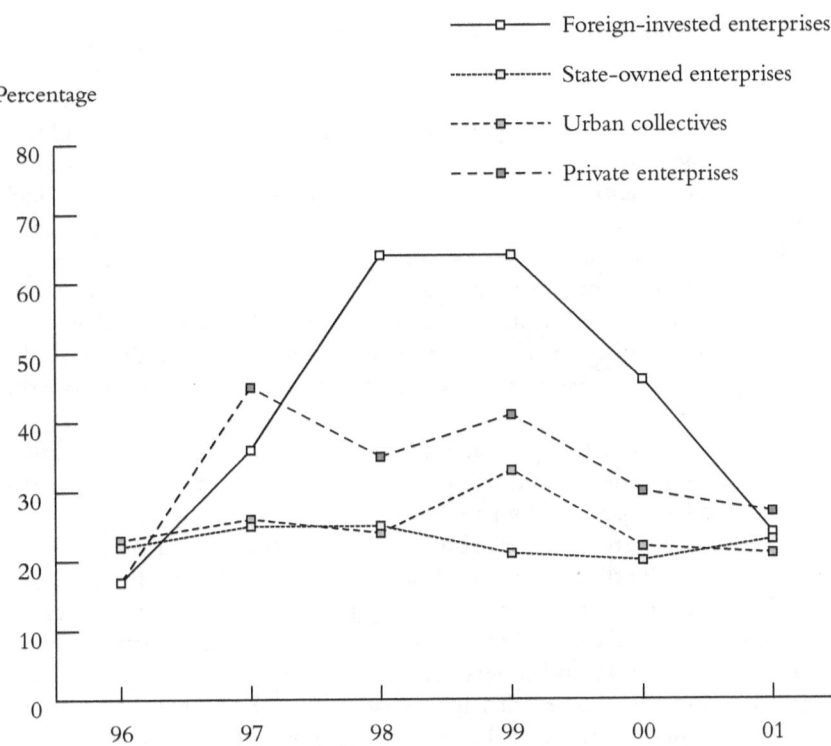

FIGURE 3.8. Percent of Labor Disputes Resolved by Other Means, 1996–2001
SOURCE: *Labor Statistical Yearbook* [Laodong tongji nianjian] (Beijing: State Statistical Publishing House), various years.

lawyers now speak of the labor dispute resolution process as a process often involving "one hearing and two appeals."[58] The hearing takes place at the LAC when an arbitral judgment is made. The appeals are held in civil court. From 1995 to 1999, the number of arbitral judgments appealed ranged from 1.7 percent in 1995 to 4 percent in 1998. Yet, by 2003, Beijing and Shanghai labor officials reported that nearly 70 percent of all arbitration decisions were appealed. A Supreme Court decision on April 16, 2001, clarified the role of courts in dispute resolution and made it easier for labor disputes to be heard in court.[59] Courts are now instructed to accept labor disputes that have been rejected by an LAC (often for reasons of jurisdiction or expiration of the time limit).

An increasing tendency to reject an arbitral judgment and to appeal to the courts is an interesting and possibly disturbing development. Since 1995, workers have routinely won over half of all labor disputes outright. (In SOEs the rate is slightly below this, at about 45 percent, and in private firms and foreign-invested firms the rate climbs to about 60 percent.) Of the other labor suits, 30–35 percent are "partially won by both sides," while employers win on average only 15–20 percent of all cases outright. Dissatisfaction with the arbitral judgment often has more to do with enforcement of the decision than with its outcome. The growing number of court appeals is thus related to weaknesses in the arbitration system. Workers go to court in increasing numbers because the arbitration system is overburdened, understaffed, and suffers from a lack of independence from local governments and powerful enterprises. These problems often lead to decisions that favor enterprises over workers as well as delays in the enforcement of arbitral judgments.[60]

These trends, taken together, indicate a growing rights consciousness among Chinese workers and a general decline in resolution processes that have been relied upon in the past. Workers are increasingly inclined to ask the state to intervene in enterprise labor relations through LACs and civil courts. Even as the state withdraws from many roles in labor administration, its new reliance on legal institutions to regulate labor requires that it remain involved. But it is unclear whether local state institutions can truly perform their job as regulatory and supervisory bodies, particularly in regions where local state–business ties are closely intertwined.[61] The increased role of the local state is also directly related to the continuing problem of worker representation. Workers increasingly go to court and arbitration because they have no effective advocates at lower levels. The ban on independent trade unions and the weakness and dependence of the official trade union has made lower-level resolution extremely problematic.

The rapid rise in arbitration and litigation is of noticeable concern to China's leaders. The Ministry of Labor is now placing greater emphasis on prevention of labor disputes through better labor law implementation and supervision. Clearly, more attention must also be paid to better implementation and enforcement of arbitration decisions. However, thorny questions of how to represent workers effectively and who should represent workers remain.

Conclusion

One of the puzzling aspects of Chinese labor and employment law is that despite severe problems of legislation, implementation, and enforcement, Chinese citizens are increasingly inclined to make use of these laws. In an important sense, workers are ignoring the widely known flaws of legal institutions, mimicking the state's own recourse to legality, and using these laws to press for their own rights and interests.[62]

In this chapter I have explored how the labor law and laws guiding labor contracts and dispute resolution have shaped legal mobilization. How these laws have been written has determined, in part, outcomes. The implementation of the labor-contract system has notably restricted what issues can be raised by SOE workers. Laws on labor dispute resolution process have opened new legal channels for workers to air their grievances and press for redress. Workers in the non-state sector seem to benefit especially from these changes. Analysis of national trends using aggregate statistical data can of course only answer these questions crudely. Other issues remain to be studied; they include better understanding of variation across regions, industries, and types of workers (for example, skilled, unskilled, male, female, migrant, resident).

The development of China's legal system has resulted in a wide-ranging debate regarding the nature of law in China, the relevance of law in an authoritarian state, and, finally, the contribution, if any, a more developed legal system will have in instituting democratic politics in China. As a general statement, it is accurate to say that the majority of Western legal scholars are pessimistic regarding the rule of law in China.[63] A dominant concern is the CCP's unwillingness to submit to legal regulations and strictures that may reduce its political power. Others point to the vast difficulties in implementation and enforcement of laws in China's diverse and often independent-minded regions. Both of these are significant barriers to achieving a less arbitrary, rule-based polity. However, the development of rule of law should not be ignored, even as it proceeds unevenly and with difficulty. In fact, the strengthening of China's legal institutions is directly related to the Party's interest in holding onto power. The pessimists might argue that the CCP will never willingly submit to laws that limit its discretion. They might be right. On the other hand, the Chinese party-state might gamble that rule through law and the added benefits of increased legitimacy both at home and abroad are worth the risk of activating social forces and enlarging the role of new interest groups. This dynamic of state–societal interaction around legal rights and obligations is one key element of China's rule-of-law project. It suggests that we adopt a perspective that understands the rule of law as an outcome of negotiation and contestation between the authoritarian state (those who make the law) and society (those who make use of it).

Why do workers increasingly turn to the law even when the rule of law remains at best a long-off goal of an overstretched central leadership and at worst a cynical attempt by the party-state to buttress its own monopoly on power with a patina of legitimacy? Related analysis of the development of citizenship norms may offer some clues. Kevin O'Brien has found that in the Chinese countryside "certain citizenship practices are emerging even before citizenship has appeared as a fully recognized status," and that citizenship "is less granted than won, less accorded than made."[64] Both of these notions, rights of citizenship and enjoyment of the rule of law, should be treated analytically as political processes rather than as gifts bequeathed or withheld from above. In this way we can begin to understand interactions between state and citizen (or worker) as one element in a contentious process of political change. This approach to change can be opposed to a dichotomous understanding of development in which China either has the rule of law (and citizenship rights) or it does not.

The codification of laws and regulations matters greatly in this process because they specify what gets included, to whom a law applies, and how disputes should be processed. Laws are significant because they shape the expectations of citizens. They are written "guarantees," and even when, or especially when, they go unfulfilled, they have important consequences for societal action. Labor laws and regulations, with their emphasis on contractual responsibilities, are particularly suited to creating and shaping societal expectations. Forming expectations and placing blame are critical steps in the initiation of disputes.[65] O'Brien finds that when rural residents make claims of citizenship, they are often voicing "popular dissatisfaction with incomplete inclusion."[66] Workers, too, when they lodge grievances, are voicing popular dissatisfaction with incomplete implementation and enforcement of Chinese laws. This type of legal mobilization should be seen as a "form of political activity by which the citizenry uses public authority on its own behalf."[67]

The rise of arbitration and litigation is a fitting example of societal dissatisfaction with ineffectual legal implementation and enforcement. The growing number of appeals to courts is particularly relevant because it is the result of weaknesses and problems with arbitration. Viewing the rule of law as a process rather than as an outcome is useful, insofar as it allows us to see more clearly at which stage law is compromised. The Chinese state has passed many laws and regulations designed to enhance the rights of Chinese workers. Workers, in turn, have responded by using the dispute resolution process to lodge grievances against their employers. But nearly a decade after the promulgation of the National Labor Law, the state's ability to implement and enforce arbitral judgments remains weak. Worker dissatisfaction with dispute resolution is growing and so is pressure on the courts.

Up to this point the formalization and legalization of labor relations has "mutually empowered"[68] the state and workers. The state garners some legitimacy, both domestically and internationally, and workers have an arena for controlled but real conflict. The development of labor and employment law has helped direct labor conflict into officially sanctioned channels, but it

"Use the Law as Your Weapon!" 77

has also made it more difficult to deny the existence of conflict, as top-down reform has met with responses from below. Companies might not pay a promised wage, a new factory might offer better wages and benefits, and a contract worker might simply leave in search of something better. Yet workers do more than vote with their feet; they also take the state at its word and use the law as their weapon.

Notes

For research assistance on this chapter, I would like to thank Juan Chen and Lyric Chen.

1. "Use Legal Weapons to Protect Your Own Rights" [Yong falü wuqi weihu zishen quanyi], quoted in "The Awakening of Workers' Rights Consciousness" [Laodongzhe quanyi yishi de suxing], *Workers' Daily*, 2 January 1997, 6. Chinese reports of labor unrest are generally circumspect but allude to large-scale collective disputes and strikes that threaten social stability; external reports are often more detailed. See, e.g., "Over 100,000 Workers Demonstrate in Mianyang City...," *Human Rights in China Press Report*, 16 July 1997; "Huge Mine Protest in China as Angry Laid-off Workers Vent Anger," 7 April 2000, http://www.insidechina.com/news; John Pomfret, "Miners' Riot a Symbol of China's New Discontent," *Washington Post*, 5 April 2000, A1.

2. These figures are conservative, including only disputes that reached local arbitration and leaving out those mediated by enterprises themselves. Inclusion of mediated disputes and informally negotiated disputes would bring the total in 1999 from 120,191 to 171,669 (*China Statistical Yearbook* [Zhongguo tongji nianjian], various years [Beijing: China Statistical Publishing House]; *China Labor Statistics Yearbook* [Zhongguo laodong tongji nianjian], various years [Beijing: China Statistical Publishing House]).

3. Ministry of Labor official, interview, 12 December 2002. E.g., see "Where There Is Conflict, They Are There" [You maodun de difang jiuyou tamen de shenying], *Xinmin Evening News*, 7 October 2003, 12.

4. Individually owned businesses with seven employees or less are the one exception. There are many reasons why small businesses have low rates, including exemptions from key labor regulations and their often family-owned nature.

5. For an analysis of labor abuse and problems in contemporary China, see Anita Chan, *China's Workers Under Assault: The Exploitation of Labor in a Globalizing Economy* (New York: M. E. Sharpe, 2001).

6. Zhao Minghua and Theo Nichols, "Management Control of Labour in State-Owned Enterprises: Cases from the Textile Industry," *China Journal* 36 (July 1996): 1–21.

7. A better way to get at problems in working conditions or labor relations in different types of firms or across regions would be to examine variation in causes of labor disputes rather than their number. For example, provinces with high levels of FDI and large, non-state sectors also tend to have high rates of disputes about labor protection and occupational safety. This would seem to indicate that workers in

these firms are more likely to be subjected to unsafe working conditions than workers in other types of firms.

8. In practice, of course, differences between workers can be stark. This is the case, in particular, for migrant workers who do not enjoy some basic rights of citizenship while employed outside their home jurisdiction. Local regulations also vary considerably in regard to migrant workers' rights. The author has visited numerous factories in which employers pay out benefits and social insurance only to workers with permanent resident permits for that locality. Local officials seem to be complicit in this practice.

9. Both these attributes are highlighted in Chinese analysis of the law. E.g., see, Chang Kai, *Labour Relations, Labourers, Labour Rights* [Laodong guanxi, laodong zhe, laoquan] (Beijing: China Labor Press, 1995); and Jiang Junlu, "Labor Dispute Handling: A System to Guarantee the Implementation of the Labor Law" [Laodong zhengyi chuli: Laodongfa shixing de baozhang zhidu], *Workers' Daily*, 21 March 1995. Foreign lawyers in China have also paid attention to them; see Hiroaki Tsukamoto et al., "Restructuring FIEs in China and Procedures to Cut Staff" [Chugoku niokeru gaisho taishi kigyonoresutora oyobi], *International Commercial Law Journal* [Kokusai shoji homu] 27, no. 5 (1999): 539–45.

10. The Ministry of Labor translates *zhongcai caijue* as "arbitration lawsuit," but I have used "arbitral judgment" to indicate that this process results in a written judgment, including who was at fault and the amount for compensation.

11. "People's Court, Procuratorate Present Work Reports to NPC Session," 11 March 2002, BBC Monitoring International Reports, http://www.lexisnexus.com (accessed 12 October 2002).

12. The fees required for arbitration and litigation are part of an ongoing debate about access to these procedures. Company representatives and labor officials tend to believe that the fees are too low, encouraging frivolous suits. Legal aid advocates and workers believe that these fees are already onerous for poorly paid workers, particularly given the increased need for legal representation due to the complexity of many issues and the use of legal representation by companies.

13. Craig S. Smith, "China Faces Problems Creating Jobs, Officials Say," *New York Times*, 30 April 2002, A14.

14. Ching-Ching Ni, "China's Booming Economy Lagging Behind Persistent Unemployment," *Los Angeles Times*, 2 May 2002, A3.

15. Detailed information on large labor protests in China are regularly provided by China Labour Bulletin, a Hong Kong NGO; see http://www.china-labour.org.hk.

16. These disputes are often accompanied by extralegal action, including strikes and work stoppages (former MOL official, interview, Beijing, 9 December 2002).

17. These figures are for the year 2000 and are calculated from data provided in the *China Statistical Yearbook* (Beijing: State Statistical Bureau, 2001).

18. In 1978 SOE workers made up 78.3 percent of the urban workforce. Most other urban residents were employed in smaller collectives. As Mayfair Yang found, however, even in small urban collectives there was a tendency to supply many social welfare benefits, albeit at a lower level than at SOEs (Mayfair Mei-hui Yang, "Be-

tween State and Society: The Construction of Corporateness in a Chinese Socialist Factory," *Australian Journal of Chinese Affairs* 22 [July 1989]: 31–60).

19. Particularly during the 1950s SOEs employed many temporary and contract laborers, who had fewer entitlements. By the late 1970s, however, many of them had been transformed into permanent state workers (see David Granick, "Multiple Labour Markets in the Industrial State Enterprise Sector," *China Quarterly*, no. 126 [June 1991] 280).

20. Andrew Walder, *Communist Neo-Traditionalism* (Berkeley: University of California Press, 1986).

21. SOE workers currently account for about one-third of the formal urban workforce. This figure has declined rapidly over the past few years due to restructuring, layoffs, and privatization (see *China in the World Economy: Domestic Policy Challenges* [Paris: OECD Publications, 2002], 541; *China Statistical Yearbook, 2001* [Beijing: State Statistical Publishing House, 2002]).

22. Gordon White, "The Politics of Economic Reform in Chinese Industry: The Introduction of the Labour Contract System," *China Quarterly*, no. 111 (September 1987): 367.

23. "Labour Law of the People's Republic of China" [Zhonghua renmin gongheguo laodongfa], *China Law and Practice*, 29 August 1994, 21–40.

24. These regulations include the December 3, 1994 "Ministry of Labor Announcement Regarding Methods of Economic Compensation for the Violation and Termination of Labor Contracts" and the August 11, 1995 "Ministry of Labor Opinion on Several Problems in the Implementation of the Labor Law," as well as other circulars on the implementation and extension of the labor contract system (*Handbook on Laws on Labor Disputes* [Laodong zhengyi falü shouce], vol. 1 [Beijing: People's Court Publishing House, 1996]). For English translations of four of these regulations, see Edward Gu, ed., "Labor Market Reforms: Central Government Policy," *Chinese Law and Government* 34, no. 1 (January–February 2001); see also Mary Gallagher and Junlu Jiang, "China's Labor Legislation," *Chinese Law and Government* 35, no. 6 (November–December 2002).

25. Yin Jizuo, ed., *2003 Report on Shanghai Society* (Shanghai: Shanghai Academy of Social Sciences Publishing House, 2003), 5.

26. See the 2002 white paper on labor relations issued by the Ministry of Labor and Social Security ("White Paper: New Labor Relations Taking Shape in China," Xinhua News Agency, 29 April 2002, http://web.lexis-nexis.com/universe).

27. "Ministry of Labor Announcement on Whether Disputes between Employer and Employee Related to the Sale of Housing and Other Problems Should Be Accepted," no. 312, 27 September 1994, republished in *Union Handbook for the Resolution of Labor Disputes*, ed. Zhou Wanling (Beijing: Zhongguo Gongren Chubanshe, 1999).

28. *Xiagang* is usually translated as "laid-off." In China, the term describes workers in SOEs or collectives who have been sent home without work but who have not yet severed labor relations with their employer. On non-acceptance of cases involving *xiagang*, see, e.g., "Mr. Zhu vs. X Metal Processing Co," in *Selected Labor Dispute Cases*, ed. Wu Guoqiang (Shanghai: Shanghai People's Publishing, 2002), 52–57.

This case was not accepted by the local arbitration commission on the grounds that *xiagang*-related disputes were not within its jurisdiction. The worker then brought the suit to court. The first court also rejected it on the same grounds. Finally, in the second court appeal, the court ruled that the company (a foreign-funded enterprise) was not permitted to lay off workers using the *xiagang* policy, nor could it lay off workers who were currently holding union positions.

29. For a discussion of the legal debate on labor contracts, see Ronald C. Keith and Zhiqiu Lin, *Law and Justice in China's New Marketplace* (New York: Palgrave Press, 2001), 109–19.

30. A related issue is workers' acceptance of the "hegemony" of the market, which may dampen their enthusiasm for legal processes of dispute resolution. Marc Blecher has argued that this has been one factor that explains the relative lack of large-scale worker protest (see Marc Blecher, "Hegemony and Workers' Politics in China," *China Quarterly*, no. 170 [June 2002]: 283–303). It is unclear, however, why SOE workers, those closest to the previous socialist system, would be more prone to hegemonic influence than other workers.

31. Common issues include early termination of the contract, changes in the contract due to restructuring, and failure on the part of the employer to implement the contract.

32. Foreign-invested enterprises also have a relatively high proportion of contractual disputes. This is partly a function of the identity of many foreign-invested joint ventures. Because the domestic partner is almost always a state-owned enterprise, the high incidence of contractual disputes may be a result of workers from the SOE shifting to the joint venture. This transition often leads to disputes about the term of the new employment contract and how to treat the worker's previous tenure in the SOE.

33. William Hurst and Kevin J. O'Brien, "China's Contentious Pensioners," *China Quarterly*, no. 170 (June 2002): 345–60. For the material dimensions of the pension and unemployment problem, see Dorothy Solinger, "Labour Market Reform and the Plight of the Laid-off Proletariat," *China Quarterly*, no. 170 (June 2002): 304–26.

34. Hurst and O'Brien, "China's Contentious Pensioners."

35. Of course, labor disputes can occur in tandem with extralegal action, such as demonstrations and strikes. I do not want to overemphasize the distinction between these actions, although in an authoritarian context the risks of demonstrating are much greater than the risks of bringing a grievance to an arbitration committee.

36. Charges by labor lawyers and researchers that LACs are overly formalistic have increased recently. It may be that underfunded and understaffed LACs are simply trying to reduce the number of disputes. For example, Thireau and Hua find in their contribution to this volume that Shenzhen labor arbitration committees refused to hear cases when a written labor contract did not exist. This is clearly in violation of the labor law. There is growing pressure from labor law experts, including well-known judges, to be less formalistic. On this point, see Guo Wenlong, "Research on Real Labor Relations," *Shanghai Shenpan Shixian* (September 2002): 12–15.

37. This delimiting is, of course, recognized by workers themselves, leading them

to emphasize not the legal parameters of the labor contract but their past (moral) contributions to socialism and the nation. This notion of "contribution" to society and the nation was mentioned frequently by workers who were interviewed about their experiences surrounding reemployment (see Yu Faniao, *How to Resolve Problems of the Reemployment Centers for Laid-off Workers* [Ruhe jiejue xiagang zhigong chu zaijiuye fuwu zhongxin de wenti] [Beijing: Jingji Kexue Chubanshe, 2000]). See also "Mr Li vs. X Glass Works: Calculation of Compensation during Discharging a Labor Contract," in Wu Guoqiang, *Selected Labor Dispute Cases*, 91–94, in which Mr. Li describes his agreement to become laid-off as a sacrifice to the firm.

38. This behavior also extends to reluctance to enter reemployment centers, which were set up to supply job training, job opportunities, and limited financial support. Often, in order to enter the center, workers are required to break off labor relations with their enterprise (see Yang Shouye, "The Laid Off Have No Guarantees, Through Arbitration Ask for Justice" [Xiagang wubaozhang, zhongcai gongdao], *Laodong Zhengyi Chuli* [July 1999]: 24).

39. Yu Faniao, *How to Resolve Problems of the Reemployment Centers for Laid-off Workers*, 15.

40. Laid-off workers' desires to remain attached to their former work unit is also related to the lack of other employment opportunities in the formal economy.

41. Yan Yuanzhang, "Astonishing On-the Spot Report: An Interview Regarding the Basic Situation of Laid-Off Workers in the Northeast Region" [Jingren jishi: Dongbei diqu xiagang gongren jiben qingkuang fangtanlu], http://www.epochtimes.com (accessed 3 February 2001).

42. Yu Faniao, *How to Resolve Problems of the Reemployment Centers for Laid-off Workers*, 197.

43. Certain policies, such as the establishment of reemployment centers, were designed to aid SOE workers specifically.

44. Some of these events are detailed by Elizabeth J. Perry, "Labor's Battle for Political Space: The Role of Worker Associations in Contemporary China," in *Urban Spaces in Contemporary China*, ed. Deborah Davis, Richard Kraus, Barry Naughton, and Elizabeth J. Perry (Cambridge: Cambridge University Press, 1995).

45. For an analysis of the role of mediation in Maoist and reform-era China, see Stanley B. Lubman, *Bird in a Cage: Legal Reform in China After Mao* (Stanford, Calif.: Stanford University Press, 1999). Diamant finds that mediation, even in the pre-reform Communist period, varied in application and was not always the dominant method of dispute resolution (Neil J. Diamant, *Revolutionizing the Family: Politics, Love, and Divorce in Urban and Rural China 1949–1968* [Berkeley: University of California Press, 2000]).

46. The data used to compile Figure 3.3 are from statistical yearbooks and data supplied in Shoichi Ito, "Changes in Labour Markets, Labour Law, and Industrial Relations in Modern China," paper presented at the 1996 Asian Regional Conference on Industrial Relations, Tokyo, 14–15 March 1996. The data show the proportion of disputes mediated by employers relative to the total number of labor disputes reported in that year. Prior to the 1993 regulations, mediation took place primarily at the enterprise level.

47. "Survey Research on Changes in the Situation of Shanghai Workers," *2003 Report on Shanghai Society* (Shanghai: Shanghai Academy of Social Sciences Publishing House, 2003), 5.

48. Neil J. Diamant, "Conflict and Conflict Resolution in China: Beyond Mediation-Centered Approaches," *Journal of Conflict Resolution* 44, no. 4 (August 2000): 523–46.

49. Lubman notes, however, that mediation was not compulsory in Maoist China but rather encouraged by many organizations, including neighborhood committees and work units (Lubman, *Bird in a Cage*, 52–53).

50. Still, even in SOEs, mediation is less popular than arbitration. For example, in the year 2000, 18,802 disputes were mediated by SOEs, but more than 32,000 SOE disputes proceeded directly to arbitration.

51. Mediation committees are responsible for dispute resolution, of course, but the presence of a union is almost a prerequisite since the union chairman must lead the mediation committee.

52. See, e.g., Trini Leung, "ACFTU and Union Organizing," *China Labour Bulletin*, 26 April 2002, http://www.china-labour.org.hk/iso/article.adp?article_id = 2265 (accessed 16 June 2004).

53. These numbers were supplied by a staff member of the Ministry of Labor, Labor Arbitration Bureau, in an interview in Beijing, 11 December 2002.

54. It seems inappropriate for the statistics to include these cases as "resolved" when in actuality they have simply been disposed of. Some of them turn up later as court cases.

55. During arbitration, the parties can agree to go through mediation (*tiaojie*) and sign a letter of agreement that settles the dispute. If this is unacceptable or unsuccessful, the parties proceed to formal arbitration (*caijue*). Such local-level mediation is classified differently than the mediation that takes place at the enterprise level; it is more formal and involves the active participation by the local LAC (Wang Quanxing, *Laodong fa* [Labor law] [Beijing: Falü Chubanshe, 1997]).

56. Japanese lawyer, interview, Shanghai, July 1999.

57. "Courts Handle More Cases of Underworld in Nature: Chief Judge," Xinhua General News Service, 11 March 2002, http://www.lexis-nexis.com/universe (accessed 11 October 2002).

58. Labor lawyer, interview, Beijing, 10 December 2002.

59. "Supreme Court Interpretation of Several Problems in the Applicability of Law in the Hearing of Labor Dispute Cases" [Zuigao renmin fayuan guanyu shenli laodong zhengyi anjian shiyong falü ruogan wenti de jieshi], issued 30 April 2001, reprinted in Wu Guoqiang, *Selected Labor Dispute Cases*, 355.

60. These problems are raised frequently by labor lawyers and Ministry of Labor officials; MOL officials often frame them as a problem of low quality cadres and government officers rather than viewing them as systemic (labor lawyers, interviews, Beijing, 9–10 December 2002; Ministry of Labor arbitration official, interview, Beijing, 11 December 2002; labor lawyer, interview, Shanghai, 14 October 2003).

61. See David Wank, *Commodifying Communism: Business, Trust, and Politics in a Chinese City* (New York: Cambridge University Press, 1999).

62. These findings are similar to those of Kevin J. O'Brien, "Rightful Resistance," *World Politics* 49, no. 1 (October 1996): 31–55.

63. Lubman, *Bird in a Cage*; Pitman Potter, "Foreign Investment Law in the People's Republic of China: Dilemmas of State Control," *China Quarterly*, no. 141 (March 1995): 155–85; Karen Turner et al., eds., *The Limits of the Rule of Law in China* (Seattle: University of Washington Press, 2000); Franz Michael, "Law: A Tool of Power," in *Human Rights in the People's Republic of China*, ed. Yuan-li Wu et al. (Boulder, Colo.: Westview Press, 1988). This pessimism is also prevalent in research on labor law (see Ching Kwan Lee, "From the Specter of Mao to the Spirit of the Law: Labor Insurgency in China," *Theory and Society* 31 [2002]: 189–228; and Chan, *China's Workers Under Assault*).

64. Kevin J. O'Brien, "Villagers, Elections, and Citizenship in Contemporary China," *Modern China* 27, no. 4 (October 2001): 408, 423.

65. William Felstiner, Richard L. Abel, and Austin Sarat, "The Emergence and Transformation of Disputes: Naming, Blaming, Claiming . . . ," *Law and Society Review* 15, no. 3–4 (1980–81): 631–54.

66. O'Brien, "Villagers, Elections, and Citizenship in Contemporary China," 423.

67. Frances Kahn Zemans, "Legal Mobilization: The Neglected Role of the Law in the Political System," *American Political Science Review* 77, no. 3 (September 1983): 690–703.

68. The concept of "mutual empowerment" was elaborated in Joel Migdal, Atul Kohli, and Vivienne Shue, eds., *State Power and Social Forces: Domination and Transformation in the Third World* (New York: Cambridge University Press, 1994). Xu Wang argues that rural elections also have mutually empowered peasants and the state apparatus (Xu Wang, "Mutual Empowerment of State and Peasantry: Grassroots Development in Rural China," *World Development* 25 [1997]: 1431–42).

ISABELLE THIREAU AND HUA LINSHAN 4

One Law, Two Interpretations
Mobilizing the Labor Law in Arbitration
Committees and in Letters and Visits Offices

Societies governed by different regimes develop different ways of expressing a sense of injustice. Hence, there often emerges a variety of spaces in which social facts are debated and denounced—spaces that can be characterized by the identity of interacting parties, established procedures and rules, and the principles and norms used to expose a given reality as unjust or unacceptable. The concept of *épreuve de justice*, or "test of justice," has been elaborated by Alain Cottereau to designate these processes during which principles of justice are mobilized and put to the test.[1]

Traditionally, and then quite differently under Mao, particular norms prevailed in China regarding what was fair, just, or correct. These norms now coexist with and are being challenged by a new economic order that has arisen over the past two decades. Analyzing the sense of injustice expressed nowadays by ordinary Chinese emerging from such a complex heritage can help us identify which norms and principles are denied, reinterpreted, or reassessed during the various tests of justice apparent today. More pointedly, such analysis can help us grasp the normative positions deemed legitimate by Chinese people as they interpret the reality they face and respond to it.

In undertaking this, it must be noted that the nature of the norms articulated during such processes depends on the specific arenas in which they are invested. Different "spaces" confer legitimacy upon different approaches to grievances. As a consequence, legal developments during the two last decades cannot help but influence the space within which such tests occur and the normative repertoire used. A sense of injustice is usually expressed by comparing what happened with what *should* have happened. Laws, which establish specific rights and duties, may thus ground the denunciation of given facts as illegal, and also as wrong, illegitimate, or unreasonable in the view of ordinary Chinese. These assessments may go well beyond the legal significance of the conduct observed.

This chapter focuses on expressions of injustice and mobilization of the Labor Law in two contexts—arbitration committees, which are formally tasked with solving labor disputes, and letters and visits offices, an administrative organ that handles people's complaints. As we will see, both of these institutions apply different "tests of justice"—the first based largely on legality and the second more on generalized appeals about injustice. Each institution also serves a somewhat different constituency. Arbitration committees in the city of Shenzhen are resorted to more frequently by employees with financial means and standing, while letters and visits offices are turned to more frequently by groups of impoverished workers. For this latter group, the offices provide not just a means to challenge specific violations of their legal rights, but more than this, are a means to draw attention to political and social norms they believe should apply in the workplace.

Our data consist of a group of 123 randomly selected files from the archives of a letters and visits office (gathered during 1996 and 1997), and a second group of 60 files (also randomly chosen) from 1998 and 1999 from an arbitration committee.[2] Both bodies fall under the Labor Bureau of the Shenzhen municipal government in Guangdong Province.

Expressing Labor Grievances in Two Different Spaces

This paper compares expressions of injustice and mobilization that deploy the Labor Law in a judicial and in an administrative organ. Such a choice, however, does not imply that these are the only means available to address labor conflicts. An aggrieved worker alternatively can move to another enterprise or locality, endure the treatment faced, negotiate with the employer or its representatives, or file a lawsuit. A survey by the Shenzhen Labor Bureau in 1996 revealed that 1,537 of 2,789 migrant workers contacted had encountered some labor-related problem during the previous year: the survey found that 4 percent of these workers had turned to arbitration committees, courts, or letters and visits offices, although the survey did not distinguish among these routes. Another 39 percent had tried to take up their problem directly with their employer, 26 percent had given up trying to improve their situation, 23 percent had initiated some form of mediation process within the enterprise, 5 percent had quit the enterprise over the problem, and 2 percent had launched an appeal in the local media.[3]

Even though turning to arbitration committees and to letters and visits offices increased in frequency during the 1990s, the above survey shows that these organs clearly do not constitute workers' only alternative when pursuing a labor dispute. We must, therefore, clarify our purpose: the aim of this paper is neither to analyze the various ways workers react when labor disputes arise, nor to provide a systematic description of legal settings in which such disputes can be resolved.[4] Rather, our focus is on the links between the expression of a sense of injustice and the use of relevant legal provisions: in one case, through a relatively new institution that possesses quasi-judicial powers; in the second case, through an institution with fewer formal powers but anchored in a longer and multifaceted history.

Officially, labor dispute resolution may be pursued through three venues: mediation by an enterprise's labor dispute mediation committee; arbitration conducted in accordance with the law by an arbitration committee external to the enterprise; and litigation, that is, filing a suit in court.[5] Since only large state-owned enterprises have mediation committees, the first method often involves discussion or negotiation between the parties within an enterprise. Arbitration committees, on the other hand, are the principal organs in charge of handling labor disputes. It should be noted that there are different views concerning the relationship between the three means of dispute resolution. Some say that plaintiffs can choose any of these methods to solve a dispute, while others argue that they are arrayed in a hierarchy. According to this second perspective, only when either party is unsatisfied with an arbitrator's decision can he or she file suit with a People's Court. In localities where such an understanding prevails, some plaintiffs may find themselves with "no doors open to express their complaint; no tears to shed although they want to cry."[6] Legal circles have recently concluded that arbitration committees can be bypassed.

By the end of 2001, China had established 3,192 labor dispute arbitration committees at the county level or above, consisting of nearly twenty thousand full-time and part-time arbitrators.[7] From August 1, 1993, when the Regulations of the People's Republic of China Concerning the Handling of Labor Disputes in Enterprises was promulgated, to the end of 2001, such committees handled 688,000 labor disputes involving some 2,368,000 workers.[8]

Arbitration committees rely on a rather large body of labor legislation, described by Mary Gallagher in her essay in this volume. We note here a few relevant points. First, although the 1995 Labor Law supersedes other laws and regulations, it was passed by the National People's Congress and not its Standing Committee, a fact often noted by some trade-union leaders to explain its low status.[9] Second, other legal provisions, national and local, limit its influence. Moreover, two features characterize the Labor Law as compared to previous labor regulations: a shift from a focus on work discipline dominant in the pre-reform era to a focus on contract procedures,[10] and a shift from labor regulations dealing only with state and collective sectors to labor legislation that covers all forms of enterprises, including the many different types of firms that have emerged out of the reform process.[11]

While the arbitration committee system is complex and varies from place to place, it does have some general characteristics. Arbitration committees established under the jurisdiction of municipal governments are supposed to be composed of representatives of labor administrative departments, trade unions at the same level, and employers. They mainly handle the three types of labor disputes (*laodong zhengyi*) that are identified by the 1993 regulations, those that:

> arise due to dismissal, discharge or resignation of an employee;
>
> are related to the implementation of state regulations concerning wages and salaries, insurance, welfare, training, or labor protection; or
>
> are linked to employment contracts.[12]

Other types of disputes (e.g., those stemming from discipline within the enterprise) tend to be neglected. In some localities, such a narrow understanding of arbitration committees' responsibilities even induces arbitration committees to refuse cases in which the two parties have not established a labor relationship based upon written contracts.[13]

Arbitration committees have the right to refuse cases. According to the applicable regulations, the complainant must state a grievance in written form to the committee within sixty days after his or her legal rights are violated. Then, within seven days, the arbitration committee must decide if it will handle the case or not. Within sixty days, a solution should be reached through mediation or arbitration.[14] Moreover, in the written claim, the complainant must state his or her name and address as well as that of the enterprise at issue, attach a copy of the labor contract, and include all available written evidence. That litigants must be willing to disclose their identity means they must be willing to run the risk of retaliation. It is impossible to remain anonymous because a main component of the procedure is confrontation between the plaintiff and the defendant.[15]

The second set of institutions is the letters and visits offices (*xinfangke*). They have a far longer history than arbitration committees. In place since the early 1950s, they have evolved and have been extended progressively down to the county level. They may be established under specialized departments—such as a municipal Labor Bureau in the cases discussed here—or under more general organs such as the Party or People's congresses. In addition to handling complaints received through letters or visits, most can now also be reached by telephone or e-mail. Such bodies have been regularly used by ordinary citizens since the beginning of the 1980s.[16]

Not surprisingly, labor grievances produce a large number of citizen complaints. In Shenzhen, official estimates show that in 2001 half of the complaints addressed to all letters and visits offices at the municipal level concerned labor issues.[17] Moreover, the number of labor grievances officially recorded in 1999 amounted to 24,528, and of these, 13,300 were deemed labor disputes. Among these 13,300 cases, only 1,649—that is, 12 percent—were ultimately handled by arbitration committees.[18]

The operation of the letters and visits offices bear some resemblance to those of a much older procedure, that of appeals of capital cases during the Qing dynasty. Under the Qing, after having exhausted all the judicial resources at the local and provincial levels, individuals could bring their case to Beijing.[19] Continuities can be observed between such appeals in the imperial era and recent complaints. For instance, as with the Qing-era appeals, today's grievances can be related to malfeasance by administrators or injustices committed by ordinary members of society. Moreover, two fundamental principles grounding this traditional institution continue to apply: complaints acknowledge the state's legitimacy, since they are addressed to its representatives and request their intervention (hence, they cannot be construed as overly confrontational); and they rest on the belief that rulers and ruled share the same understanding of right and wrong, of just and unjust. These two facts are crucial, as we shall see, in understanding the tone and the content of the letters examined here.

At the same time, the 1995 national regulations governing letters and visits procedures also recognize a changed relationship between state and society compared to the past. They specify that these organs should accept citizens' reports of malfeasance, but that citizens may also express criticisms, comments, and wishes. More pointedly, these institutions today play a wider role than they did during the imperial era insofar as they are implicitly assigned five broad aims: to preempt social protests, monitor administrators, provide information about social problems, maintain a channel of communication between "the government and the masses," and offer a means for citizens to participate in legitimate public action.[20] Besides these, the offices also have more specialized functions. In 1989, for instance, the Letters and Visits Office of the Labor Department of Shenzhen municipality was assigned responsibility for labor inspections (*laodong jiancha*).[21] This example was picked up on by many local governments when, in 1993, a labor inspection system was implemented nationwide. Such a system had been deemed unnecessary when the state was the main employer, and was developed to supervise implementation of labor provisions as the ownership of enterprises became more diverse. The Shenzhen office has now also been assigned the duty of issuing legal documents and regulations regarding labor issues.[22] It does so by developing information through its inspection tours of local firms and by handling complaints it receives.[23]

It should be added that citizen complaints, mobilized in a range of situations,²⁴ are conducive to the emergence of different tests of justice. Many factors matter, including: the identity of the persons accused (members of the administration or ordinary citizens); the extent to which complaints are individual or collective; the degree of distance among complainants and whether they are anonymous; the ability of the involved parties to mobilize connections (*guanxi*); and the rank of the letters and visits office in the administrative hierarchy.²⁵ All these affect the nature of the space that emerges as a consequence of the expression of citizen complaints.

As far as labor disputes are concerned, important procedural differences can be observed between arbitration committees and letters and visits offices. While visitors to a letters and visits office must state their identity, written complaints may remain anonymous. In addition, the office must accept a complaint submitted to it. Hence, there are no formal provisions that complainants need to take into account to ensure that their grievances will be accepted; the facts they expose do not need to fit into specific categories. Thus, lodging a complaint at the letters and visits office is a personal decision that has a margin of freedom associated with it. Yet the individuals turning to these bodies face one important formal constraint: they must have *witnessed* what they report, although they do not have to be direct victims of the action denounced. Moreover, victims may report past unfair treatment and suggest a reform that would prevent such situations from recurring, rather than request immediate and individual justice.²⁶

Despite such procedural differences and despite the differences in duties and responsibilities of arbitration committees and letters and visits offices, the two systems often overlap. Many contributions to this volume stress the blurry boundary between legal and administrative bodies in China. The two institutions discussed here are no exception. Besides the historical and political reasons for this, it should be noted that the main purpose of letters and visits offices is to localize conflicts and prevent them from escalating into threats to social order. Hence, the offices often intervene in ongoing collective conflicts or act as mediators. There is also much crossing over from one body to the other, and it may happen that a letter and visits office resolves a labor dispute when the plaintiff refuses to resort to arbitration committees because such a process is too protracted or expensive.²⁷ Still, arbitration committees and letters and visits offices both offer venues that provide different ways to "name, blame, and claim," depending on the resources complainants have and the problem they have identified.²⁸

Who Complains About What? A Comparison

These two bodies serve somewhat different ends and have their own procedures. Their limitations and the opportunities they provide are strongly related to the identity of the appellants and the nature of the injustices exposed. So, let us first consider: Who are the complainants?

In the sixty arbitration committee files we have, all of the cases were initiated by employees[29] and 25 percent of them concerned collective disputes.[30] All of the complaints to the letters and visits office were also presented solely by workers or employees, and 10 percent of them were signed by more than thirty persons.

Workers in state-owned enterprises were more inclined to lodge complaints with an arbitration committee: that is, to appeal to the state to incriminate an enterprise. Whereas 17 percent of the firms named in the arbitration committee files were state-owned enterprises,[31] there was only a single case involving a state firm in our letter and visits files, and in this case the grievances related to a subcontracted canteen. Collective enterprises account for only 8 percent of the arbitration committee cases and fewer than 2 percent of the letters and visits office files. The remaining cases relate to private Chinese or foreign-invested enterprises and to all kinds of mixed-ownership firms.

Notably, too, arbitration committees' plaintiffs in Shenzhen are often skilled employees. If we put aside collective disputes, which often provide incomplete information about the positions held by complainants in the firm, 33 percent of the plaintiffs who approach arbitration committees are non-manual employees, and significantly, the mean monthly wage of all arbitration committee litigants amounts to a relatively high 1,444 yuan. On the other hand, those who lodge complaints with the letters and visits office are primarily migrant and manual workers with a mean monthly wage of 578 yuan. One might add that, while lodging a complaint with the letters and visits office is free, the average expense for arbitration, not including private lawyers' fees, totaled 2,361 yuan. These costs were shared among the parties at the final settlement. This expense may deter workers who are struggling to make ends meet from turning to arbitration committees. Finally, it should be stressed that arbitration committees' plaintiffs have worked an average of more than three years for the company involved, and 31 percent of them enjoyed a three-year contract.[32] Although no information is provided regarding their household registration permit, they seem to have possessed enough resources to have settled in Shenzhen, become involved in a long-term struggle, and perhaps to have developed a local "support structure," to use Charles Epp's term (see the Introduction).

Such is not the case for those who turn to letters and visits offices: most of them identify themselves as migrant workers or *dagongzai* who come from all parts of China. Their time spent in the firm, when mentioned in the dossiers, is usually expressed in terms of months. Only two complainants said that the situation they faced was all the more unfair because they possessed a permanent right of residence in Shenzhen.

This brief description clarifies some key differences between both groups regarding their relations with employers, the positions they hold in the firm, and the material and non-material resources they possess to gain entry to these two institutions. Although such differences influence the nature of the facts exposed and the norms mobilized, there is one other important factor common to those turning either to arbitration committees or to letters and visits offices: Shenzhen is a city that relies on huge migration flows and for most of the complainants the nature of lodging a complaint differs considerably from what prevails in the rural districts from which they hail. Complainants in the countryside normally make claims against local officials (see O'Brien and Li's chapter). But in the city, as workers, their grievances are directed against a factory's management rather than local officialdom. In addition, they are not embedded in particularistic ties, that is, in a world where personal connections prevail or are easy to mobilize. Collusion can be observed in Shenzhen between employers and the labor administration,[33] but in these files the relationship between the parties involved is often characterized by some distance and lack of familiarity. This is even more evident in the relationship between workers, on the one hand, and the two government organizations, on the other. This affects not only the means available to settle a dispute, but also the nature of the principles or arguments that can be mobilized.

Moreover, these migrant workers, unlike the state workers, pensioners, or veterans analyzed elsewhere in this volume, do not enjoy any commitments from the government regarding material benefits or professional opportunities. They therefore cannot rely on charges of broken promises to bolster their claims, but instead must identify other arguments.[34]

What types of evidence do they muster and on whose behalf do complainants speak? The files reveal that workers who turn to arbitration committees focus on events that happened to them: cases are centered, by virtue of the legal process, on specific actions or decisions that can be dated. Moreover, the facts exposed fit the classifications listed earlier in the paper: they concern the lack of legitimacy of a worker's dismissal and inadequate severance pay (58 percent of the cases), unpaid wages (25 percent), work accidents and claims for fair compensation (10 percent), and unpaid childbirth allowance and premiums (7 percent).

In contrast, written or oral complaints addressed to letters and visits offices are more diverse and can be classified as follows: wages paid too late or only partly paid (65 percent), excessive overtime (40 percent), refusal to sign a contract (15 percent), arbitrary dismissal (10 percent), unpaid social security

(3 percent), intense collective conflicts (3 percent), job accidents (1 percent), requests for more legal information (1 percent), and other causes (20 percent). However, these categories do not adequately illustrate the large variety of grievances mentioned in the letters. They include, for instance, employers resorting to violence, poor living conditions in dormitories, employers' untrustworthiness, illegitimate enterprise rules, and the inability of workers to perform their filial duties due to an employer's lack of humanity.

Migrant workers' complaints to the letters and visits offices also reveal a strikingly different pattern of abuses than what gets presented to an arbitration committee. Most notable is that two-thirds of all the letters bring a charge of unpaid wages, compared to only a quarter of the plaintiffs who approach the arbitration committee. Moreover, the migrant workers do not enjoy social benefits or expect severance pay if a right is infringed, unlike the better-off employees who go to arbitration committees.

Analytically, the facts divulged in the workers' complaints are diverse, multiple, and general. They expose a more complex reality than that discussed in arbitration committees. In addition, a letter of complaint often discloses a range of abuses, as if to show that the treatment faced is unjust not only in one particular aspect but from many perspectives. Further, the charges do not usually pinpoint isolated incidents or specific events; on the contrary, the violations are described as recurrent and therefore difficult to date. Among the 123 letters, only 32 are related to specific events affecting individuals who ask for personal redress and state their names. The rest of the complaints implicate general rules and practices that employers try to impose in the workplace. It should be added that in many letters the situation exposed is egregious and calls for immediate action.

In these documents we can thus see a contrast between the *particularization* of the facts presented to arbitration committees—attaching the grievance to specific individuals—and what might be called a process of *generalization* observed in workers' complaints to the letters and visits office. In the cases brought before arbitration committees, specified individuals or groups seek redress for personal and particular offences. Each administrative file includes personal information regarding the name, address, gender, professional activity, and salary of the plaintiffs. In other words, the resolution process involves two parties, clearly identified, who are going to meet and confront each other during mediation and, eventually, arbitration. Close to half are accompanied by lawyers or other representatives, a pattern that reinforces the uniqueness of each case.[35]

In comparison, among workers' complaints at letters and visits offices, 20 of the 91 written complaints regarding general working and living conditions were written by a worker who took the initiative, but who was speaking on behalf of a wider group; 20 grievances bear the signatures of their authors (consisting of from two to seventy-five names); and 4 are written by individuals claiming to be representatives of the workers. In the remaining 47 cases, the letters end with a general and anonymous collective formula, such as "Written by all the workers of company X" or "Signed by many tens of workers of company Z." Moreover, complainants often shift from personal to shared situations or feelings. The following quotations illustrate how the dividing line between the author or authors of the complaint and the people they represent is often blurred: "I arrived from Sichuan to work in Shenzhen, and I have been working in Company Z for almost one year. The friends and workers who work with me all share the same feeling: it is impossible to go on like this!" Or, "We are all angry and this is why I write to you to denounce a situation that violates the Labor Law."

In short, the complaints usually concern a group of workers hired by the same employer and affected by the same difficulties, although the extent to which that group constitutes a collective actor is often unclear. The generalization process can also sometimes be expanded to include workers beyond the limits of the concerned workshop or enterprise, such as all migrants facing the same working conditions, as in the following poem written by a female worker:

> A woman without any strength left speaks with an exhausted voice to the honest administrators.
> She asks them to be just and help her solve her grief.
> She will be grateful to them for intervening and restoring justice.
> Their names will be carved forever in the history of *dagongzai*.

The aggrieved workers sometimes also identify themselves using terms such as "the people," "the workers," or "the masses." The legitimacy of workers' complaints seems therefore to rest in part on their capacity to expose recurrent and general abuses and to speak on behalf of a larger group. Moreover, in the absence of formal commitments regarding the status assigned to them, they try to characterize themselves as members of social groups who had enjoyed a privileged status under the Maoist era—at least ideologically speaking. Such a process can be observed in the way workers appeal to the office's officials as their protectors. Complainants often identify their interlocutors as "uncles," "fair judge," "protective god," "comrades," "directing comrades," "servants of the people," and "father and mother of the people."

Finally, the differences between the two bodies are also illustrated by the type of justice that can be expected from both institutions, which in turn influences the ways in which the Labor Law is mobilized and, more generally speaking, the sense of injustice expressed.

Although the outcome of a dispute handled by an arbitration committee cannot be anticipated, the disputants can assume that a verdict will be rendered. In other words, the dispute will inevitably conclude at some point in the legal process when, either through mediation or arbitration, a common understanding of the facts will be reached and made public to all the parties. The decisions are often couched in explicit references to legal rules. It should be added that arbitration committees offer, through mediation or arbitration procedures, a solution that often favors the plaintiffs. In half of the disputes reflected in our data, the plaintiffs obtained what they sought; in 35 percent of the cases, they won but the amount of compensation received was slightly lower than requested because of diverging interpretations of the applicable legal provisions; and in 13 percent of them, the mediators or arbitrators apportioned responsibilities in the dispute and the plaintiffs' requests were only partly granted. The defendant was discharged in only one case.[36] Notably, plaintiffs mainly requested and obtained money through arbitration committees. That is, they were paid past wages, allowances, or bonuses, or received compensation for damages caused by illegal behavior by their employer.

The administrative response of the letters and visits office to the complaints received was much more diverse and uncertain. Informing, convincing, mediating, inquiring, sanctioning: these are some of the choices that members of the office can make, according to their interpretation of the situation. In labor disputes, these bodies must contact the employer and address the complaint in one of three ways: by informing both parties and convincing them of their wrongdoing; by organizing mediation, if possible; or by sanctioning the employer. If repeated mediation fails, labor disputes are supposed to be forwarded to arbitration committees. In our files, the response to the 123 complaints was that the facts they contained were recognized as true or partly true in 40 percent of the cases; alleged facts were found to be untrue in 3 percent of cases; the dispute had already been resolved by the time the bureau became involved 11 percent of the time; negotiations between both parties succeeded in 2 percent of the cases; the case was sent to an arbitration committee 2 percent of the time; the case was sent to a court 2 percent of the time; the case was sent to mediation 2 percent of the time; it was sent to another section of the Labor Bureau 7 percent of the time; the case was sent to another administrative unit 5 percent of the time; the office was unable to reach one of the parties in 12 percent of the cases; the nature of the dispute was deemed uncertain in 2 percent of the cases; and the administrative decision was simply to archive the file in 11 percent of the cases.

These figures call for several comments. First of all, although complaints are usually dealt with and not ignored by the letters and visits office, the administrative response cannot be predicted. The criteria for deciding to con-

TABLE 4.1

Comparison of Arbitration Committees with Letters and Office Visits

	Arbitration Committees	Letters and Office Visits
Overall approach	To apply the law	To resolve problems
Legal style	Legally formal	Informal
Posture	Reactive	Reactive and proactive
Appellants' identity	Specific, clearly identified	Loose collective actors
Facts alleged	Particular events	General conditions
Cost for appellant	Relatively high	Free
Outcomes	More predictable	Less predictable
Remedies	Monetary damages	Diverse administrative means

duct an immediate investigation by the office are unclear, though an administrative intervention is more likely to occur when disputes are believed to be intense and collective.[37] Moreover, the ultimate decision is not justified by an explicit reference to given rules or norms, but rather it is discussed in terms of the veracity of the facts disclosed. Consequently, uncertainties remain regarding the legal rules and social norms mobilized to interpret the facts in question, a situation that reinforces the tendency toward generalization discussed above.

Table 4.1 summarizes the discussion and distinguishes the various factors that interact to create two distinct spaces where tests of justice are carried out.

Mobilizing the Labor Law to Express a Sense of Injustice

Analysis of arbitration committee files reveals that injustices are exposed and settled according to a well-known process: legal categories and rules shape the selection of events and actions considered to be relevant and their characterization. From the moment an arbitration committee decides if a case is to be accepted to the moment when it delivers a judgment, a process of legal translation takes place. This process appears to be rather simple because the legal rules deemed applicable are selected from rather general and abstract legal provisions, including the Labor Law and related regulations. Moreover, no explicit mention is made of settlements in similar cases and no precedents are invoked. The committee's judgment usually begins by quoting from the letter written by the plaintiff. For example:

The plaintiff, Mrs. Zhong, has written to us and noted: "I am a contract worker of Electricity Company Z, my contract is three years old now, and even though the contract has not expired, the company has fired me, giving reasons such as difficulty selling its products, the need to protect the company and help it survive, and the need to cut expenses.... I cannot accept the reasons put forward to justify this early termination of my contract. I request that the company pay all of what it owes me from the day I was dismissed to the day when the contract officially expired, or to hire me back."

And as a second example:

The plaintiff has explained: "On 18 November 1997, I was asked by my supervisor to do overtime. I was soldering when chemicals nearby exploded and I was burned. When I was in hospital, a portion of the medical expenses were paid by my employer but then I never received my October salary nor the following months' wages. I therefore request payment of the salary due to me (6,000 yuan), the remaining hospital expenses (4,000 yuan), the medical expenses I have had since I left hospital (10,000 yuan) as well as 100,000 yuan for the physical damage inflicted."

The files typically continue by quoting arguments provided by the defendant and with a narration of facts believed to be true and relevant by the arbitration committee members. Then, after mentioning that mediation failed (in these two particular cases), the arbitration judgment is rendered and quoted. Each stage is thus characterized by a process of choosing facts considered to be relevant and evaluating them according to existing legal categories. (The rather overt illegality of the facts often dealt with by arbitration committees may partially explain why appellants have recently been inclined to choose arbitration rather than mediation, as shown in Mary Gallagher's essay.)

Although litigants mobilize existing labor provisions to express their sense of injustice and arbitrators frame their resolution in the same manner, this does not mean that the discussions and solutions provided are mechanistic, or that they do not influence local understandings of labor rights in China. On the contrary, a process based on the simultaneous interpretation of facts and legal norms is invoked, which often leads to stressing certain norms and neglecting others, to creating a hierarchy among them, and to clarifying their meaning.

One of the cases already mentioned provides an example. The plaintiff, a female contract worker, was fired in 1998 by the state company, although her contract had not ended. She was forced to sign documents printed by the Labor Bureau stating that both parties had agreed to terminate the contract. In exchange, the company committed to take all necessary steps for the municipal administration to deliver her a *daiye zheng*—a certificate indicating that she was a former state employee who had become redundant and was waiting for a job—and related compensation. The proceedings concentrated on answering two questions and ignored all other issues: Could the above events be considered a "bilateral termination of the contract," as the documents signed seemed to imply? And, if not, was the unilateral breach of the contract legitimate? The evidence, as assessed under various legal rules, suggested a reality different from that described by either of the parties. The arbitration committee discussed, for example, the extent to which the signing of the documents terminating the contract had been done in conformity with the principle of "equality, freedom, and negotiation" stated in the Labor Law. The answer was negative: the signing had been forced upon the plaintiff, and this amounted, in fact, to a unilateral breach of contract. The issue in question here is the freedom that was supposed to be enjoyed by the worker to refuse to sign the document. The relevant article in the Labor Law is based upon the principle of negotiation on an equal footing between employers and employees on such issues as the contents of a contract and the internal rules of the enterprise. However, no procedure has been established to verify the nature of the consent provided by workers. In practice, such consent is almost always coerced. By discussing the extent of freedom effectively enjoyed by the worker to refuse to sign, the arbitration committee was actually making a creative leap.

Was this breach of contract legitimate? It was stated that even in a state-owned enterprise financial pressure was not a legitimate reason to fire a worker. Article 14 of the "Provisional directives regarding the dismissal of workers for disciplinary violations in state-owned enterprises" was noted to point out that this enterprise had not gone bankrupt, nor was it facing "an unanticipated situation due to changes in production, management, or technical conditions" that could justify a breach of contract. Moreover, the appellant could not be considered a redundant worker, since the same state company had recently hired fifty-six workers on a temporary basis. It had thus clearly violated existing legal provisions. As a consequence, the dismissal of the plaintiff was judged to be illegal.

As seen, the need for the arbitration committees to interpret both facts and legal norms provides room for a process of interpretation and legitimization of legal rules. Moreover, the process also offers an opportunity to observe which elements of a general normative judgment will eventually be mobilized to support a juridical judgment. For instance, in one case, the willingness of both parties to avoid escalating a dispute was judged to be "reasonable and correct" by the members of the arbitration committee, which explicitly called for a more lenient approach toward the employer. Nonetheless, the process generally employed is one in which the use of legal provisions is central, but there is also a narrowing of the social injustices identified and addressed.

At the letters and visits offices, mobilization of the Labor Law follows a rather different pattern. In these letters, the plaintiffs' main concern is to find relevant and shared normative arguments in order to convince the members of the office that the situation faced is unacceptable and unjust to such an extent that intervention is required. Lodging a complaint with the office is usually based on the assumption that rulers and members of society share a similar perspective on what is just and unjust. Complainants, however, are faced with uncertainties regarding the nature of the norms and principles of justice shared today within Chinese society, and they also continue to confront an authoritarian state. In their letters, they accordingly tend to rely on two sets of principles whose relevance and validity cannot be publicly denied by the office. The first set is composed of formal elements of the official discourse which they adopt as their own criteria of justice. In doing this, they are engaging in a partly institutionalized, partly legitimate form of contention that Kevin O'Brien has called "rightful resistance."[38] It is within this context that they appeal to legal provisions such as the Labor Law, whose legitimacy no one can contest, and which is equally applicable to all. Yet, legal arguments are not so much mobilized here to protect legal rights as to argue that a given threshold between the acceptable and the unacceptable, the tolerable and the intolerable, has been crossed. What is stressed is the distance between what is legal (and thus supposed to be fair) and the lived reality, rather than mere transgressions of the law. As such, the legal arguments pave the way for a shift to wider normative arguments.

The Labor Law is used by those lodging complaints in very specific ways. First of all, although 90 out of the 123 letters do mention legal provisions to support the complainants' allegations, only 25 of them rely exclusively on the Labor Law to characterize their own situation as unjust. The other complaints combine different kinds of principles, norms, or rules. Moreover, the law is often used in a rhetorical fashion, the alleged violations simply described as being contrary to the law or as violating the workers' legal rights and interests. Only 10 letters demonstrate a detailed understanding of the various articles of the law. When the links between legal provisions and the lived reality are made explicit, a winnowing process occurs: some provisions are emphasized, such as those linked to wages and work hours, while others are ignored, such as those linked to social security benefits or the minimum wage. In addition, the provisions that are stressed are mobilized not simply to show that they have been violated, but that they have been violated to such an extent that the resulting situation is unacceptable. In other words, it is the gap existing between what "should be" according to the law—a norm that can be considered by definition as fair or reasonable—and what actually "is," which supports the complainants' determination that their situation is unbearable.[39] The following letter provides an example:

The Labor Law notes that working time should be 8 hours per day.... But we work here 30 days a month, we do overtime every night until one or two o'clock in the morning, and we are not even offered dinner before going to sleep. If you are tired and rest for a few minutes, a fine of 100 yuan is imposed; if you complain about the work, you have to pay 20 yuan.... How can we go on with such inhuman treatment?

Moreover, complainants tend to describe as "illegal" situations that are not covered by the law. They do so for a variety of reasons: to establish a link between general and abstract legal provisions and their particular situation, to fill in gaps in the law, and to make explicit norms that are taken for granted and therefore not couched in the law. Situations depicted as illegal can be related, for example, to housing provided by the employer (an issue on which the Labor Law is silent), the multiplication of fines, loans imposed on workers, the lack of implementation of an enterprise bonus system, or the requirement that some workers carry out public self-criticism. Norms whose transgression is described as "illegal" range from resorting to violence against workers, to the lack of morality of employers who fail to provide a good reason for imposing punishments, to forgetting past oral commitments, to ignoring basic tenets of procedural and distributive justice. In other words, the law is not only selectively mobilized, it is also reinterpreted and assigned a new and broader content. More importantly, by exposing a range of situations as legal transgressions and by stressing the extent to which such transgressions have gone beyond mere legal provisions, complainants aim to expose the lived reality as unacceptable rather than simply illegal.

Come and save us! If we go on like this, we are going to die from being too tired here in Shenzhen where no compassion is shown. We cannot stand it anymore and this is why we write to you, to beg you to come and help us! ... We work in a garment factory 14 hours a day, with 65 minutes' rest only for the two meals together. ... More than 80% of the workers here have health problems.... We are not very clear about the Labor Law but we heard on the radio that we should work 48 hours a week. In addition, wages are paid very late, in June we still had not received our New Year's bonuses.... All these violations of the law show, and this is the worst thing, that we are not considered human beings.... But the law is there to protect our security, to prevent us being treated as machines, to force the boss to follow moral rules and act in accordance with his oral commitments.

It should be added that the letters often depict two types of victims: both the workers and the state itself, whose decisions are not obeyed. Hence, letters contain expressions noting that "workers' legal rights and interests should be protected as well as the state's dignity." Thus the implication of some complainants that the local state was responsible for the poor implementation of the central government's legal provisions. Forty of the letters denounce legal missteps, administrative inaction, or collusion with employers.

Mobilizing formal elements of the official discourse also entails resorting to state ideology and the government's professed objectives. In other words, official commitments made by the government, when popularized, provide a legitimate and shared language to express feelings of injustice. They originate from specific orientations toward public action concerning all citizens and encompass a given understanding of the "common good," whatever the nature of the policy implemented. About 40 letters thus resort to expressions that had been used by the Party to denounce the pre-1949 situation: "exploitation," "capitalists," "increase in value," "slaves," "buffaloes," "running-dogs," and "proletarians." Yet these concepts are invoked in a new context and reinterpreted to expose the present situation: if this situation is unjust and unacceptable, it is precisely because it resembles circumstances that the Party officially claims to have abolished. Here, it is not so much the distance between "what should be" and what actually "is" that is exposed, but rather an inversion: what "is" is what has been condemned in the past:

> The Labor Law gives us sacred rights that no one can deny to us. However, although we work on Chinese territory, we have the feeling that the government just does not care about us. What differences exist between the situation that prevailed in the French and British concessions before 1949 and the situation we are facing today? ... Chinese bosses protect foreign bosses, they are their running dogs and consider us to be slaves! They protect the capitalists and harm our interests, they exploit us.

Admonitions are expressed, sometimes implicitly: "We want to participate in the glorious construction of socialism," sometimes more directly: "Do not forget that the 'mass line' should prevail in a socialist country."[40] And:

> We are all without a cent, we do not know where we going to sleep this evening. ... We have no choice but to wait for death or shed blood. ... How is it possible that today, in the socialist country led by Comrade Jiang Zemin, in a region as economically developed as Shenzhen,[41] that employers can be allowed not to pay workers for six months?[42]

In another letter, the government's commitment to protect the health of the Chinese people is called upon:

> Chinese authorities have been discussing the "plan to protect the health of the population." Such a plan concerns all the residents of the People's Republic of China, but it does not seem to have any impact in those factories where profit is the only goal. ... In an enterprise, both parties must act reasonably and protect their interests. The nation, the society, and the human being must be respected!

Most of these letters link political decisions, legal provisions, and ideological commitments. Complainants argue, for example, that the Labor Law should "support the building of socialism," or that all efforts should be made to create a "socialist legal system." Many of them stress that legal transgressions are even more intolerable because they create situations resembling those that existed under the "old society."

A second set of principles, combined in most letters with legal references, is composed of moral and social norms. A fundamental principle of justice is stated in 70 grievances: the necessity to respect human life and treat others as human beings. It is expressed through the denunciation of given actions or situations as inhuman or lacking humanity, and also through demands to be treated with dignity or according to the "laws of humanity." One letter states:

All the female workers of Company Z are turning to you through this letter. We want to lodge a complaint against our employer who violates the Labor Law, tortures his employees, and does not pay our salaries. . . . We are required to work until 3 or 4 in the morning, and sometimes we work through the night. . . . This has been going on for four months, and most of our sisters have gotten sick, some are in the hospital; those who work at night cannot sleep or eat anymore. . . . We don't look like human beings anymore, but fines are levied if we refuse to do overtime, so no one dares say anything. . . . They consider us to be buffaloes, slaves, or machines! Is it fair that we are deprived of all freedom? It is fair that we work for nothing? We cannot go on like this. This is why we make the five following requests . . .

Such disclosures of inhuman conditions are supported by descriptions of the risks to workers' mental and physical health, the lack of basic means of survival, and the absence of freedom, a grievance that is sometimes literal because the doors of the factory are locked during working hours. They write about a feeling of extreme powerlessness: "We cannot accept what is inflicted upon us but how can we refuse it?"

If we examine the various references to the term "human," we can distinguish four dimensions, often coexisting in the same letter.[43] One refers to the rather traditional concept of *renqing*. Employers are, for instance, depicted as lacking *renqing wei*, or "human touch": they ignore human feelings and the necessity to consider others' needs or circumstances. Another use of the term "human" relates to the notion, present in Marxist ideology, of "human dignity": complainants say that they are no longer "human figures" because they suffer under working conditions which violate "human dignity." A third is related to the recent emergence of the notion of inherent rights as a human being, or *rengequan*. In contemporary China, these officially recognized rights include the rights to life and health, and the protection of one's name, reputation, and private life.[44] Migrant workers thus appeal to their right to life and to basic means of survival. Finally, a rather Confucian interpretation is sometimes asserted: an employer's role as a human entails conformity to moral and social norms. Employers' lack of morality thus demonstrates their lack of humanity and their incapacity to treat others as human beings. Complainants often do not choose among these various understandings but draw on all of them to express a fundamental principle of justice that any ruler should observe and protect.

When complainants combine abiding moral norms with other social and moral touchstones (such as distributive justice, trustworthiness, and the necessity to justify one's decisions), they are denouncing transgressions and inhuman treatment as unjust in the sense of unacceptable rather than merely illegal. Complainants appealing to the state administration thus feel compelled to anchor the expression of their sense of injustice in normative orientations shared by the rulers and by the ruled. The normative uncertainties facing Chinese society today, combined with the unpredictability of eliciting a satisfactory response and the marginality of many complainants (in terms of status and resources) contribute to the couching of such appeals in terms of generalized but fundamental notions of injustice rather than more specific legal violations.

Conclusion

China's Labor Law is employed to support different tests of justice when appellants approach arbitration committees and letters and visits offices. In arbitration committees, legal provisions and concepts are assigned a central part in the expression of injustice and in the resolution of labor disputes. The decisions reached may not always be legally correct, but they will be framed in legal categories. Workers' complaints to letters and visits offices, on the other hand, display an inclination to use the Labor Law as a legitimate *point d'appui*, as leverage to elaborate a much more general normative discourse. Complainants may sometimes mobilize specific legal provisions, but the dominant pattern is one in which the content of the law is reinterpreted and rather loosely used to discuss broader normative issues. A fundamental question is raised in such appeals: What sort of behavior is acceptable and unacceptable in contemporary Chinese society? By posing this question, by testing the legitimacy of given arguments and principles at the same time that they express them, migrant workers are participating in the rebuilding of a "normative habitat"[45] embedded in both history and culture.

The prevalence of such an approach by letter writers illustrates how much a need there is in Chinese workplaces today—and in other settings—to clarify and reshape existing situations and norms. As a consequence, "complaints spaces," whatever their form (letters-to-the-editor, website chat rooms, visits to lodge appeals) or their underlying motive (seeking justice or just expressing one's views) have been expanding of late, and are invested as places in which normative perspectives can be expressed and confronted. Relevant legal provisions are used within such spaces, because notions of right can often be extrapolated from legal texts. However, in many cases, the links established with the law are so loose that the main objective of such rhetorical legal references seems to be to ground the legitimacy of wider normative discussions.

Legal arguments become associated in workers' complaints with ideological commitments and claimed national objectives. The characteristics of what Kevin O'Brien has called "rightful resistance" can thus be extended from contention involving specific grievances to normative debates. We must pay attention to the differences in the ideological or political content chosen by various types of complainants, since different social groups may anchor the legitimacy of their grievances in terms of the state's declared rhetorical commitments while pursuing divergent interests. Still, such a process has important social and political consequences. The relevance of state regulations or plans is continually being reassessed by those who are affected by them, as their content is reinterpreted, refashioned, and placed in a new context. Hence, the state is brought under pressure to act in conformity with its rhetoric and policies that are familiar but that have also been reshaped.

As just one example, the Chinese government has decided, largely in order to protect its legitimacy, to stress political continuities, and this has enlarged the repertoire of available discourses. For instance, migrant workers can mobilize Marxist and Maoist principles to express their grievances. In contemporary China such principles are regularly put to the test against workers' lived reality. Ultimately, as shown in our files, the paradoxical outcome of such a process, which involves resorting to state action in order to legitimate the expression of a sense of injustice, draws together political and normative debates. This will in turn help to shape the development of both political culture and social norms in China.

Notes

We would like to thank Robert Kagan, Stanley Lubman, Kevin O'Brien, Neil Diamant, Jonathan Unger, and Anita Chan for helpful comments made on an earlier draft.

1. On "tests of justice," see Alain Cottereau, "'Esprit public' et capacité de juger," in "Pouvoir et légitimité: Figures de l'espace public," *Raisons Pratiques* 3 (1992): 239–74.

2. The Labor Bureau of Shenzhen municipality administers the Special Economic Zone, as well as two districts located outside the zone.

3. "Shenzhen shi laowugong sixiang daode zhuangkuang diaocha" [Survey regarding the ideological and moral situation of migrant workers in Shenzhen Municipality], June 1996, unpublished internal report of the Shenzhen Municipality that was provided to the authors.

4. A preliminary comparison of legal proceedings involving labor disputes within arbitration committees and people's courts has revealed discrepancies that have led

us to exclude the people's courts from this discussion of mobilization of the Labor Law.

5. Zhang Buhong and Zhang Nühao, eds., *Laodongfa xinleixing anli jingxi* [A careful analysis of a new compilation of cases related to the Labor Law] (Beijing: Renminfayuan chubanshe, 1997), 51.

6. *Shenzhen fazhibao* [Shenzhen Legal Daily], 1 June 2001.

7. For a detailed analysis of the increasing number of labor disputes handled by arbitration committees, see the essay by Mary Gallagher in this volume.

8. *Renmin ribao* [People's Daily], 5 June 2002.

9. *Gongren ribao* [Workers' Daily], 9 March 2001.

10. Mirjan R. Damaska (*The Faces of Justice and State Authority: A Comparative Approach to the Legal Process* [New Haven, Conn.: Yale University Press, 1986]) distinguishes between the reactive State and the activist State. The first is characterized by the creation of a legal framework within which citizens pursue their goals. As a consequence, the contracting mode is central to it. The second is characterized by the importance of state problems and state policy. State decrees dominate over notions of contract. It would be interesting to analyze legal developments in China using such categories. We note here that, surprisingly enough, as far as labor regulations are concerned, the Chinese government has adopted a mixed attitude, which stresses the centrality of the contract concluded between both parties.

11. This last shift has not been easy: from 1978 to end of 1995, forty-nine labor laws and regulations were passed. They often concern different types of enterprises: thirteen have to do with state enterprises, two with joint ventures, five with foreign-invested firms, and one with private firms. Of the twenty-eight laws or regulations concerning all types of enterprises, which therefore affect all workers, sixteen were promulgated rather recently, between July 4, 1994, when the Labor Law was promulgated, and May 10, 1995 (see Alexandre Morin and Thierry Pairault, *La Chine au travail*, vol. 1, *Les sources du droit du travail* [Paris: GEC, 1997]).

12. Article 2 of the *Zhonghua renmin gongheguo qiye laodong zhengyi chuli* [Rules of the People's Republic of China on the handling of enterprise labor disputes] (1993). This document can be found in many sources; see, e.g., Wang Xueli, *Gongzi yu gongzi zhengyi chuli* [Salaries and the resolution of disputes linked to salaries] (Beijing: Renmin fayuan chubanshe, 1997), 459–63.

13. *Chuangyezhe* [Pioneers] 193 (2000): 16–17.

14. More exactly, the existing provisions indicate that the complainant must write to the arbitration committee within sixty days after a violation occurs.

15. It should be pointed out that interpretations vary also regarding the part assigned to mediation. Some believe mediation is a compulsory step before arbitration, while others believe that the decision to resort to mediation is left to the parties and the arbitrators (*Chuangyezhe* [Pioneers], 196 [2000]: 44).

16. For instance, the various letters and visits offices of the Guangzhou municipal government handled a total of 43,332 letters and visits in 1999. There were 4,612 visits alone, and most of them involved large groups, since the total number of visitors was 16,869 (the urban population of Guangzhou amounted to 4,054,958 during that same year) (*Guangzhou Yearbook 2000* [Guangzhou: Guangzhou nianjian chubanshe,

2001], 82). On the historical development of letters and visits institutions, see Laura M. Luehrmann, "Facing Citizen Complaints in China, 1951–96," *Asian Survey* 43, no. 5 (2003): 845–66.

17. *Nanfang Dushibao* [Southern Metropolis Daily], 14 June 2002.

18. *Shenzhen Yearbook 2000*, 528; Lu Bianqian, interview, Shenzhen, 16 November 2001.

19. Jonathan K. Ocko, "I'll Take It All the Way to Beijing: Capital Appeals in the Qing," *Journal of Asian Studies* 47, no. 2 (1988): 291–315.

20. *Renmin ribao* [People's Daily], 2 September 2001; *Shenzhen fazhibao* [Shenzhen Legal Daily], 26 December 2001.

21. Shenzhen Municipal Labor Bureau, ed., *Shenzhen tequ laodong zhidu shi nian gaige licheng* [Historical process of ten years of reforms of the labor system in the Special Economic Zone of Shenzhen] (Shenzhen: Haitian chubanshe, 1991).

22. The number of letters and visits offices has increased as a result of institutional proliferation. For instance, nowadays in Shenzhen, labor complaints can be transmitted to forty addresses. At the top of the hierarchy, the letters and visits office, which is attached to the "labor inspection brigade" of the municipal government, is divided into five departments and employed fifty-three persons in 2001. Each of the six districts forming the municipality has its own labor administration. Beneath the district level, there are various "stations of labor administration."

23. Labor inspection campaigns are regularly carried out, such as one organized in Shenzhen from May 11 to June 11, 2001. When the campaign ended, it was reported to have inspected 3,590 enterprises employing 780,000 workers. The inspections revealed that 99,000 persons had not properly registered at the Labor Bureau and 55,000 workers had not concluded a contract with their employer. An amount equaling 6,420,000 yuan of unpaid salaries was recovered on behalf of employees (see *Shenzhen shangbao* [Shenzhen Commercial Daily], 7 June 2001).

24. On citizen complaints, their dynamics, and the role of *guanxi*, see the papers written in this volume by Kevin O'Brien and Lianjiang Li, Mark Frazier, and Neil Diamant. See also Kevin J. O'Brien and Lianjiang Li, "The Politics of Lodging Complaints in Rural China," *China Quarterly*, no. 143 (1995): 756–83; and Ying Xing, *Dahe yimin, shangfang de gushi* [Migrants from the Great River: A story of collective protest] (Beijing: Sanlian chubanshe, 2001).

25. Such offices, for instance, do not exist below the county level, and rural complainants often have to work their way through other organs before reaching letters and visits offices.

26. Not only have letters and visits offices expanded since the beginning of the 1980s, but complaint centers and hotlines have increased as well, both within and outside administrative realms. "Complaints" as a category is also present on many Internet forums.

27. In November 1998, for instance, the letters and visits office discussed here received a written complaint from a worker who had been seriously injured at work in 1996. Just after the accident, an agreement was reached by both parties stating that the employer would pay 220,000 yuan in medical expenses and 100,000 in living expenses. Two years later, the worker complained that the compensation received was

far too low compared to the damages inflicted. Encouraged by the letters and visits office to apply to the arbitration committee, he refused, arguing that he had no money to resort to such a procedure. As a consequence, a new mediation process was initiated and the company ultimately offered 55,000 yuan as compensation (*Shenzhen shangbao* [Shenzhen Commercial Daily], 22 June 2001).

28. William Felstiner, Richard Abel, and Austin Sarat, "The Emergence and Transformation of Disputes: Naming, Blaming, Claiming . . . ," *Law and Society Review* 15, nos. 3–4 (1981): 631–54.

29. In 1999, 5 percent of cases accepted by arbitration committees were appealed by employers (*China Labor Statistical Yearbook 2000*, 462).

30. In 1999, 7.5 percent of the cases accepted by arbitration committees were collective (*China Labor Statistical Yearbook 2000*, 461).

31. National figures for 1999 show that 22 percent of cases were appealed by state-owned enterprises (*China Labor Statistical Yearbook 2000*, 461).

32. In 1999 the total population of Shenzhen municipality was 4,051,300 persons, of whom 70 percent possessed only provisional residence cards. On migration to Shenzhen, see Thomas Scharping and Sun Huaiyang, eds., *Migration in China's Guangdong Province* (Hamburg: Mitteilungen des Instituts für Asienkunde, 1997). In 1999, 36 percent of workers were employed in the state sector and 5 percent in the collective sector (*Shenzhen tongji xinxi nianjian 2000* [Shenzhen statistical information yearbook 2000] [Beijing: Zhongguo tongji chubanshe, 2000], 69, 277).

33. For instance, 12 percent of the complaints in our files received no administrative response, on the grounds that one of the parties could not be reached, an outcome that often hides collusion between the letters and visits offices and employers.

34. Our files thus focus on a specific type of complainant: migrant workers hired in non-state enterprises. Such workers form the majority of the labor force in Shenzhen. As a consequence, the local response to their problems certainly differs from other places. As discussed above, this municipality was the first one to establish a labor inspection system, and arbitration committees appear rather active, as compared to Guangzhou, for instance. However, as far as the expression of injustices is considered, migrant workers' complaints in Shenzhen do not appear to differ greatly from those filed by migrant workers in other localities such as Foshan, Dongguan, and Guangzhou, or complaints accessed via the Internet. See, for instance, migrants' complaints on Zhujiang luntan (the Pearl River Forum), http://www.chat.ycwb.com/forum/index.

35. In our files, 56 percent of the litigants appeared alone, while the others were assisted by either one or two lawyers, or by non-legal representatives.

36. The files contained no information on the implementation of such decisions. On this issue, see Stanley B. Lubman, *Bird in a Cage: Legal Reform in China after Mao* (Stanford, Calif.: Stanford University Press, 1999).

37. *Shenzhen shangbao* [Shenzhen Commercial Daily], 10 February 2001.

38. Kevin J. O'Brien, "Rightful Resistance," *World Politics* 49, no. 1 (1996): 31–55. See also Shen Yuan, "L'affaire du tirage au sort: Principes de justice des commerçants d'un marché du nord de la Chine," in *Disputes au village chinois*, ed. Isabelle Thireau and Wang Hansheng (Paris: Editions de la Maison des Sciences de l'Homme, 2001).

39. For this point, see O'Brien, "Rightful Resistance," 55.

40. On the use of Maoist symbols and defunct regime norms to anchor resistance, see Elizabeth J. Perry, "Crime, Corruption, and Contention," in *The Paradox of China's Post-Mao Reforms*, ed. Merle Goldman and Roderick MacFarquhar (Cambridge, Mass.: Harvard University Press, 1999), 308–32; Lianjiang Li and Kevin J. O'Brien, "Villagers and Popular Resistance in Contemporary China," *Modern China* 22, no. 1 (January 1996): 45–47; and Ching Kwan Lee, "From the Specter of Mao to the Spirit of the Law: Labor Insurgency in China," *Theory and Society* 31, no. 2 (2002): 189–228.

41. The main differences between complaints in Shenzhen and complaints lodged by migrant workers in other places center on (1) the extent to which Shenzhen is such a "special" place that people there can ignore national laws and (2) the contrast between Shenzhen's economic prosperity and the treatment of some workers.

42. See also Ching Kwan Lee, "The 'Revenge of History': Collective Memories and Labor Protest in North Eastern China," *Ethnography* 1, no. 2 (2000): 217–37.

43. For a more detailed analysis of the content of this body of written complaints, see Isabelle Thireau and Hua Linshan, "Le sens du juste en Chine: Enquête d'un nouveau droit du travail," *Annales* 6 (2001): 1283–1312.

44. Liu Fengjing, *Rengequan* [The rights of the human person] (Beijing: Zhongguo shehui kexueyuan chubanshe, 1999).

45. Alain Cottereau, "Dénis de justice, dénis de réalité: Remarques sur la réalité sociale et sa denegation," in *L'expérience du déni*, ed. Pierre Gruson and Renaud Dulong (Paris: Editions de la Maison des Sciences de l'Homme, 1999), 159–89.

MARK W. FRAZIER 5

What's In a Law?
China's Pension Reform and Its Discontents

Recent protests by pensioners in Chinese cities have arisen over specific, largely local demands, but the protests also possess an abstract, nearly universal grievance. Pension reform, in China as elsewhere, threatens to undermine an implicit social contract between the state and a specific, usually loyal group of beneficiaries. John Myles and Paul Pierson have observed of pension reform in the American and West European welfare states that "pension systems are *essentially a code of laws* stipulating who may make claims on the state and under what conditions. Reneging on past contracts by unilaterally reducing benefits creates a profound problem of legitimacy for governments."[1] In their study of Chinese pensioners and laid-off workers, William Hurst and Kevin O'Brien offer empirical support for the notion that public pensions in China carry an implicit social contract. The authors conclude that pensions "appear to be considered a truly sacred right in the eyes of both workers and the state."[2]

When the Chinese government in the 1990s introduced fundamental changes in how pensions were financed and distributed, it changed the unstated "code of laws" regarding who may claim benefits from the state and who pays for these benefits. In effect, pension reform transferred the costs and responsibilities for financing and distributing retiree benefits from the "work-unit," or state enterprise, to the abstraction of "society." The latter term (*shehui*) is routinely used by officials and ordinary Chinese to emphasize the point that pensions are no longer administered, as they were for almost fifty years, by state enterprises on behalf of their retirees. As suggested by the vague notion that pensions are now handled in "society," pension reform has spread the financial and administrative burdens from state enterprises across a broad swath of employers, workers, national agencies, and local governments. Successive regulations issued since the early 1990s have done little to resolve a fundamental problem that emerged when pensions were moved from the enterprise to "society": namely, the diffusion of powers and responsibilities over pension fund collections and administration to local governments that face incentives both to comply with and to evade national pension regulations. As a result, today's pensioners, like the 1950s veterans whose plight Neil Diamant discusses in this volume, face a state that once glorified them politically but that has now abandoned them financially.

The abundant and growing literature on China's pension reform has stressed the difficulties of financing benefits for retirees from a dwindling base of state firms, as well as problems associated with collecting sufficient social security revenues. With few exceptions, most analyses of pension reform have tended to underemphasize the critical fact that China's "pension system" does not come under a singular institution but is an agglomeration of some two thousand "social pools" (*shehui tongchou*) under the local control of provincial, city, county, and prefectural governments.[3] Nelson Chow and Yuebin Xu have discussed in broader studies on social welfare in Guangzhou how the evolution of pension reform in the 1980s and 1990s created fragmented coverage and benefits depending on ownership categories (state, collective, etc.) and on employment status (full-time, temporary, etc.).[4] This fragmenting of pension administration occurred in virtually all urban areas of China. Fragmentation of pensions and social welfare more broadly was a legacy of the planned economy, which created sharp regulatory divides between rural and urban areas, across state and non-state enterprises, permanent and temporary labor, and others. As Linda Wong has shown, the pattern of social welfare reforms mirrors closely in its coverage the categories created under the planned economy.[5] In the case of pensions, for example, only registered urban residents remain eligible for coverage.

The decentralized, locally based structure of pension administration evolved gradually over the course of pension reform in the 1980s and 1990s, when municipal governments began pooling funds of local enterprises in order to spread the costs of retirement benefits across groups of firms. Still, large deficits exist between how much a given pension pool takes in and how much it expends on benefits for retirees. Only a few pension pools have managed to operate without a deficit. The source of this deficit problem is a subject of some debate among researchers and policy analysts. Studies by Peter Lee and Jiang Chunze and by Yaohui Zhao and Jianguo Xu point to various problems in coordination and collective action as cities and provinces continually look to one another or to the central government to plug the gap between what a given locality collects in pension fees and what it pays out in benefits.[6] In this article, I show that the portrayal of urban governments'[7] operating pension pools as the lackadaisical agents of the center do not square with recent observations showing the great lengths that local officials have gone to in order to apply pressure on local enterprises to remit pension fees to local pools. There is no doubt some mileage to be gained in analyzing China's deficit-ridden pension system from a principal–agent perspective in which local governments duck and evade the orders of the central government to collect sufficient social security revenues. Such an emphasis on agency problems, however, overlooks important patterns in how officials, enterprise managers, and workers utilize a confusing patchwork of pension regulations in a protracted policy struggle over the future structure and content of China's pension system.

The findings presented here are based in part on open-ended interviews with twenty-three officials, enterprise managers, policy analysts, and others in two provincial capitals and in Beijing and Shanghai during the summers of 2001 and 2002. Over the course of these interviews, many officials and scholars, especially those associated with the Ministry of Labor and Social Security, whose task it was to collect payroll taxes from enterprises to finance pension benefits, consistently took the position that their work was severely hampered by the absence of a social security law.[8] These officials and analysts made the point that passage of such a law would clarify ambiguities in current regulations and would elicit greater compliance from employers reluctant to remit payroll taxes. This argument, flawed though it might be, reveals an important perception about law in China and the potential uses of "law as a weapon": they are not used by disaffected workers, as the chapters in this volume by Mary Gallagher and by Isabelle Thireau and Hua Linshan reveal, but by state officials themselves, who must implement complicated pension rules. As I show in this chapter, current regulations on pensions and their enforcement by local agencies have elicited a surprising degree of compliance among some enterprise managers. Nor has the lack of a formal law prevented pensioners and workers from pursuing claims and redressing grievances associated with pension funding and benefits. In general, the fixation among many officials and analysts on the passage of a social security law distracts attention from the underlying issue of the heavily decentralized structure in which local governments and their preferences can easily override the goals of pension regulations (or legislation, if it were to be enacted in the future).[9]

The essence of pension reform in China, and in many other transitional economies, is to replace a retirement benefit provided by state enterprises with benefits linked to the amount that an individual worker contributes to a retirement account while employed. This process of turning a guaranteed state benefit into individually funded accounts (with partial state support) involves current or soon-to-be retirees drawing upon public coffers since they lack sufficient job tenure to build up funded accounts. As in other public pension programs, employers are required to make contributions to pension funds through a payroll tax, which social security agencies collect and administer as part of a broader social security fund. (In China this fund includes benefits paid for unemployment, illness, workplace injury, and maternity leave, in addition to pensions.)

In many countries the politics of pension reform involves extensive debates among interest groups and political parties representing, inter alia, business associations and trade unions. The ability of these groups to muster resources and their access to political institutions has resulted in different types of pension reforms being passed into law.[10] In Hungary and Poland, constitutional courts and constitutional advisory panels intervened to modify proposed pension reform legislation to endorse the "legal concept of acquired rights to benefits."[11] In Poland, legislation had to be revised so as to include a state guarantee to cover pension deficits between collections and payouts.[12] In China, by contrast, pension reform has taken the path of incremental adjustments to administrative regulations through successive measures by the central government. Central government regulations can be modified significantly by local governments when they issue their own local rules and regulations to implement the center's directives. Pension administration over time has thus become heavily localized, meaning that the mechanisms for dismantling old policies, collecting funds for new accounts, and supporting the pension needs of the transitional cohort have all been left to local governments. A not so far-fetched comparison may be made to the American federal government's passage of ambitious social legislation that it then leaves to the states and cities to finance: the central government in China has given localities the "unfunded mandate" to finance a new pension system based on the parameters laid down by the center. This approach to pension reform has left pensioners heavily dependent on the efforts of local government agencies to collect sufficient payroll deductions from firms within their jurisdiction.

Without a nationally administered, or at least regionally consolidated, pension system under more direct central government control, retirees' claims to benefits and other disputes over pension administration are channeled through the enterprise and local officialdom. The lack of a pension or social security law does little to hamper local governments from collecting payroll taxes or individual pensioners from making claims to retirement benefits, but the more crucial absence of a centralized social security apparatus has meant that pension politics in China remains a distinctly local affair.

Writing in 1991, Donald Clarke noted that the "vast quantity of legislation produced by the central government since 1978 represents [a] centralization effort," with Beijing seeking to regain controls over economic policy that had been devolved to local governments and enterprises. Clarke observed that "in many respects central legislation has failed to achieve its goal because it was an effort to put new wine—new substantive rules about what enterprises and local governments could and could not do—in the old bottle of pre-reform legal institutions, which remain in many ways unchanged in the position they occupy in the Chinese polity."[13] Clarke's observation over a decade ago applies likewise to efforts by the central government during the 1980s and 1990s to introduce a less costly pension program and to create a uniform social safety net. New rules about the funding and administration of pensions were poured into the "old bottles" of enterprise-based pension arrangements dating back to the 1950s.

The Trajectory of Pension Reform

Most full-time workers in state enterprises and urban collectives have received basic medical, workplace injury, maternity, retirement, and accidental death benefits since 1951, when the fledgling PRC government issued "Labor Insurance Regulations of the People's Republic of China."[14] These measures, including pensions, were financed by each enterprise setting aside 3 percent of its wage bill to union committees locally and within the enterprise. Upon reaching age 60 for men and age 50 for women, workers were entitled to receive a certain percentage (about 50 to 70 percent) of their final year's base wage as pension benefits. By the early 1970s, such benefits were paid out directly by enterprises to their retirees. However, since enterprises remitted profits as taxes and received their budgets from government coffers, ultimate financial responsibility for supporting pensioners remained with the state.

When the national leadership initiated industrial reforms in the mid-1980s, granting greater autonomy to enterprise managers was a central objective. While the reforms permitted state-enterprise managers to retain profits, enterprises continued to provide, and even expanded, their welfare function as "small societies." Retirees, as before, received pensions and medical benefits directly from their enterprises. Only in the 1990s, when state enterprises faced enhanced competition from non-state enterprises, did reductions of the workforce, and the comprehensive welfare programs administered through the enterprise, come to the forefront of reforms. In recent years, the pension system has been used to "retire" a significant portion of the 20 million state-enterprise workers who have left the state sector since the mid-1990s. The ranks of retirees have grown from 31 million in 1995 to an estimated 40 million by 2002, an expansion that contains a large portion of "early retirees," according to several informants from the Ministry of Labor and Social Security.

Experimental measures introduced by selected cities in the mid-1980s created citywide pension funds (also known as "social pools") that were intended to distribute the burdens of supporting retirees more evenly across all of the enterprises in the pool. As often is the case in the evolution of public policy in China, experiments with pension pools in several selected cities served as the basis for subsequent administrative regulations. The most significant regulations covering full-time state-enterprise workers came in 1991, when the State Council announced a nationwide policy to finance pension obligations through "three pillars." These provided for a defined benefit, that is, a basic pension for retired state-enterprise workers; an individual account to which workers would contribute during their active work years and draw upon in their retirement (a "defined contribution" in pension policy parlance); and an optional supplemental pension insurance that enterprises and individuals could purchase for additional income during retirement.[15] Significantly, the regulations did nothing to alter the benefit structure from the 1951 regulations, meaning that retiree benefits remained a function of years of service and past wage earnings. In effect, the new financing arrangements had to support pre-reform benefit packages for a growing retiree population.

The State Council's 1991 decision contained several other areas of ambiguity. While generally calling for pension pools ultimately to come under the administrative control of provincial governments, the regulations did not specify which level of government should regulate pension pools. The 1991 decision stated that "those areas that have not yet implemented provincial-level pools for basic pension insurance funds must actively create conditions for them, and current city and county level pools must gradually be transferred into provincial pools."[16] Moreover, the regulations did not standardize "contribution rates," or how much firms and individuals should remit as a percentage of their wage bills. As a result, urban governments were left to set their own payroll tax rates. Urban governments had to ensure that they collected enough to provide local retirees with pension benefits equivalent to a percentage of the average local wage.[17]

Subsequent State Council regulations issued in 1995 and 1997 attempted to bring greater uniformity across the locally based pension pools. A 1995 circular (*tongzhi*) was significant for expanding pension coverage from state-enterprise workers to all urban employees, regardless of the type of their employment status or their enterprise's ownership form. Yet these regulations did little to standardize contribution rates, and in fact permitted urban governments to adopt one of two types of methods for calculating local contribution rates. The 1997 regulations, technically a State Council decision (*jueding*) renewed the central government's effort to standardize the collection of pension fees and the distribution of benefits, but these measures stopped well short of unifying pension administration under one level of government.[18] Local governments had their options narrowed by these regulations, but they nonetheless exercised a great deal of leeway in designing and implementing their own pension funds.

For central-government regulations to be substantially modified, and even to encounter resistance at local levels, will come as no surprise to those familiar with Chinese bureaucratic politics. Implementation of laws and directives from central-government ministries and other agencies can be postponed, compromised, or even ignored under certain conditions by various sub-national layers of government. This pattern of local government preferences mediating central legal-administrative power is consistent with Kenneth Lieberthal's model of "fragmented authoritarianism."[19] Nonetheless, the center does retain important levers over the regions and under certain conditions can structure incentives in order to gain compliance. Some argue that Beijing's willingness to centralize a policy area depends on the salience or importance of the issue.[20] One of the most commonly cited examples is that of fiscal policy reforms in 1994, when the central government, encountering shrinking revenues, unified tax collection and established national tax collection agencies at local levels.[21]

Pension policy logically seems an area in which the central government would desire to assert greater controls. It is highly consequential, vital for the future reform of state-owned enterprises, and politically sensitive, in that it presents a threat to the Party's highly prized goal of social stability. In 2000 the central government accordingly established a National Social Security Fund, but to date the fund acts as little more than a mechanism to subsidize deficit-ridden provinces, which in turn redistribute funds to prefectures, cities, and counties. In short, there is a compelling rationale for regulations—or legislation, as many PRC analysts and officials assert—that would standardize payroll tax rates, consolidate pension pools at national or regional levels, and distribute benefits to retirees in a more uniform fashion.

Significance of Regulations and Other Rules

One could make the case that, in broad terms, the rights of retirees to pensions were guaranteed in Articles 44 and 45 of the 1982 Constitution, in which the state promises to ensure the livelihood of retirees from enterprises, institutions, and state agencies, and to provide insurance for the elderly, ill, and disabled. Moreover, the 1995 Labor Law contains an article (No. 73) stipulating that employees are entitled to pensions and other forms of social insurance, with specific provisions to be spelled out in "laws, rules, and regulations."[22] Pension regulations issued in the 1990s by the State Council, some of which preceded the Labor Law, attempted to fulfill this legislative mandate by enumerating precisely how the state would finance and support retirees.

The Chinese state in the reform era has frequently issued regulations on the assumption that they will accumulate until conditions are considered "mature" for formal legislation.[23] "Maturity" generally connotes that multiple agencies whose functions and staffing might be affected by a new law have reached a consensus on the draft legislation. Some informants explained that bureaucratic politics among agencies with clashing interests have prevented passage of pension or broader social security legislation to date.[24] However, law or no law, it is worth considering the heavily decentralizing effects that nearly fifteen years of accumulated regulations have had on the ability of the Chinese state to administer a coherent pension system.

China's 1982 Constitution (Article 89) gives administrative regulations (*xingzheng fagui*) issued by the State Council the status of legal documents, superseded in their authority only by formal legislation passed by the National People's Congress or its Standing Committee.[25] According to most interpretations, State Council "decisions" (*jueding*) and "orders" (*mingling*) are of a subordinate status compared with State Council documents labeled as "regulations" (*tiaoli*), "rules" (*guiding*), and "measures" (*banfa*).[26] The original 1951 labor insurance regulations, and a subsequent revision in 1953 that enumerated benefits for urban-enterprise workers, were *tiaoli*. However, the 1991 State Council directive that dramatically altered pension financing arrangements ("Decision on Pension System Reform for Workers and Staff of Urban Enterprises") was, by virtue of its labeling as a "decision," arguably among a subordinate class of State Council administrative regulations. Subsequent pension regulations, for example, a 1997 "decision," also possessed by their labels an implicitly subordinate regulatory–legal status, and therefore, some PRC legal analysts argue, signaled to local levels a secondary priority in terms of implementation.[27]

In the final analysis, of course, the label that State Council regulations bear matters less than their real consequences, intended and otherwise, when they are implemented. In 1998, in response to the mounting deficits in pension funds created in part by letting firms reduce what they owed in contributions to local funds, the State Council issued a "circular" that ordered local social security offices thenceforth to collect in full what enterprises owed to pension funds, and prohibited firms from deducting what they were ostensibly going to pay in benefits to their retirees. The circular also urged provinces, prefectures, and cities to "actively create the conditions and hasten the social [e.g., local government's] distribution of basic pension funds to enterprise retirees."[28] These measures signaled a renewed effort by the central government to move the distribution of pension benefits once and for all out of the enterprise and into "society." These and other policy directives in 1998 had important consequences for pension administration, according to the provincial officials and enterprise managers that I interviewed. Prior to the 1998 circular, enterprise managers bore some legitimate responsibility to distribute pensions to retirees. Thereafter, the obligation to finance pensioners lay with city officials, because the social security agencies of local governments were now the sole providers of pension distributions. Any disputes over pension payouts could now be placed at the doorstep of city hall, rather than the firm itself. Cities thus assumed both the financial and political risk of funding pensioners.

One year after local governments had assumed the responsibilities of delivering pensions to retirees, the State Council issued another important directive, this time a "provisional regulation" (*zanxing tiaoli*) that strengthened the hands of local governments in collecting pension and other social insurance fees from employers. Among the most significant clauses in this regulation was an article that gave courts the ability to issue compulsory measures if an enterprise manager or responsible persons refused to comply with social security agency orders to remit delinquent payments.[29] A subsequent Ministry of Labor and Social Security measure stipulated fines and legal remedies for dealing with enterprises that failed to remit social insurance fees.[30] Fines were levied directly at the "principal personnel and others directly responsible" for an enterprise, and fines ranged from 1,000 to 20,000 yuan.

This gradual ratcheting up of regulatory measures in the 1990s came with a growing sense that the incremental approach to pension reform was inadequate to finance benefits for current retirees, not to speak of future cohorts. A spate of protests by unpaid pensioners in the late 1990s offered dramatic proof that many cities were collecting less in pension contributions than they needed to distribute as benefits. Yet, despite the urgency with which pension policy was discussed at various national conferences, the central government stopped short of consolidating local pension funds into a national account. Such a move would have entailed a major budgetary commitment that the central government was not willing to make at that point, explained several PRC policy analysts in interviews. Even though State Council pension regulations of the 1990s made repeated calls for consolidation of local pension funds at provincial levels, they had the effect of further localizing an already fragmented pension system by giving local officials more powers and incentives to collect and to retain funds they raised from local enterprises.

LOCAL ENFORCEMENT

Since the late 1990s and early 2000s, provincial and city governments have issued dozens of local laws and regulations on pension and social insurance reform.[31] These local measures emerged as a result of new pressures placed on local governments to collect pension and other social insurance fees now that such benefits were in practice supposed to be distributed by "society" rather than the enterprise. Local governments responded in different ways, but generally provincial and municipal governments have issued rules and regulations that enhance their authority to go after delinquent employer-contributors.

According to legal commentators, the 1999 "Provisional Regulations"[32] gave legal backing to efforts by local governments to collect social insurance fees from enterprises and a legal basis to efforts to deal with social insurance remittances that fell into arrears. First, the 1999 "Provisional Regulations" allowed urban governments to use the tax collection agencies, with their relatively greater abundance of personnel and other administrative resources. Local tax authorities reputedly have more accurate and reliable information about local firms' employment and wage bills. They can check management's tax filings against information submitted with social insurance fees. Knowing that the same officials will be examining both sets of documents, managers are much less likely to reduce their pension fee remissions by underreporting the number of employees and the size of the wage bill on social insurance forms, a Beijing policy analyst explained. The Chinese press has noted with some frequency the success of transferring social insurance fee collection to tax authorities.[33]

Second, urban governments have used their leverage over licenses and inspections to pressure firms to comply with pension regulations. Annual renewals of business licenses, tax compliance certifications, public health certifications, family planning compliance (for the one-child policy), etc., might be delayed or denied if a firm falls into arrears on pension fee remissions, as several officials noted in interviews. Within the social security bureaucracy, which is also responsible for workplace safety inspections, wage policy compliance, labor contract certifications, and other licenses, officials are likely to apply stricter standards or even delay renewal of certifications. According to local social security officials as well as enterprise managers who have faced sanctions, enterprises have been turned down in their applications to retire workers, meaning that the firm must support would-be retirees until managers come up with a plan to remit unpaid pension fees. One enterprise in Jilin Province claimed that its retirees were placed in limbo and not able to retire because local authorities were punishing the entire enterprise group to which this firm belonged after one of its member firms had accumulated a large amount of unpaid pension and other social insurance fees. Contrary to claims made by advocates of a social security law, the absence of formal legislation has not prevented state officials from pursuing measures against firms that evade or cannot remit pension fees.

Third, urban governments have made frequent use of the media in their pension collection efforts. Many local broadcast networks run investigative reports naming the enterprises and the managers that have fallen behind on their pension contributions to local pension pools. Reporters show up at an enterprise unannounced for an "on-the-spot" interview with the enterprise director, seeking to elicit an embarrassed explanation for why the firm has fallen behind. When a group of firms in the city of Rongcheng in Hunan Province were exposed in this way, none of the managers conceded before the cameras that they would pay back fees, and all reacted with disdain at being the target of reporters' questions. However, half of the managers paid their fees after the reports were broadcast. A commentator in *China Social Security* magazine concluded, "Even though . . . some [managers] cover the camera lens, use foul language, and cause injuries, this media exposure is not one bit inferior to official inspections and other forceful measures."[34] Several informants noted that urban governments frequently publish in local newspapers the names of enterprises that have fallen behind on pension fee remissions, along with the amount that they owe. In Beijing, the Ministry of Labor and Social Security routinely releases a list of enterprises that owe more than 10 million yuan in back payments to pension funds (the number of these firms reached thirty-three in early 2002). While the actual number in arrears is larger, the Ministry names enterprises that reportedly "have the ability to pay their fees but still fall into arrears on basic pension insurance fees."[35]

Finally, in addition to issuing regulations, a number of provincial-level governments have produced local legislation (*difang lifa*) to further pension collection efforts. Hunan Province in the mid-1990s passed local legislation on social insurance that established a Social Insurance Tribunal. It was said that foreign-invested enterprises in the province ignored the "red letterhead" documents of the local government agencies, but upon receipt of a subpoena from the Hunan Social Insurance Tribunal, enterprise managers actively pursued out-of-court settlements to remit their unpaid pension fees to local social security offices.[36] The Standing Committee of the Shanghai People's Congress passed a measure in 1998 giving Shanghai authorities the legal backing to work with local courts to authorize the auction of enterprise assets and to collect pension fees from the proceeds.[37] According to one social security specialist, local legislatures have taken such initiatives—and done so to an excessive degree—because there is no national law on social insurance.[38]

Despite these steps by local legislatures, the overriding preference by urban governments has been not to use formal judicial procedures based on legal norms to pressure enterprises and employers into remitting pension fees. This preference was explained in remarks by a social security official in Sichuan Province, who stressed to me the broader implications if his agency pushed existing measures on pension remittances to the letter of a law. "We have to be careful here about overall economic development and social stability—it's possible to do this to death [*gao dao gaosile*]. So we're reluctant to use judicial and bankruptcy channels."

ENTERPRISE PERSPECTIVES ON LOCAL REGULATION

The emergence of local pension administration in the 1990s had the effect of pitting large state enterprises against local governments in fights over contributions to local pension pools. This was the case because the larger the firm, the larger its wage bill and hence its potential contribution to local social insurance coffers. In an interview, a labor and social security official in Sichuan recounted a vivid example of one such dispute. The city government of Panzhihua, a "company town" in Sichuan, faced fierce resistance from the leaders of Panzhihua Steel, a large, integrated mill with over 100,000 employees and relatively few retirees. This firm had the distinction of tallying the largest amount in unpaid pension and other social insurance contributions of any firm in China—over 300 million yuan by 1998. Ultimately, it took an order from the CCP's Central Committee to force it to pay up. In a similar case pitting a large enterprise with national political clout against a local government, the managers of Baoshan Steel engaged in a protracted dispute with the Shanghai municipal government over 2 million yuan in unpaid pension contributions in 1999–2000, according to a researcher at a local think-tank. In both instances, it took pressure from the upper reaches of the CCP hierarchy through the enterprise Party committee to get management to comply.

This struggle between employers and local officials is not limited to large state enterprises. False reporting of payroll records, usually by understating the number of employees and their wage levels, is commonplace, and more readily accomplished in private firms. Smaller, scattered firms are inherently difficult to monitor. As one county-level official wrote of enterprise managers: "In order not to remit pension insurance fees, some enterprises rack their brains, giving every thought to how they might play tricks on the collecting agencies and engage in a see-saw battle with them."[39]

From the perspective of enterprise managers, administrative measures since 1998 have given municipal governments far too much arbitrary authority to compel firms to remit the fees. The manager of an SOE in Changchun explained during an interview that "the municipal government prevents us from falling behind on pension collections. They say to us, 'If you fall into arrears then we won't give out pensions to retirees from your enterprise.' They shouldn't do this because if an enterprise falls behind on pension payments, why make things worse?" A manager in Chengdu asserted, in strident tones, that it is social security authorities that violate the Labor Law and existing regulations entitling retirees to pension benefits. Social security officials, he felt, used heavy-handed methods. Particularly galling to this manager was the practice of social security authorities to turn down applications for would-be retirees—in short, forcing them to continue working and drawing upon the enterprise for their pensions.

If workers have reached retirement age, it's not the social security authorities' business to decide if they can retire. That's the law, not a social security regulation. When workers reach retirement age, they shouldn't have to seek permission from the social insurance authorities to retire. If an enterprise owes the social insurance office back contributions, it's a matter between these two parties, not the employee. If I was a worker wanting to retire and the social insurance office wouldn't permit it because my company hadn't paid its social insurance contributions, I would take the matter to court and charge the social security authorities with violating the law.

The same manager, who said that his firm had not been a target of social security agency sanctions for delaying its pension contributions, argued that current regulations were too vague because they gave local social security officials the ability to pick and choose which enterprises they might pursue for falling behind on social insurance remittances: "If the social insurance departments can decide which companies can put off their social insurance payments and which companies must pay, it's not fair. Social insurance departments should have some power, but not arbitrary power." Local social security authorities in Sichuan confirmed to me that they use "flexible methods" in permitting enterprises to apply to delay social insurance payments and to extend payments over periods of time.

The battle over pension contributions has seen local governments gain the upper hand over state enterprises that could once have sought out protection from bureaucratic patrons in central government commissions and ministries. This shift in power toward local governments is illustrated in the case of the actions taken by a municipal government in Sichuan in the late 1990s toward a large enterprise that I will label "National Engine." National Engine, which had 14,000 employees in mid-2001, was part of an enterprise group owned by a central government agency. National Engine had accumulated a 100 million yuan social insurance debt because of a transaction that the municipal government had arranged with another state enterprise ("City Steel") that was under the ownership of the city government. City Steel was a supplier firm to National Engine, and after some years of selling steel to National Engine on a credit basis, the latter had racked up a 100 million yuan debt to City Steel. However, at the same time, City Steel had amassed a debt of its own, in unpaid social insurance contributions of 100 million yuan. When the city government decided to convert City Steel into a shareholding corporation in 2000, city officials wanted to make City Steel's shares more attractive to investors by first cleaning up the firm's social insurance debt. They did this by going to National Engine and offering to cancel its 100 million yuan debt to City Steel, in exchange for National Engine taking on a 100 million yuan in debt to the local social security office. This transaction removed City Steel's social insurance debt and repackaged National Engine's 100 million yuan debt as payable to the local social security office rather than to City Steel. As a National Engine manager I interviewed put it, "*Their* delinquent payments to the social insurance office became *our* delinquent payments to the social insurance office."[40]

The transfer of pension distributions to urban governments in the late 1990s created new conflicts between the local officials and firms whose bureaucratic masters had once been powerful industrial ministries. "We're now under local government rule," the National Engine manager explained. "It's hard for us to go even to the provincial government [for dispute resolution]. The reason is that local governments have to think about social stability and the political problem of disturbances by workers and retirees."

Through new regulations and the sense of urgency with which central government officials have treated pension protests, local governments by the early 2000s have generally gained the upper hand in disputes with enterprises over delinquent payment of pension fees. The decentralized, fragmentary structure of China's pension administration has thus opened a new front in the ongoing battle between local governments and firms (a battle in the past that was primarily waged over taxation). China's localized pension structure has also influenced how retirees have pursued various claims regarding pensions.

Pension Disputes and the Use of Courts

State agencies, enterprises, and individuals appear to show some reluctance to use courts or arbitration committees to resolve disputes over pension fee remittances or pension benefit distributions. To date, it remains rare for pensioners or others to resolve pension disputes via legal channels. While officials from Ministry of Labor and Social Security and the All-China Federation of Trade Unions note with frequency the rising "legal consciousness" among workers, there does not appear to be active litigation or arbitration involving disputes over pension administration. Partial evidence of this comes from Jilin, where despite a doubling in the number of arbitration cases at municipal and provincial levels between 1997 and 1999 (to 1,008 cases), only 10 percent were over pension matters, according to a Jilin informant. These pension arbitration cases usually arose from an enterprise failing to distribute benefits to pensioners. Given the rapid increase in protests by pensioners nationwide since the late 1990s, it is clear that pensioners preferred to air the grievances in public rather than using arbitration channels. For their part, managers have frequently threatened to take local social security agencies to court for violating laws that protect firms from agencies that "chaotically extract fees," but the public record reveals few instances of enterprises actually following through with such threats. A Sichuan informant explained that from a legal perspective it can be very difficult to pursue enterprises that have fallen into arrears on pension or other social insurance fee contributions. Even if a law were passed to strengthen enforcement in this area, the prosecutors would have to show evidence that the persons in charge of the enterprise had willfully violated the law. Since it is difficult to show intent in cases where a firm is already deeply in debt, urban governments have relied on administrative action rather than recourse to the courts.

Local courts in some provinces, when they have been invoked, have demonstrated a willingness to uphold administrative sanctions or work in conjunction with urban governments to force compliance. A recent ruling by an intermediate court in a prefecture in Henan upheld administrative enforcement measures taken by a county government against two local enterprises that owed more than 1.5 million yuan in unpaid unemployment and pension insurance fees.[41] In two other cases in Henan, the city government of Zhengzhou turned to local district courts to confiscate land of state enterprises that had fallen behind on pension contributions over a period of several years. The court auctioned the land and then turned over proceeds—over 5 million yuan in one instance—to the city's pension pool.[42]

Despite this support in the courts for administrative actions taken by local governments, workers face daunting obstacles in attempting to seek legal redress over pension disputes with their employers. As with any labor dispute, an individual or group of workers faces the threat of punishment or firing by reporting on an employer in violation of a labor regulation. While workers may seek out arbitration committees and the courts to redress labor violations over issues such as unpaid wages, workplace injuries, or unsafe working conditions, the failure of an employer to remit social insurance fees is far less likely to represent the sort of infraction that a worker would pursue in a legal case. Since payroll deductions for pension and other social insurance apply to both the employer and the employee, the latter might gladly collude with the employer to avoid reducing take-home pay, according to one Shanghai-based policy analyst. When workers do report on employers that falsely report wage earnings or otherwise avoid paying pension fees, they usually make anonymous reports to local Labor and Social Security offices rather than openly accuse the employer.[43]

By contrast, groups of workers whose contracts have been terminated have shown some willingness to pursue legal action against their former employers, and they have found sympathetic officials on labor arbitration committees. In Hunan Province, 13 released contract workers at a Xinhua bookstore took the latter to arbitration in 2002 after they discovered that store management had not remitted pension fees on their behalf during the course of their three-year employment contracts. Despite the fact that the store's management had paid each worker well in excess of the 300 yuan per month agreed to in their employment contracts, the labor arbitration committee found in favor of the ex-employees. The store was ordered to pay three years of unpaid pension fees amounting to over 25,000 yuan.[44] In another case, a group of 180 construction workers in Hefei took their former employer, the Anhui Provincial No. 2 Construction Company, to court over a disputed amount of pension contributions. A local court eventually compelled the firm to contribute 183,200 yuan toward the workers' pension accounts.[45] Companies have emerged victorious as well. In a case involving construction workers, this time in Shenzhen, a group of 189 employees from the Jianye Construction Company lost their battle to recover money that Jianye had deducted from their wages over a ten-year period for pension contributions to individual accounts. The "pension fee deductions," at 8 percent of each worker's wages, had in fact been sent back to a company in Sichuan that had transferred the workers to Jianye. The employer won in an appeal after the court sided with Jianye's argument that the workers were not technically Jianye employees. "The laws are good, but the legal system doesn't work," one of the workers told a foreign reporter. "If we had to do it again, we would just protest."[46]

Although courts can exert a significant amount of pressure on firms to remit social insurance fees, local governments, which control the staffing and budgets of the courts, can strongly attenuate the courts' autonomy, particularly in sensitive bankruptcy proceedings. According to the provisions of the Bankruptcy Law of 1988 and a subsequent State Council Notice in 1994, an enterprise going through bankruptcy proceedings must clear up its unpaid wages and accumulated pension fees. This means that the workers displaced by the bankruptcy get a payout from the sale of enterprise assets that represents their "pension," a loosely defined term since those displaced are not necessarily older than the legal retirement age. But since urban governments have a strong financial interest in—and the ability to reap personal economic gains from—corporate restructurings of state firms, the most valuable assets get transferred to the new corporate entity, while creditors, including workers and local pension funds, wind up with piecemeal distributions from bankruptcy proceedings.[47] The numerous accounts of pension protests suggest that disputes often arise when retirees and laid-off workers receive these paltry sums. Large-scale protests in Chongqing, Baotou, and Daqing in 2002, and at a mine in Yangjiazhanzi in 2000, arose because laid-off workers and retirees received what they felt were small severance packages and were then compelled to remit social insurance fees to their individual accounts from these payouts.[48] In other words, retirees in both cases were not demanding actual pensions (as was often reported) but an adequate amount of severance pay, from which no pension or other social insurance fees should be deducted.

Conclusion

Given the ambiguities and complications arising from China's fragmented, locally administered pension funds, many PRC policy analysts and officials, as well as the World Bank, have called for legislation that would standardize payroll taxes and benefits and centralize pension administration.[49] National pension regulations currently in place, this argument goes, fail in several respects to provide the coercive and normative underpinnings necessary to ensure compliance with payroll tax collection efforts and to provide adequate fund management that would secure the timely provision of benefits. This argument offers some insight into how officials and public policy analysts view the law, yet it is clear that repackaging existing regulations as legal statutes would not ipso facto resolve problems of fee evasion by employers and underpayment of benefits to retirees and laid-off workers. A pension or social security law would increase the likelihood of local governments using the courts rather than relying on their current strategy of sanctioning firms that fail to remit payroll taxes. However, it is also likely that the conflict between enterprises and local governments would intensify rather than recede. The patterns of behavior that take place now under a system of pension regulations would replay themselves, with greater involvement by the courts, under a legally codified pension regime.

The preceding discussion of local efforts to finance and administer pension funds also shows that local governments and officials respond to central government incentives, as a principal–agent perspective would predict. Yet for those interested in how officials and citizens mobilize and utilize legal and regulatory institutions in China, the customary emphasis in the public policy literature on getting incentives right in games between principals and agents overlooks the important issue of ideas and practices that lie beneath policy choices. Further research might usefully explore the role of ideas and norms regarding support for the elderly, and how such ideas have influenced implementation at local levels.

The provision of public pensions, in China as elsewhere, represents an implicit social contract in which the state guarantees a basic level of old-age income to its citizens. Pension reform in China has diluted this social contract considerably. Employers resist or evade payroll taxes needed to finance pensions, and local governments stubbornly avoid transferring their pension funds to higher levels for consolidation. Pensioners are often left to fend for themselves, though as the limited number of court cases in the public record shows, some employees and retirees have sought to redress grievances through the courts. The fact that central authorities have balked at consolidating pensions into a national framework suggests that the central government is not yet prepared—financially or otherwise—to make an explicit pledge to support some minimum level of old-age income for urban workers, not to mention rural inhabitants. Until the fundamental question of what the state owes its citizens in terms of guaranteed basic pension benefits is resolved, the debate over the necessity of pension legislation to supplant the current patchwork of national and local regulatory controls is largely academic.

Notes

1. John Myles and Paul Pierson, "The Comparative Political Economy of Pension Reform," in *The New Politics of the Welfare State*, ed. Paul Pierson (New York: Oxford University Press, 2001), 321 (emphasis added).

2. William Hurst and Kevin J. O'Brien, "China's Contentious Pensions," *China Quarterly*, no. 170 (June 2000): 360.

3. For discussions of pension reform in China from a public-policy perspective, see Peter Whiteford, "From Enterprise Protection to Social Protection," *Global Social Policy* 3, no. 1 (2003): 45–77; Estelle James, "How Can China Solve its Old Age Security Problem? The Interaction Between Pension, State Enterprise, and Financial Market Reform," *Journal of Pension Economics and Finance* 1, no. 1 (March 2002): 53–75; Yan Wang, Dianqing Xu, Zhi Wang, and Fan Zhai, "Implicit Pension Debt, Transition Cost, Options, and Impact of China's Pension Reform: A Computable General Equilibrium Analysis," World Bank Policy Research Working Paper Series, 2000; Loraine A. West, "Pension Reform in China: Preparing for the Future," *Journal of Development Studies*, no. 35 (February 1999): 153–83; and World Bank, *Old Age Security: Pension Reform in China* (Washington, D.C.: World Bank, 1997).

4. Nelson Chow and Yuebin Xu, *Socialist Welfare in a Market Economy: Social Security Reforms in Guangzhou, China* (Burlington, Vt.: Ashgate, 2001), 89–104. See also Nelson W. S. Chow, *Socialist Welfare with Chinese Characteristics: The Reform of the Social Security System in China* (Hong Kong: Centre of Asian Studies, University of Hong Kong, 2001), 108–21.

5. Linda Wong, *Marginalization and Social Welfare in China* (New York: Routledge, 1998).

6. Yaohui Zhao and Jianguo Xu, "China's Urban Pension System: Reforms and Problems," *Cato Journal* 21 (Winter 2002): 395–414; Zhao Yaohui and Xu Jianguo. "Zhongguo chengzhen yanglao baoxian tizhi de zhuangui wenti" [Transition problems in China's urban pension system], Working Paper, China Center for Economic Research (CCER), 1999, http://old.ccer.edu.cn/workingpaper/workingpaper99c.htm (accessed 13 June 2002); Jiang Chunze and Li Nanxiong [Peter N. S. Lee], "Zhongguo yanglao baoxian shengji tongchou yihou de maodun: Fenxi yu duice yanjiu" [Contradictions in China's pension insurance after provincial-level pooling:

Analysis and research on countermeasures], Working Paper, CCER, 1999, http://old.ccer.edu.cn/workingpaper/workingpaper99c.htm (accessed 13 June 2002).

7. China's subnational administrative structure consists of 31 provincial-level units (including the four provincial-level cities of Beijing, Tianjin, Shanghai, and Chongqing), 333 "prefectural-level units" (including 259 municipalities), and 2,074 counties (including 400 county-level cities) (see Ministry of Finance, *2000nian quanguo dishixian caizheng tongji ziliao* [Nationwide financial statistics on prefectures, cities, and counties, 2000] [Beijing: Zhongguo caizheng jingji chubanshe, 2001]). "Urban governments" refers to the largely urban centers whose governments have established such pension funds. Pension funds do not exist below the county level (townships and villages), though some prosperous villages are beginning to establish pension funds for residents.

8. This argument can also be found in several articles from the publication *China Social Security*, which is funded through the Ministry of Labor and Social Security. For examples, see Feng Lanrui, "Cengceng fenjie jinpozhe xian chutai" [Resolving things level by level, starting with what's most pressing], in *Zhongguo shehui baozhang: Lunwen zhuanji* [China social security: Special collection of articles] (Beijing: Zhongguo shehui baozhang zazhishe, 2002), 205; Chen Hengming, "Dangqian qiye canbao jiaofei renshu chengfu zengzhang de yuanyin ji duice" [Causes and countermeasures of the negative growth in the number of enterprise participants in insurance and contributors of fees], in *Zhongguo shehui baozhang: Lunwen zhuanji*, 174.

9. Given the limited fiscal capacity of the central government, the ill health of the banking system, and the current preference to reduce government personnel, it is difficult to imagine that a social security law would come with adequate funding from Beijing and sufficient staffing. Estimates of China's implicit pension debt—what the state in theory owes to current workers in the form of future benefits—vary widely, with most estimates in the range of from 2 to 7 trillion yuan.

10. Katharina Müller, *The Political Economy of Pension Reform in Central-Eastern Europe* (Northampton, Mass.: Edward Elgar, 1999); Moisés Arce, "The Politics of Pension Reform in Peru," *Studies in Comparative International Development* 36 (Fall 2001): 90–115; Mitchell A. Orenstein, "How Politics and Institutions Affect Pension Reform in Three Postcommunist Countries," World Bank Development Research Group, Policy Research Working Paper, no. 2310 (Washington, D.C.: World Bank, 2000).

11. Joan M. Nelson, "Pension and Health Reforms in Hungary and Poland," in *Reforming the State: Fiscal and Welfare Reform in Post-Socialist Countries*, ed. Janos Kornai, Stephan Haggard, and Robert R. Kaufman (New York: Cambridge University Press, 2001), 251.

12. Ibid., 252.

13. Donald Clarke, "What's Law Got to Do With It?" *UCLA Pacific Basin Law Journal* 10 (Fall 1991): 15.

14. These provisions were based on the 1951 regulations, with revisions in 1953, 1958, and 1978 to expand the scope of coverage and to adjust the way pensions were calculated (see Han Liangcheng and Jiao Kaiping, *Qiye yanglao baoxian zhidu de tongyi yu shishi* [Unification and implementation of the enterprise old-age insurance sys-

tem] [Beijing: Zhongguo renshi chubanshe, 1997], 4–7; Xie Jianhua and Ba Feng, *Shehui baoxian faxue* [Social insurance legal studies] [Beijing: Beijing daxue chubanshe, 1999], 119–33).

15. "State Council Decision on Pension System Reform for Workers and Staff of Urban Enterprises," State Council Document No. 33 (1991). This and other regulations cited in this article can be obtained in Chinese at http://www.molss.gov.cn/trsweb_gov/mainframe.htm (accessed 19 June 2002). Chinese policymakers adopted pension reforms generally consistent with recommendations of the World Bank, which promoted pension reform in many developing and transition economies in the early 1990s (see World Bank, *Averting the Old Age Crisis: Policies to Protect the Old and Promote Growth* [Washington, D.C.: World Bank and Oxford University Press, 1994]).

16. Han and Jiao, *Qiye yanglao baoxian zhidu*, 82.

17. Ibid., 58.

18. A concise English-language summary of these and other regulations can be found in Chow and Xu, *Socialist Welfare*, 39–54.

19. Kenneth G. Lieberthal, "Introduction: The 'Fragmented Authoritarianism' Model and Its Limitations," in *Bureaucracy, Politics, and Decision Making in Post-Mao China*, ed. Kenneth G. Lieberthal and David M. Lampton (Berkeley: University of California Press, 1992), 1–30.

20. Jae Ho Chung proposes the hypothesis that the central government will recentralize control over implementation when "the policy concerned is a national priority with high stakes for the regime" (see Jae Ho Chung, *Central Control and Local Discretion in China: Leadership and Implementation during Post-Mao Decollectivization* [New York: Oxford University Press, 2000], 12).

21. Susan H. Whiting, *Power and Wealth in Rural China: The Political Economy of Institutional Change* (New York: Cambridge University Press, 2001); Le-Yin Zhang, "Chinese Central–Provincial Fiscal Relationships, Budgetary Decline, and the Impact of the 1994 Fiscal Reform: An Evaluation," *China Quarterly*, no. 157 (March 1999): 115–41.

22. Text of the Labor Law, available in Chinese and English, can be found in *Labour Law of the People's Republic of China*, trans. Legislative Affairs Commission of the Standing Committee of the National People's Congress (Beijing: Zhongguo laodong shehui baozhang chubanshe, 2000).

23. Perry Keller, "Sources of Order in Chinese Law," *American Journal of Comparative Law*, no. 42 (1994): 730.

24. As of early 2003 the draft of a social security law remained within the National People's Congress Standing Committee, with several ministries weighing in for and against the draft, according to a policy analyst who has observed the progress of the legislation closely. Among those opposed to it are the Ministry of Finance, which fears the fiscal consequences, and the various agencies with ties to SOEs whose economic performance would be further jeopardized by the envisioned social security tax. The Ministry of Labor and Social Security generally supports passage of a social security law, though with some reservations if it means MOLSS loses regulatory authority over social insurance fee collections.

25. Keller, "Sources of Order," 743; Jan Michiel Otto and Yuwen Li, "An Overview of Law-Making in China," in *Law-Making in the People's Republic of China*, ed. Jan Michiel Otto, Maurice V. Polak, Jianfu Chen, and Yuwen Li (The Hague: Kluwer Law International, 2000), 3–4.

26. Otto and Li, "An Overview of Law-Making in China," 3. In 1987 the State Council passed a "regulation" on how it enacted administrative regulations. Since that time, administrative regulations have to carry one of three designations: "regulations," "rules," or "measures."

27. Xie Ai, "Woguo shehui baoxian lifa qushi" [Legislative trends in China's social insurance], in *Zhongguo shehui baozhang: Lunwen zhuanji*, 209.

28. "State Council Circular on the Relevant Issues in Implementing Provincial-Level Basic Pension Insurance Pools for Enterprise Workers and Staff and the Transfer of Sector Pools to Local Management," State Council Document No. 28 (1998).

29. "Provisional Regulations on the Collection of Social Insurance Fees," State Council Document No. 259 (1999).

30. "Measures for the Supervision and Inspection of Social Insurance Fee Collections," Ministry of Labor and Social Security Document No. 3 (1999).

31. At the provincial and municipal level, one finds the same overlap in lawmaking functions as at the national level. That is, "people's governments" of provinces and large cities can issue different types of "local administrative rules" (*difang zhengfu guizhang*), while local "people's congresses" of the same units can pass "local regulations" (*difang fagui*). These local lawmaking powers are limited by the requirement that rules and laws not contravene those of higher-level bodies such as the State Council and the NPC. However, the same ambiguities that arise in distinguishing the legal effect of the State Council's administrative regulations and the formal laws of the NPC take place at local levels (see Otto and Li, "An Overview of Law-Making in China," 4–5).

32. "Zhang on Improving Social Insurance System," *Renmin ribao* [People's Daily], 12 April 1999, in Foreign Broadcast Information Service, China (FBIS-CHI-1999-0423); "Qingdao dui 26 jia wugu qianfei qiye tichu jinggao" [Qingdao issues warning to 26 enterprises owing fees without cause], *Zhongguo shehui baozhang* [China Social Security], no. 55 (January 1999): 41.

33. "Guangdong shehui baoxianfei zhengjiao xingshi kanhao" [Guangdong social insurance fee collection improves], Xinhua [New China News Agency], 22 August 2000, http://www.peopledaily.com.cn/ (accessed 19 June 2002); "Hubeisheng shebaofei mingqi quanmian shixing dishui zhengshou" [Hubei Province social insurance fees to be comprehensively collected as local taxes], Xinhua [New China News Agency], 30 June 2001, http://www.peopledaily.com.cn/ (accessed 19 June 2002).

34. Song Houzhen, "Yanglao baoxianfei zhengjiao nanti zenyang jie" [Resolving difficulties in the collection of pension insurance fees], *Zhongguo shehui baozhang* [China Social Security], no. 59 (May 1999): 13.

35. "Laodong he shehui baozhangbu gongbu qianjiao jiben yanglao baoxianfei qian wan yuan yishang qiye mingdan" [Ministry of Labor and Social Security announce list of enterprises that owe more than 10 million yuan], 8 January 2002, http://www.molss.gov.cn/news/2002 (accessed 19 June 2002).

36. Song, "Yanglao baoxianfei zhengjiao nanti zenyang jie" (see note 34), 12.
37. "Shanghai 40wan ren ling yanglaojin bu chu shequ" [400,000 in Shanghai pick up pensions without leaving the residence committee], *Zhongguo shehui baozhang* [China Social Security], no. 55 (January 1999): 41.
38. Xie Ai, "Woguo shehui baoxian lifa qushi" (see note 27), 209.
39. Liao Yihai, "Qingli qiye qianfei renzhong daoyuan" [Shouldering heavy responsibilities in clearing up enterprise fee arrears], in *Zhongguo shehui baozhang: Lunwen zhuanji*, 161.
40. When asked why they didn't go to their bureaucratic superiors in Beijing for support in the matter, National Engine's managers countered, "Oh, we *did*. And they not only refused to give us any financial support, but they scolded us for agreeing to the transaction in the first place."
41. "Sunhai zhigong liyifa burong Zhoukou zhijie jujiao shehui baoxian an" [Harming the legal interests of workers is not permitted by law: Zhoukou wraps up a refusal to remit social insurance case], 29 March 2001, *People's Court Daily*, http://www.rmfyb.com/public/detail.php?id = 21496 (accessed 7 November 2002).
42. "Qianjiao laodong tongchoujin yifa paimai ni tudi" [Owing payments to labor pools: Your land is auctioned in accordance with the law], 5 November 2001, Henan Baoye Wang [Henan News Web], http://www.hnby.com.cn/papers/hnfzb/200111/05/3110/3119.html (accessed 16 September 2002); "Qianjiao yanglaojin; fayuan qiangzhixing" [Owing payments on pensions: Court forces compliance], 26 December 2001, Henan Baoye Wang [Henan News Web], http://www.hnby.com.cn/papers/dhb/200112/26/26447/26450.html (accessed 16 September 2002).
43. Fan Jun, "Shaobao manbao: Rechu shifei duoshao" [Underreporting and falsely reporting: How much trouble is stirred up?], *Zhongguo shehui baozhang* [China Social Security], no. 81 (March 2001): 10.
44. "Wode gongzi wo gaina: ni bujiaofei ni fanfa: shisan mei yifa weiquan" [I should draw my wages; if you don't remit fees then you break the law: 13 sisters protect their rights in accordance with the law], *Zhongguo laodong baozhangbao* [China Labor Security Report], no. 2629 (29 October 2002).
45. Fan Jun, "Shaobao manbao" (see note 43), 10.
46. Philip P. Pan, "Chinese Workers' Rights Stop at the Courtroom Door," *Washington Post*, 28 June 2002, A1.
47. "Qiye qianjiao yanglao baoxianfei yuanyin fenxi" [Analysis of reasons that enterprises owe pension insurance fees], *Zhongguo laodong baozhangbao* [China Labor Security Report], no. 2522 (20 June 2002).
48. "Retrenched Workers in Sichuan Get Organised for Legal Action," *China Labour Bulletin*, 17 September 2002; John Pomfret, "China Cracks Down on Worker Protests," *Washington Post*, 21 March 2002, A21; James Kynge, "Chinese Miners Riot Over Severance Pay," *Financial Times*, 3 April 2000, 9; Keith Bradsher, "Factory Dispute Tests China's Loyalty to Workers' Rights," *New York Times*, 18 July 2002, A3.
49. World Bank, *Old Age Security: Pension Reform in China*, 56, 63, 66. Views of central government officials can be found in Liu Zhongli, "Zhongguo shehui baozhang zhidu gaige de moshi yu fazhan" [Models and development of China's so-

cial security system reform], 102; and Zhang Zuoji, "Zhongguo shehui baozhang tizhi gaige de jinzhan" [Progress in restructuring China's social security system], 97; both in *Zhongguo shehui baozhang tizhi gaige* [Restructuring China's social security system], ed. Wang Mengkui (Beijing: Zhongguo fazhan chubanshe, 2001). For views of policy analysts, see note 8, and Li Jinyan, "Shehui baoxianfa de qicao, fazhi yuanze he guoji jingyan" [The drafting, legal principles, and international experience of social insurance law], in *Zhongguo shehui baozhang tizhi gaige* [Restructuring China's social security system], ed. Xu Dianqing, Yin Zunsheng, and Zheng Yuxin (Beijing: Jingji kexue chubanshe, 1999).

NEIL J. DIAMANT 6

Hollow Glory

The Politics of Rights and Identity among
PRC Veterans in the 1950s and 1960s

In April 2002 a group of approximately twenty thousand veterans—most of them retired People's Liberation Army (PLA) officers—descended upon Beijing in order to file a collective petition to the Ministry of Civil Affairs for better treatment. Around many of their necks hung a placard with the words, "I am a veteran" on its front, and on its back, "I want to eat." The veterans made two key demands: to be provided jobs with decent salaries as they were promised by state policy, and to be allowed to establish a national veterans association. Coming not many years after the gathering of close to ten thousand adherents of the Falun Gong spiritual movement in 1999, the size and audacity of the veterans' petition was shocking to the central government. According to one source, the government met the veterans' first demand by issuing orders to local governments to pay the veterans no less than what they were paid in the army, regardless of whether they were assigned a job (whether this order was implemented is difficult to ascertain). However, their second demand—to establish a national veterans association—was flatly turned down. Soon after, the leaders of the petition movement were arrested. This incident was ignored in the official press and received no coverage in the international press. Veterans apparently had no contact with the media and did not pursue their claims in some of the more official and institutionalized channels, such as the courts and letters and visits offices, which are now being promoted as antidotes to the more "chaotic" forms of social protest.[1]

This was not the first incident in the reform period in which veterans mobilized to secure improved benefits, unfulfilled rights, and status. Veterans, as useful as they are during their service to the state, can become thorns in the side of the regime after their discharge, particularly if their expectations are not met and they encounter a citizenry divided about the value and importance of their contribution to the state. In several incidents of rural unrest during the 1980s and 1990s, for example, veterans assumed leadership roles at great personal risk.[2] Even when dead, veterans are troublesome for the regime that recruited them into state service. In 1998 a report about a letters and visits office in Beijing focused on the plight of a woman from Northeast China named Dong Xiulan. Dong had been married to an ex-serviceman who was beaten to death by Red Guards during the Cultural Revolution for being a "capitalist roader." "Bureaucratic mistakes" resulted in her being denied the pension to which she was entitled by State Council regulations. She moved to Beijing permanently in 1983, and in the early 1990s she was living under a bridge close to the Beijing letters and visits office, and survived by begging and eating discarded food. Clutching old letters and her dead husband's discharge card, Dong complained: "I'm not asking for another life in return for the life of my husband. I'm just asking for the compensation my husband was entitled to. My husband fought for the revolution for many years, but now nobody has any sympathy for my misfortune." According to the report, her case had been held up because the appeals court had demanded better supporting documents and she could not afford to procure them. Dong did not go to, nor was she approached by, any legal aid office or law firm; she had been forced to pursue her husband's case on her own. And unlike workers who can seek a modicum of justice using the Labor Law (see Gallagher's and Thireau and Hua's contribution to this volume), or abused women who can seek the protections of the state on the basis of the Marriage Law, Dong could not appeal to the state or seek redress in the courts on the grounds of violation of a "Veteran's Law," since none has been legislated or even considered by the National People's Congress.[3] In two PRC Constitutions (1978 and 1982, Articles 50 and 45, respectively), there are clauses that address the right to livelihood for disabled soldiers who fought in the pre-Liberation PLA and family members of revolutionary martyrs and mobilized soldiers, but none that mention veterans. This statutory and constitutional gap appears to have been filled in by other forms of lawmaking: there are policies, administrative regulations, and "decisions" galore. In 1983, the government published a collection of policy documents regarding veterans—most issued by the State Council and the Interior Ministry between 1950 and 1982—that runs over 1,000 pages long.[4] There is also no lack of quarterly and annual summary work reports, internal Party investigations detailing policy errors and ways to correct them, as well as documents of a more hortative nature that spell out the state and society's moral responsibilities to veterans.

The gap between veterans' feistiness, moral standing (having served the state and the revolution), and the absence of a "Veteran's Law" is all the more glaring given that veterans have occupied a central place in PRC politics for well over half a century. The PRC government stated on many occasions that veterans, having proven their loyalty and mettle in battle and wartime deprivation during the revolution, or having exhibited a willingness to risk the loss of life, limb, and livelihood by volunteering for military service after 1949,[5] deserved to be placed in positions of authority. There were "veterans committees" at several levels of the state hierarchy, and they were over-represented in people's congresses. According to many regulations issued by the State Council and the Interior Ministry, veterans were entitled to free or discounted medical care (depending on their rank and degree of illness) and tuition, and industrial firms and state offices were expected to take affirmative steps to hire them if they met minimal requirements. These policies should not have been problematic to implement given that veterans were backed by numerous state agencies and were associated with a sentiment that supposedly formed the zeitgeist of both the Maoist and reform periods: patriotism.[6] These sentiments notwithstanding, and despite thousands of circulars, guidelines, directives, and investigations by the State Council, intra-Party reports reveal numerous instances in which veterans felt a keen sense of rights denied, injustice, and a concomitant willingness to take action locally and nationally, often framing their protests in the language of state policy and rhetoric about veterans' role in society. As in the 2002 Beijing protest, in the 1950s groups of veterans made their way to the State Council and Communist Party headquarters in Beijing from remote areas of the countryside to petition for better benefits and treatment,[7] while some participated in anti-state rural collective action[8] or filed "collective petitions" with county- and provincial-level governments.[9] In 1956, in a four-month period alone, veterans from several counties in Anhui Province traveled to Beijing 362 times.[10] During the Cultural Revolution, hundreds of veterans from around the country broke into military bases and even Chinese Communist Party (CCP) headquarters in Beijing to request recognition for a national, independent veterans association that would enable them to counter widespread discrimination. This request was categorically denied, and several independent veterans associations were declared "counterrevolutionary."[11] Still, despite this impressive record of political participation, activism, and awareness of rights unfulfilled, the state failed to promulgate any statute or institutionalize any formal legal process whereby veterans would be able to voice their complaints.

There is an interesting puzzle here. Throughout PRC history, the Chinese state—like most others, regardless of regime type—has been concerned about veterans, as seen in the policies awarding them preferential treatment in employment and political representation. On paper, they had privileges few other citizens enjoyed.[12] From the 1950s until the 1970s, veterans were elites in the official pecking order, and were extolled as exemplars of patriotic sacrifice who deserved the nation's gratitude. But if this was the case, how did it happen that there was a critical mass of veterans willing to resort to high-risk political activism during both the Maoist and reform periods? Why would an officially privileged group exhibit the same repertoire of political protest as more marginal groups, such as contract workers?[13] Did military service and the granting of special privileges lead to the enhancement of their sense of citizenship, and willingness to take action? And, when they took action, were veterans motivated by the absence of procedural or distributive justice?[14] How did state institutions—ranging from local authorities to the Center—deal with their polical activism during these years? This essay draws upon recently opened archival sources from the 1950s and 1960s—a period, unlike today, when veterans were a key regime constituency and therefore on the receiving end of a great deal of state attention—to answer these questions. It is, to the best of my knowledge, one of the only accounts of veterans' politics, "rights" consciousness, and identity published since the reform period began.[15] Although this chapter deals with the 1950s and 1960s, I argue that many of my conclusions are equally applicable to veterans during the reform period.

None of these questions can be adequately answered unless we employ two perspectives on law and society in China. First, the case of veterans highlights the imperative to look at legal and policy implementation in China in a highly *disaggregated* perspective. Central state regulations and policies regarding veterans appear to be well intended; central state leaders took an active role in administration and invested significant state material and symbolic resources. Still, somewhere along the line, many veterans did not succeed in taking advantage of their privileges. Such evidence might lead us to propose an interpretation along the lines suggested by Gerald N. Rosenberg in *The Hollow Hope*: laws unsupported by political and administrative follow-through, citizen support, and inducements for compliance cannot lead to significant social change.[16] While we might not be surprised to find such failure among relatively marginalized groups in the PRC[17] (Rosenberg focuses on African Americans and women), it is somewhat striking that veterans, who were lauded by the state, given resources and representation, failed to secure privileges that were promised to them by the state. Second, questions about access to privileges and legal implementation cannot be answered without paying significant attention to the way entitlements are embedded in historical, cultural, and political contexts, all dimensions which long have been at the heart of the law-and-society literature. In the case of Chinese veterans, the arresting but simple facts that (1) throughout Chinese history military personnel have generally been accorded *low* social status, and (2) the People's Liberation Army was comprised of poor and often illiterate peasants in a society that discriminated against the poor and uneducated, proved to be critical impediments to the implementation of preferential policies.

In this chapter I will argue that although PRC veterans as a group were the beneficiaries of preferential policies and were therefore usually (but not always) better off than those who either opposed the revolution or did not participate in it, a substantial number of them—mainly soldiers, NCOs, and junior officers—were acutely aware that their status was quickly eroded by economic, political, and socio-cultural forces that were beyond their control. Granting veterans privileges and political representation, and placing them in a position of fostering popular nationalism and patriotism, frequently backfired, as civilian officials and ordinary citizens contested the extent to which veterans deserved these benefits. Particularly in the 1950s and 1960s (but in the reform period as well), granting veterans entitlements and status worked at cross-purposes with other state goals and policies, most notably modernization and industrialization, and they also inadvertently threatened the political status quo. Modernization, after all, requires individuals with technical skills, which veterans often lacked. Modernization also requires urban development, and most veterans in China were recruited from the countryside. So, while one facet of veteran identity was their embeddedness in the symbols of state power and patriotic commitment, another, and ultimately more salient one for many, was their status as representatives of economic backwardness. Politics also worked against veterans' successful integration into the state and society not *despite* their official classification as "revolutionaries" but *because* of this. Many local officials considered veterans a substantial threat to their authority and legitimacy precisely because of their patriotic credentials, and they used many different methods to discredit them. As a result, in their day-to-day life many veterans felt betrayed by the revolution they helped usher in and the regime they helped defend, and the gap between entitlements on paper and the lofty rhetoric praising veterans' "glorious" service to the revolution and the way they were actually treated by bureaucrats, politicians, and ordinary citizens grew larger. Finally, the story of veterans in the PRC reveals the limitations of an approach that awards privileges but anchors them not in statute but in policy, regulation, and bureaucracy. Lacking a "law," veterans could not access courts (which, as an arm of the state, would be charged with carrying out state law), and the Civil Affairs bureaucracy (which was the bureaucracy responsible for veteran affairs) was unable to protect them because they, like veterans themselves, were "outsiders" as far as the villages, townships, and firms were concerned. As a result, veterans learned to rely on themselves and hoped that the Center would begin to live up to its promises.

Modernization

The story of how the Communist Party emerged from the countryside, conquered the cities, and then turned its attention to economic reconstruction based on urban development is well known and need not be repeated here. Far less known, however, is how this transition played out in the lives of those who devoted years of their youth to the revolution and war, who returned to their villages or cities as changed individuals, with either different bodies, owing to disability, or different conceptions of their role in the polity. Nor do we know much about how former GMD (Nationalist Party) soldiers who were absorbed into the PLA fared in the post-1949 period. Whether having joined the revolution in the early 1940s in a revolutionary base area or in 1946 during the Civil War, these soldiers and officers were frequently hailed both in the official press and in central and local policy directives as exemplars of patriotism and sacrifice who deserved preferential treatment in employment and political representation. Despite this (and, in many cases, precisely because of this), a substantial number of veterans in the postwar period nevertheless found themselves at the mercy of officials and bureaucrats whose priorities and preferences often conflicted with veterans' interests and rights.

For the returning veteran who had spent several or many years of his life away from agriculture or, in rarer cases, industry, the nitty-gritty issue of employment was by far the most salient and vexing problem, far more important than the question of political representation or procedural and distributive justice. This was a question of survival: many veterans were recruited from the impoverished North China countryside and earned very little during their years in the military. Demobilization was further complicated by the wartime devastation of many rural communities in North China, as well as by recurring natural disasters after 1949. Nonetheless, the thrust of state demobilization policy was to return veterans to the areas "from which they came [*yuanji anzhi*]."

Acutely aware that cities offered more opportunities than the countryside, many veterans attempted to avoid complying with state resettlement policy.[18] Some simply lied, telling their army unit personnel directors that they had been "born in a city" (even though they moved out of the city when they were very young), or that "all of their relatives in the countryside were dead" (even though some were alive), or that they "had a relative in the city willing and able to support them."[19] Personnel directors, too busy or uninterested in checking on the facts or clearing the assignment with the municipalities, issued them the proper documentation.[20] Other veterans turned military and state policies and rhetoric to their advantage. For instance, some veterans justified their urban relocation by claiming that they were simply being good soldiers: "The army agreed that we should come to Shanghai; we're just following orders."[21] In other cases, veterans were dispatched to cities by rural cadres, who claimed, perhaps correctly, that their villages were "overpopulated" and that the veterans would be a strain on local resources.[22]

A 1957 investigative report on 469 veterans who "aimlessly came to Shanghai" provides us with a closer look at the causes and responses of urban officials to veterans' desires for upward mobility via urban residence.[23] Not surprisingly, given that the army had recruited soldiers from the North China countryside, the report found that 77 percent of the veterans living without permits in Shanghai had come from the northern part of Jiangsu Province (Subei), an area that had always been looked down upon by Shanghainese as uncultured and poor.[24] The veterans' claims of homelessness notwithstanding, the report found that 74 percent of them had family in their native place; moreover, 34 percent were members of the CCP or Communist Youth League (CYL). Still, many of the veterans were barely getting by: only 2 percent had formal factory positions, while 37 percent had temporary positions in construction, factories, the service sector, or on the docks; 21 percent were peddlers selling vegetables, firewood, peanuts, and used odds and ends. Another 20 percent of the veterans were unemployed, relied on government aid, or engaged in some form of illegal means (usually theft) to get by, which resulted in arrests (one veteran had been caught eighteen times stealing chickens).[25] Not a few had been forced to beg, eat scraps out of garbage bins, or sleep in police pillboxes or adjacent to sewers.[26]

Having come to the city to seek employment, to escape the "bitterness" of peasant life and natural disasters (these constituted some 90 percent of arrivees in 1956 and 1957), or the harsh treatment by local officials in their hometowns,[27] veterans were not going to return without a fight. Some were aware of the fact that they were unwanted but took the chance that at least some citizens might treat them better if they could be made aware of veterans' contributions to the revolution. Lacking the media resources that some groups are now able to employ, veterans tried to mobilize public opinion in other ways:

Some veterans deliberately disregard the political impact of their actions. They wear their uniforms and adorn them with medals and decorations and then go out on the street to polish shoes, sell peanuts and pickled vegetables. When policemen request that they move along, they ignore them. Some even demand money from PLA officers at the train station or on the street, or go to homes of martyr and military families to ask for money and food.[28]

Others tried to mobilize public opinion by stressing their own rectitude and the government's callousness:

After arrival, veterans are approached by residence committees, the police, the district committee and Bureau of Civil Affairs who demand that they get a Shanghai residence permit to stay in the city. If they have had a hard time doing this, they get into heated arguments with the cadres and rail against the government. They publicly complain that "You've become an upright person and still end up like this; you go home [to your native place] and can't make a living and Shanghai doesn't give you any work either."[29]

When mobilizing public opinion was ineffective, some adopted other strategies to call attention to their plight, such as taking their bedding to the reception office of local authorities and refusing to leave, initiating hunger strikes, threatening to commit suicide ("I'll commit suicide if I can't stay in Shanghai; the Huangpu River will be my home!"), or even forfeiting their hard-earned Party membership.[30] Other veterans, long accustomed to violence, pummeled officials who harassed them.[31] Some mustered whatever writing skills they had acquired in the army and wrote impassioned letters to politicians at higher levels of the state apparatus, such as city government officials, Marshal Zhu De, and Chairman Mao.[32] These efforts were largely fruitless, and veterans were said to be "very dissatisfied with the government" for trying to expel them from the cities.

For municipal authorities, the experience of dealing with veterans as real people with real-life problems and not merely as abstract symbols of the revolution, was eye-opening. It was, after all, unprecedented in Chinese history to have such a large-scale demobilization and to have thousands of peasant veterans enter cities. It was not an easy predicament: veterans were elites in their formal status and in the privileges they were awarded, but many of them were "outsiders" (in the countryside as well, since they had been away for many years), and their lack of technical skills made them a burden on local resources. Policy reflected their multivalent identities: municipal agencies were instructed to differentiate among those who had failed to make it in the city (they should be the first to go), those who were dependent on poor friends and relatives, and those who had established a foothold. Those who managed to attain formal residence status, stable work, or "really have no family or production capacity in their native villages" would be allowed to stay.[33]

Veterans were not alone in their pursuit of preferential treatment. Veterans committees, established at the district and municipal levels in cities and the district and county levels in the countryside, were expected to intervene on their behalf with local employers, as were employment offices attached to each department of Civil Affairs. Party branches and unions in factories were explicitly instructed to give preference to veterans who had appropriate skills. During the Korean War, a massive propaganda campaign emphasized the importance of veterans to the national cause and society's role in helping them out. If mobilization of state law and regulations partially depends on a group's organizational capacity, it would seem that veterans—who had significant organizational heft behind them—would have been in a good position to take advantage of the benefits they had coming to them.

Such support notwithstanding, economic development required people with certain skills and veterans were frequently lacking in this department. Prior to 1949, skilled workers commanded higher salaries than non-skilled labor, and as Elizabeth J. Perry has pointed out, they were also the backbone of the underground Communist Party leadership and came to occupy many key posts in the labor unions after the revolution.[34] What's more, these officials tended to hail from areas south of the Yangzi River. In Shanghai, many veterans were the opposite: they were unskilled, political novices, outsiders, and northerners to boot, and these biographical attributes proved far more important to officials charged with day-to-day administration than the veterans' role in the revolution and the entitlements they were granted by the state.

From the earliest years of the PRC, veterans encountered tremendous difficulties. These problems were deemed serious enough to warrant State Council–mandated investigations, which were filed almost annually to municipal and central state authorities. The critical mass of these reports, however, were filed in the period 1956–57, as part of a nation-wide effort to check up on the implementation of the State Council's 1955 "Decision" regarding veteran benefits and treatment, which in itself was an attempt to reverse discrimination veterans had faced in previous years.[35] In a report on veterans in Shanghai's Hongkou District, for example, veterans assigned to work in a printing factory all received apprenticeship salaries and were experiencing financial difficulties. They complained to the factory, which promised that their salaries would be adjusted in six months. When the six months were over and their salaries remained unchanged, the veterans went to the Bureau of Light Industry to complain. When the factory heard about this, it put a disciplinary note in their files.[36] The problem of setting veterans' salaries too low was widespread, since many factory managers—fearing that higher salaries for veterans would alienate other workers—refused to give veterans any credit for their years of military service[37] and often did not differentiate among rank, age, or disability; in a factory in Xincheng District, every single one of the forty-five incoming vets in 1956 received a salary of 39 yuan per month.[38] In many other cases, veterans were assigned to positions that completely disregarded their physical condition and made their employment unbearable. In the Shanghai Railway Bureau, an investigation found that more than eighty veterans who were assigned to do road and rail maintenance work had been unable to fulfill their work quotas.[39]

For veterans who had been discharged at relatively low rank (private to lieutenant), probably the easiest position to obtain was in the security field.

But this also proved problematic. In factories, workers heaped ridicule on veterans who were assigned to guard the gates by calling them "guard dogs" and by identifying their military insignia as "dog tags" (in Chinese culture, calling someone a "dog" is a particularly noxious curse). Some Korean War veterans were scorned as "POWs."[40] Relegated to menial jobs such as security officers, cleaners, temporary laborers, and apprentices, veterans found that their salaries were often much lower than those they had received in the military (this was apparently a cause of the 2002 protest as well). According to one report, this was because "their rank and skill in the military does not necessarily match the needs of individual firms." The veterans, reports noted, "have raised quite a few objections" to this matter,[41] and these resulted in several veteran strikes in factories, even in sensitive military industries such as the Jiangnan Shipyard in Shanghai.[42] These problems continued throughout the pre-Cultural Revolution years. For example, at the same time that the PLA was being touted as the model for political awareness and revolutionary values, 68 percent of the complaints at the Shanghai Veteran Resettlement Committee in 1963 were salary-related. Most emphasized the injustice of local officials who violated central state policy by not accounting for the length of veterans' military service or the widespread practice of unlimited apprenticeship periods.[43] As one veteran wrote sarcastically to the State Council, "If I were a counterrevolutionary I'd be sent off to labor reform—at least that way I'd have some work!"[44] Since positions with the state provided sinecure only to a minority of veterans (according to the Guangdong gazetteer, only 2 percent of 118,000 discharged veterans in 1955 received state positions in the rural sector[45]), many veterans felt that their contributions were undervalued and that those who had contributed and risked less were unduly rewarded.

These intra-Party documents reveal several patterns in the way many veterans were treated by the state and community. First, despite the organizational muscle veterans could muster on their own behalf, and despite the existence of numerous state regulations regarding employment and benefits, individual union directors, factory managers, or personnel directors could often foil veterans' access to preferential rights. Second, there was a gap, perhaps an inevitable one, between military and civilian remuneration systems, and this led to a very strong sense of injustice. In the military, after all, evaluation of individual merit is based on contribution to the collective—the unit, and in a larger sense, the state. This currency was devalued in an economy where production was the most important goal and skill and experience determined salary and status. While not unusual in military demobilizations, this situation became morally repugnant when veterans continued to be the subject of frothy propaganda at the same time that they were being denied medical care, consigned to apprentice status for years, and paid lower wages than other workers. Finally, it also appears that well before the reform period and the current emphasis on law, veterans were cognizant of their status and the rules that granted them privileges and were capable of organizing collective action on their own behalf.

Politics

By most any measure veterans were part of the governing elite of the PRC. Their revolutionary credentials, access to institutional support, and preferential policies were all designed to help ease their way back into civilian life and leadership positions in the regime. State campaigns and propaganda were expected to remind a country at peace that sacrifices had been made, and continued to be made, on behalf of the common good. Particularly when compared with the lot of various "enemies" of the regime, veterans, having good "class status," were in a favored position. This view has been articulated implicitly or explicitly by many political scientists, sociologists, and feminist scholars.[46] The notion that the officially privileged might have encountered experiences similar to those of the politically disenfranchised does not square with much of the established literature on China, or with the political science and legal literature about privilege and access to rights. That such discrimination could have taken place when the central state's veteran's commission was staffed by high-ranking veteran revolutionaries who were familiar with veterans' problems and often pushed for better treatment of them is even more surprising. The case of Chinese veterans shows that officially designated political status, preferential policies, and benefits did not ensure even minimal assurances of decent treatment in the absence of a formal law and corresponding levels of cultural, social, or financial capital.

For most Chinese—rural and urban—firsthand contact with PLA veterans came only after 1949, when PLA peasant armies swept down from their North China base areas and conquered the rest of the country. Personal exposure to veterans (as workers, security officials, cadres, and ordinary citizens) coincided temporally with the outbreak of the Korean War in 1950. In response to the war, the state unleashed a nationwide propaganda campaign centered on the importance of patriotism and the key roles that veterans, soldiers, revolutionary martyrs, and their families played in the establishment and protection of the state. Veterans, as the "corporeal manifestation" of patriotism, were expected to benefit from this surge in patriotic agitation and sentiment.

Unfortunately for veterans, state efforts to increase patriotic sentiment during the Korean War often fell on deaf ears; new archival evidence suggests that few were persuaded that the war was necessary or important, or even that the United States was China's enemy. In Shanghai's working-class

Penglai District, factory cadres claimed they were "too busy with production" to even read state documents, newspapers, and magazines. "Propaganda work," they complained, was a "burden," and contradicted other objectives, particularly production. The North Koreans, they proposed, "should liberate themselves."[47] School officials reportedly took no action against accusations that Mayor Chen Yi refused to lead the troops in Korea (at Mao's request) because he "wanted to rest and spend time with his thirty wives." "Why," they asked, was "China fighting the West when it should be trying to join NATO?" Nor were ordinary workers and citizens swept up in patriotic fervor. Many were quite content to have the North Koreans fight the United States by itself.[48] Most workers and citizens, reports from Penglai and elsewhere complained, either "greatly admire" the United States because of its medicine ("the U.S. invented penicillin"), material comforts, high cultural level, and technology, or they feared American military might. But no matter how fearsome the United States might be, its brand of "imperialism" still paled against what the Japanese had recently done to China. For these reasons, many were convinced that China was being used by the Soviet Union for its own purposes. "China will burn and then the USSR will come and pick up the millet," some said.[49]

If the regime hoped that veterans would bask in the reflected glory of a successfully prosecuted war against a dangerous superpower with imperialistic intentions, it was undoubtedly disappointed. Looking at patriotic sentiment from the ground up—at hundreds of actual statements made by ordinary people and officials—there is little evidence pointing to a real appreciation of the role soldiers and veterans played in the polity, even during wartime.[50] But, as the war ended, international threats receded, and the state demobilized many PLA soldiers and officers, civilian views toward veterans assumed an even harsher tone. One view of veterans was particularly nasty and widespread, and had direct and sometimes fatal implications. This was that former soldiers became "veterans" only because the PLA no longer wanted them or because they were old, sick, weak, or had been "purged" for some offense or problem; they were, in essence, "PLA refuse" and therefore unworthy of assistance or privileges. At the Shenxin No. 1 textile mill, Zhang Shimin, a workshop leader and deputy union chair, told a group of veterans: "You're all so young! Why were you discharged? You must have had some sort of problem!" A common sentiment—appearing both in archives and in recently published gazetteers—was that "among veterans there isn't a good person, and there's no good person who's a veteran."[51]

In many villages there were also many veterans who suffered, albeit for a different reason. In the city, veterans appear to have been genuinely disliked and feared by officials and citizens alike. In the countryside, however, reports indicate that peasants respected veterans for their patriotism and toughness, and for this reason local officials made their life difficult. Veterans were a threat to their status, since many village officials had risen to their posts not from military service but from less highly regarded activities. During local elections in the early 1950s, for instance, many veterans appeared on candidate lists, and they were often preferred by villagers over officials who had come to power through activism in land reform. Nevertheless, village officials sometimes undermined the veterans by spreading rumors that they had been "purged from the PLA." One cadre, for example, said: "The army didn't want him, so why should we give him a position?"[52] Not a few veterans were punched, kicked, and otherwise abused by village cadres.[53] In 1955, in Guangxi Province, investigations revealed the case of a veteran who had resorted to eating corpses to fill his empty belly; others had sold sons, daughters, land, and farm equipment to raise money when local officials refused to give them food allotments or scarce political positions.[54] As might be expected in the countryside, land was another source of tension. PLA veterans who returned to their villages often found that local officials had already appropriated the best plots and controlled whatever land that remained. As a result, many veterans were assigned rocky or otherwise difficult-to-till plots, making their everyday existence in the village very difficult and forcing many to leave for the cities. Upset by this reception, some veterans were not even on speaking terms with their village cadres.[55] This sort of behavior also occurred in the early 1960s. In Songjiang County, a 1963 report cited one commune where twelve returned veterans had been accepted into the local political establishment, albeit at low rank (none had a position outside of the village). At the same time, however, officials continued to believe that veterans had been discharged mainly because "they were sick, weak, or have problems," this despite many State Council circulars telling them otherwise.[56]

It is, of course, difficult to know if these claims represented local cadres' true beliefs about veterans or if they were mainly a rhetorical weapon used to prevent veterans from gaining power at cadre expense. It is also unclear whether such comments masked a different version of patriotism: perhaps local officials believed that one served the country best by increasing production, and that by *not* hiring veterans they were behaving patriotically. My own suspicion, based on reading hundreds of texts, is that local officials genuinely feared and disliked veterans, and did not behave as they did because of an alternative understanding of patriotism. Managers' comments about veterans were viscerally negative, focusing almost exclusively on just how problematic veterans were as a population.[57] In some ways, this is not surprising. The army, after all, *is* a demanding institution and not a few have trouble accepting the level of discipline required. Individual dossiers that were transferred from the PLA to civilian units may have included negative reports, which local officials could then pounce on to malign all veterans.[58] Whatever the reason for such negative attitudes, however, the result was the same: ad hoc efforts—sometimes successful and sometimes not—to prevent veterans from joining unions, the Party (if they had not already joined in the army), the Communist Youth League, and rural political institutions.

As it turned out, this was relatively easy to accomplish, given veterans' outsider status and local officials' near monopoly over information and ready access to the coercive machinery of the state, particularly the police and courts. In Shanghai, many union branches made it very difficult for veterans to join by requiring, in violation of party regulations, long-term "trial periods." This led some veterans to complain, "Getting into the union is harder than getting into the Party."[59] For union officials, veterans' revolutionary credentials just were not adequate, particularly when compared to their own; the revolution, having lasted for so long, had given hundreds of thousands of people an opportunity to contribute something, and this diluted veterans' claims to high status. The statement—"I participated in the revolution"—was indeed true for many, but at the same time, its vagueness blurred the difference between different degrees of participation, risk, and sacrifice; surely there are differences in the contributions of the front-line combat soldier and the worker on the "home front" who stays in the factory an hour longer three times a week for the war effort.[60] Union officials at a boat repair factory, for example, told veterans: "It took thirty years of bloody struggle for us working-class people to establish the union; you can't enter just like that and enjoy power and benefits."[61] While the reference to working-class struggle is a direct reflection of Communist Party history, the notion that veterans do not deserve benefits and privileges is not unusual. In the United States after World War I, for example, "liberals and conservatives alike . . . denounced the one time heroes as 'mercenaries of patriotism,' . . . and to many servicemen who sought hospital benefits, the nation seemed to respond with the attitude, 'better dead than in bed.'"[62]

Faced with such ostracism, veterans looked back on their army service with great nostalgia, recalling it as a time of warmth and camaraderie, and they cried "in deep sorrow" about their present circumstances.[63] Some complained: "In the army we were the most loved [zui ke'ai], but now we are the most pitiable [zui kelian]." Some even thought seriously about reenlisting;[64] others did: in 1962 the State Council issued orders to cease "casually allowing" veterans to return to the army.[65]

Injustices such as these, however, paled in comparison to those instances in which local officials decided to use the police and courts against the veterans. For instance, in 1954, at the Shenghua Pharmaceutical Factory in Shanghai's Hongkou district, a veteran named Wang Hongnian was known to be "creative" in his job and was chosen to represent the veterans at the district level. One day he inadvertently caused a work accident that resulted in several hundred yuan's worth of damage. Shenghua officials, however, resented Wang because he had had the audacity—like many veterans—to file a complaint against factory officials during an earlier political campaign. They reported to the Public Security Bureau that Wang had "intentionally" caused damages in the amount of 7,600 yuan, and that this constituted a "counterrevolutionary incident." In October 1954 Wang was arrested. He stewed in prison without a hearing until November 1955, when the Hongkou District Court formally sentenced him to two years of incarceration. Wang appealed to the Shanghai Intermediate Court, which investigated and then cleared him of all charges. Factory officials, however, refused to reemploy him. Suffering from poverty and stress, Wang was said to have lost his mind.[66]

This case might be considered a particularly horrible travesty of justice, but other reports confirm that it was not exceptional. A 1956 report noted:

In state-owned firms leading cadres take revenge on veterans who dare to raise objections and criticisms. They do this by fabricating charges of "violating labor discipline" or some other offense and then reporting them to the police and judiciary. As a result, there are many cases of mistaken arrests, verdicts, and other miscarriages of justice.[67]

When cases such as this happened, the state machinery that was set up to protect veterans rarely intervened in a timely fashion. My evidence shows that lower-level courts were more likely to prosecute veterans than to protect them. Veterans might be able to obtain relief from appellate courts but only *after* they had suffered significantly. Such cases came to light only after dozens of complaints filtered up through the system (usually by way of family members, veterans committees, and the Bureau of Civil Affairs) and an investigation was finally undertaken.

Exploiting the machinery of the state was not the only weapon local officials could deploy. Access to privileged information was another. Because of their relatively long history of service and because of the enlistment selection process, veterans had a relatively long paper trail. On more than a few occasions, a veteran's individual circumstances were quite complex, reflecting the realities of war, the circumstances surrounding particular units' incorporation into the PLA, and the shifting alliances between the CCP, Nationalists, and even warlords and secret societies, as well as divided family allegiances. In the Shanghai area, thousands of Nationalist soldiers crossed over to the PLA in the last year of the Civil War. Even though these veterans were "red" by virtue of having served in the PLA, their tangled histories could easily be used against them by political enemies. Sometimes "red" was not red enough, and veterans might be ostracized to the same degree as some of the "black classes."

Several reports issued by state agencies throughout the 1950s and 1960s provide a good sense of how veterans could fall prey to officials' access to personal histories and the insistence on class purity. In 1956, for instance, the Shanghai Labor Bureau analyzed forty-four cases in which PLA veterans were unable to find work (and suffered a great deal of economic deprivation as a result) because personnel directors weeded out any veteran whose "complicated" biography made him even slightly suspect. Work-units, the report complained, "ignore that these veterans have already come clean and have undergone a trial by fire in the army and instead overemphasize the importance and uniqueness of their units and refuse to hire them."[68]

In some military units, very many veterans had some sort of "complication." The PL Navy, for instance, was almost entirely composed of former GMD officers and sailors, many of whom had switched allegiances during the Civil War. When 129 naval veterans from the East China Military Region Navy were sent to Shanghai, 74 of them (57 percent) were said to have "serious political history problems and complicated social relations." But rather than emphasizing the veterans' service to the PLA, the Bureau of Civil Affairs asked that district governments avoid assigning them to any sensitive post.[69] As a result, some veterans had been unemployed for 3–4 years and were said to be extremely poor, depressed, and "very dissatisfied with the Party and government." In response to such reports, the State Council and Ministry of Interior issued a policy document instructing local units to separate "historical problems" from "current ones"; so long as the veterans were working well and had come clean, they should be treated with honor and respect.[70] There is little evidence, however, to suggest that this directive was implemented.

As these reports make clear, many veterans returned to civilian life with heavy social and political baggage. While state propaganda frequently held up veterans as exemplars of patriotic sacrifice, in many instances, other, much less flattering, identity markers—whether social (most were peasants or the working poor) or political ("impure" political histories)—deflected the patriotic spotlight the state shined upon them. Because veterans were still alive, and because their lives were complex, they could not effectively serve as the regime's "agents of memory," to use Paloma Aguilar's useful term.[71]

It would be both simplistic and misleading, however, to depict urban and rural local officials as the only culprits in this story. While very few veterans were "counterrevolutionaries," some *did* behave badly. Three issues frequently appear in these reports and others: theft/corruption, sexual offenses, and overt challenges to authority.[72] If we consider PRC veterans' experiences and life circumstances, it is easy to understand why many veterans who came from poor villages were then discriminated against in a job market that favored people with technical skills. The temptation to steal or embezzle must have been overwhelming. And, given that many veterans were poor Northerners, uneducated, and occupied low-status positions in the security establishment, it also makes sense that they might have difficulty establishing a family and might resort to prostitutes, affairs with married women, "casual flirting," or common-law marriages.[73]

The state did what it could—in the mid-1950s the Bureau of Civil Affairs even proposed that the Women's Federation take upon itself a matchmaking role for veterans who had difficulty getting or staying married—but these sorts of solutions were ad hoc and of limited effectiveness.[74] It also makes a good deal of sense that veterans would be accused of overtly challenging local authority. Both during their military service and afterward veterans were frequently told that they were fulfilling a sacred patriotic and glorious duty to the state, and many—ultimately to their misfortune—took these words to heart. BCA officials were the first to call attention to this issue when they repeatedly emphasized that PLA veterans were "unrealistic," "arrogant and self-satisfied [*jiao'ao ziman*]" when it came to job expectations, and that some of them thought of themselves as "people with outstanding service records [*yiding de gongchen*]" who would accept nothing less than a very good position.[75] In factories, many managers complained that veterans were "difficult to control," "seek status," "hard to manage," "unruly [*tiaopi*]," "disobedient and undisciplined," and prone to solving problems through violence.[76] In Qingpu, veterans who returned from the Korean War refused to take orders from local officials, telling them, "I've been abroad! Who are you to tell me what to do?"[77] The state thus placed veterans in an untenable position: it taught them to appreciate their contribution to the state and the revolution, but failed to support them when this new sense of entitlement translated into political action. Accusations of "unruliness" masked the local political establishment's inability to accommodate the change in veterans' identity and behavior as empowered and privileged citizens.

The yawning gap between their expectations (generated both by state policy and propaganda) and everyday political, social, and economic realities generated a powerful sense of alienation and desperation among many veterans. In the mid-1950s, for instance, Civil Affairs reports from the provinces pointed to an increasing number of veterans who had resorted to suicide. In Shanxi, Jiangsu, and Zhejiang provinces, veterans committed suicide using a variety of methods, including poison, throwing themselves down village wells, and hanging and shooting themselves. County-level investigators who were dispatched to the villages discovered that maltreatment at the hands of local officials and ridicule by other villagers often precipitated the series of events leading to suicide.[78] Similar reports surfaced in the late 1950s as well, with investigators noting that among suicide cases (including attempts), "a considerable proportion" were of veterans with chronic illnesses who lacked the means to secure medicine, even though they were entitled to discounted or free medical care.⁷⁹ A Qingpu report found that veteran suicides resulted from "chronic illnesses," "marriage disputes," "political history problems," and "unsubstantiated accusations against them."⁸⁰ In Shanghai, an investigation into forty-three suicide attempts (eleven of them successful) from 1954 to 1956 revealed the following major causes:

Corruption and sex-related charges, post-homicide fear and stress	7
Stress over political history problems	6
Marriage problems/unrequited love	13
Mental illness, chronic disease leading to "abnormal behavior"	9
Financial difficulties	2

Two cases flesh out some of the political, economic, and social causes that led some veterans to take their own lives (or at least threaten to). In Shanghai, a veteran named Jin Guangming worked in an underwear factory as a maintenance worker. Jin, however, suffered from chronic stomach ulcers and was unable to work. He requested some time off in order to see a physician, but the factory refused. When he finally secured permission, the factory refused to reimburse his expenses. Jin, like many veterans, refused to take this sitting down. Disobeying factory orders to remain at work, he returned to the hospital. The factory then called the hospital and informed them that Jin was not sick at all but had "ideological problems [*sixiang wenti*]." Jin was incensed when he heard this, and immediately proceeded to the rooftop of the infirmary of the No. 1 People's Hospital. Luckily, he was pulled to safety before he leaped.⁸¹

Politics and the lack of appreciation of veterans' contribution were behind the suicide of Wu Hongji, who in 1955 jumped into the Huangpu River and drowned. According to the investigation, Wu killed himself because he "had serious problems" and had been "exposed during the *sufan* campaign." The investigators, however, failed to find any evidence of "serious" problems in Wu's dossier, only indications that his "social relationships were complicated." What precipitated the suicide, they found, was not his past history but his recent political actions: Wu had written a letter to the city government accusing a workshop director of "bureaucratism." When factory officials got word of this, they launched a counteroffensive.⁸²

Allies

Veterans were not expected to face local officials' obstructionism and indifference alone. They were awarded privileges upon which claims could be based. A large bureaucracy—the Veteran Resettlement Division (*anzhi chu*) of the Interior Ministry—was responsible for helping them secure these benefits, and senior officials (such as Zhou Enlai and Liu Shaoqi) were put in charge of their affairs. Given their official status and their high level of sponsorship, one might expect that many of the problems veterans encountered could have been avoided. And yet, during the 1950s, the early 1960s, the Cultural Revolution, and the reform period, it is clear that there existed a critical mass of veterans who suffered at the hands of the local state. In the end, the veterans were also betrayed by the Center when they tried to establish their own representative association to counter discrimination. Below, I examine veterans' interactions with the organizations that were supposed to be "on their side"—local bureaus of civil affairs and the Center.

As veterans were demobilized throughout the 1950s, they faced two concrete problems: the lack of money and jobs. BCA officials—many of whom were veterans themselves—were responsible for arranging financial aid when veterans needed it and work when they applied for it. Official guidelines notwithstanding, throughout the 1950s and 1960s reports on the administration of aid to PLA veterans often complained about the wide gap between central state guidelines and what happened on the ground. The first signs of difficulty were noticed early on, when state investigators (in Beijing and Shanghai) complained that local BCA officials all but ignored the "preferential" feature as a criterion for distributing aid. According to the official guidelines, PLA veterans' living standards should either be "equal to or above the average denizen of an area." But what sort of people did "average" include? In many cases, this average was calculated purely from an economic standpoint, and did not take into consideration class status or sacrifice for the revolution. As a result, preferential treatment programs for veterans were often administered as if they were welfare programs (not very surprising, given that the BCA was responsible for these programs as well), and PLA veterans were often treated as if they were "ordinary" poor. The absence of a sharp distinction between the two programs made the political position of veterans particularly problematic, since many people had become recently impoverished as a result of having become politically disenfranchised.[83] Among these were former GMD officers, landlords, and political prisoners. According to a BCA report from Beijing, local administrators sometimes "forgot their class standpoint" because they felt excessive "sympathy" for these people. Ironically, former Nationalist officers received the same amount of aid as PLA veterans, simply because both were considered "needy poor."[84] The result was Kafkaesque: in work-units, veterans were subject to abuse because of "complicated" political and family backgrounds, while veterans working in the Bureau of Civil Affairs routinely ignored class considerations when distributing financial aid. A constant refrain in the

BCA's internally circulated gazette, *Minzheng jianbao*, was the need to enhance local officials' (BCA and non-BCA) "political thought" so that they would appreciate the veterans' past contributions rather than their (sometimes problematic) current disposition and behavior.

Employment was no less an issue. Veterans expected officials in BCA offices to help them find employment and then assist them—through direct intervention or job transfers—if they encountered problems on the job. Here again, they were frequently disappointed. Despite explicit guidelines that veterans were to receive preferential treatment in job assignments, in day-to-day hiring they were often lumped together with other job seekers and had to wait until a "suitable" position opened up.[85] Moreover, BCA officials, many of whom were new to their jobs, unfamiliar with the local labor market, and often unmotivated, were rarely proactive in locating open positions.[86] One report charged low-level BCA clerks with "assigning jobs for assigning jobs' sake"—to prove to their superiors that they were actually doing something—and then "relaxing" and not doing any follow-up investigation after telling the veteran where he needed to go; "inappropriate" assignments were thus a common problem.[87] Once veterans were assigned to factories or to townships, they then "belonged" to those units and there was little the BCA could do to help. In one telling exchange, a workshop deputy director told a veteran: "I can tell you to spin cotton your entire life. Let's see what you can do about it!" To which the veteran replied, "Sir, I ask that you treat me according to the veteran resettlement policy guidelines of the State Council." The official shot back, "The State Council is the State Council—what do they have to do with me? You'll always be working for me, so you'd better do what I tell you."[88]

This comment was largely true, even though it reflected a bit of braggadocio. Once they left the PLA, veterans found themselves at the mercy of local organizations and officials. It was not surprising, therefore, that veterans clamored for justice by seeking to be re-embraced by the Center, which they saw both as a counterweight to local power and as the only "slice" of the state apparatus that appreciated their contributions, or by appealing to political bodies that had a certain percentage of veterans in them, mainly people's congresses. In the mid-1950s, as in the events of April 2002, reports noted that veterans in the countryside had traveled all the way to Beijing (from as far away as Sichuan Province) to request audiences with central leaders, clearly believing that their benefits and political rights should reflect their high political status. Beijing complained that repeated visits by veterans to the capital constituted a "disturbance of the public order" which also "harmed agricultural production," but they placed the blame squarely on the shoulders of local officials, not veterans.[89] Others veterans wrote to Zhou Enlai, Mao, Zhu De, and the National People's Congress.[90] In Shanghai, the preferred address for filing complaints in person or in the mail was the Municipal People's Congress; it comes up in a number of reports from the mid-1950s.[91] It appears that, as far as the veterans were concerned, "the state" that owed them a modicum of respect and economic benefits was the *Center*, just as in the contemporary period the Center is often seen as a generally benevolent power whose intentions are consistently thwarted by evil local officials.[92] Given that central governments are largely responsible for declaring and waging war, as well as for the legislation and policies awarding benefits to those who fight in its name, this appeal to the Center is quite understandable. Nor is it unusual: the ideological foundation of all pension programs for veterans is that when men sacrifice for the state—regardless of their motives for joining the military in the first place—the central government should assume responsibility for their benefits and care. Central governments therefore are the targets of protests when rights and benefits are not forthcoming.[93]

Assessing the success of such appeals is inherently difficult, given the limitation of sources from this period; it is almost impossible to trace a particular petition (*shangfang gaozhuang*) from beginning to end. My own estimate is that the chances of success were moderate at best, and that not a few veterans came back empty-handed. Unlike the case of citizens' requests to letters and visits offices, examined by Thireau and Hua in this volume, veterans' requests do not appear to have received the same level of response. A letter from a Qingpu veteran to Premier Zhou Enlai requesting a job transfer, for instance, was simply stamped by the letters and visits office of the State Council and then returned to provincial and county authorities, who promptly denied his request and directed him to "work single-mindedly in your current post." Absent effective intervention from the Center, many veterans remained at the mercy of local officials, waiting for an opportunity to claim what they felt was rightfully theirs: power, respect, and economic opportunity. The Cultural Revolution provided this, as veterans fled their units, set up fledgling veterans associations, and broke into CCP headquarters demanding—futilely, as it turned out—that they be officially recognized.

Conclusion

Two issues formed the core of veterans' conceptions of justice (and its opposite): state hypocrisy and violations of procedural and distributive justice. The hypocrisy of the state—the wide disjuncture between the highfalutin rhetoric of heroism, sacrifice, and promises of preferential treatment emanating from the Center and the many instances of intentional distortion of policies and regulations on the part of local officials—was keenly experienced by individual veterans in their struggles to survive in the postwar environment, as well as by veterans as a collective when they mobilized to protect whatever rights and status they could salvage. For a substantial number of veterans, but particularly those in the lower ranks, hypocrisy was not, as Judith Sklar has suggested, simply one of life's many "ordinary vices."[94]

Given that the state was attracted to the bright lights of patriotism at the same time that both its administrators and Chinese society were very much divided on veterans' importance, it is entirely possible that this hypocrisy was inevitable. It is also quite possible that hypocrisy is deeply embedded in the state-making process itself: the qualities that create states (bravery, willingness to sacrifice oneself) are not nearly as useful in generating revenue, creating "legible" populations (to use James Scott's term), and attaining other state goals. One scholar of international relations, in fact, has coined the term "organized hypocrisy" as a defining feature of sovereignty—states frequently violate long-standing norms to which they pledge adherence.[95] Nevertheless, veterans are a special case; most governments recognize this when they provide them with special rights and privileges and refrain from rewarding other groups in this way.[96] Very few citizens are willing to sacrifice their youth, their marriageable years, and life and limb for the state, or at least endure the rigors of long-term military service. Contrary to the conventional wisdom about the popularity of military service in the countryside, documents show that rural families in China were well aware of these risks (especially during the 1950s and 1960s, when it seemed on several occasions that China would go to war) and frequently discouraged young people from joining up, unless they were to be well compensated. Structural problems in the economy certainly made it difficult to provide veterans with a sense of distributive justice, but for many the procedural justice issues were just as important: if the state said you were important, you should be treated as an important person, not as someone with serious political problems. This suggests that if governments are not able to provide good jobs or ensure decent treatment, they would do well to turn down the volume of the rhetoric. To put it bluntly: states that cannot put up would be better off shutting up, as it is the gap between expectations and reality that is often the most galling to returning veterans. In 1956 one lieutenant wrote in an impassioned letter to the Minister of Interior, warning him that discontent among veterans would result in widespread disobedience in the event of mobilization for war:

> Glory, glory, glory, really glorious. To our ears, "glory" is an empty, meaningless and detestable word because we've had far too many "glories." When we signed up during the war, which was "glorious"; fighting is "glorious"; sacrifice is "glorious"; shedding blood is "glorious." . . . Nowadays, "glory" is the voice of the hungry and bitter people.[97]

In addition to calling attention to veterans' experience of hypocrisy, this essay has also focused on veterans' conceptions of justice, which appear to have been shaped by notions of fair or "reasonable" distribution of rewards and treatment comparable to their status and contributions. As far as the central state was concerned, veterans received a fair shake in the package of benefits they were provided: preferential access to jobs, welfare funds, power, political participation, and medical benefits were seen as giving veterans the rewards they deserved. Unfortunately, the state was either unwilling or unable to provide what many veterans wanted most of all—urban residence and a salary that was both commensurate with their contributions and at least equal to the salaries of others who, in their minds, had contributed a lot less. As I have argued, both of these goals worked at cross-purposes with other state objectives, most importantly, limiting the growth of cities and industrial development. This problem was recognized by the central government, which tried to compensate for these policies by highlighting veterans' political virtues. But this effort also fell flat, as local officials used a vague discourse on class status as a referendum on veterans' entitlements. Given the complexity of China's modern wars and tangled family allegiances, this was rather easy to do. Add to this the low status of soldiers and illiterate peasants in Chinese society and you have a very inhospitable soil in which to plant new entitlements.

Given these obstacles to the implementation of veteran benefits, would a "Veteran's Law" have made much of a difference? I think it would have.[98] Here, the case of women and the 1950 Marriage Law is instructive. The Marriage Law proved surprisingly effective in empowering rural women within their families, largely because it gave them access to courts and local governments for redress. The law provided women a place to confront their husbands and access to an official who was not embroiled in their dispute. And confront they did: in the early 1950s courts were flooded with marriage-related cases, more so in rural than in urban areas.[99] Judging by the contributions of O'Brien and Li, Gallagher, and Thireau and Hua in this volume, laws and legal institutions matter, even if the former are not fully implemented and the latter do not function even close to optimally. Workers in state-owned enterprises, for instance, experience a similar sense of hypocrisy as veterans do—they are exalted in state propaganda and in the very definition of the regime but are laid off without severance pay or pensions—and they are using the Labor Law, sometimes successfully, to claim rights due to them. Given that even in the 1950s—not a period known for rights consciousness and citizens' ability to assert claims against the state—veterans, much like women, proved to be aware of rules and willing to fight for them, providing them access to courts probably would have helped a great deal, if only by improving the probability of success by increasing the number of entry points to the polity. What the case of veterans shows is that in China it is very difficult to secure benefits—even for the officially privileged—if these are grounded only in "policy" and not in "law," nor backed up by what Charles Epp has called a "support structure" in society.[100] This structure was absent in the 1950s and 1960s, and it has not developed much in the reform period either. While laws and policies can certainly be ignored, having a law would have provided an institution that might have provided a counterweight to unsympathetic officials and citizens, and it would have reduced the pressure on the Center to make up for the failings of local authorities. Given all that we have seen about the way many veterans were treated, it certainly would not have done any greater harm.

Notes

1. Personal communication with a scholar in Beijing, December 2002.
2. Mo Yan, *The Garlic Ballads*, trans. Howard Goldblatt (New York: Viking, 1995); Kevin J. O'Brien and Lianjiang Li, "The Politics of Lodging Complaints in Rural China," *China Quarterly*, no. 143 (September 1995): 756–83.
3. Erik Eckholm, "In Beijing, a Long Wait for Indifferent Justice," *International Herald Tribune*, 8 November 1998.
4. These documents have been collected by the State Council's Veteran's Resettlement Office in the volume *Junren ganbu zhuanye fuyuan gongzuo wenjian huibian* (Beijing: Laodong renshi chubanshe, 1983) [hereafter cited as *JGZFG*].
5. In addition to fearing disability and death, veterans were also afraid of losing their fiancées while they were in the service. The state's claims in this regard were not inaccurate. Archival evidence reveals that peasants were often reluctant to join the military because they feared death, disability, and family problems. In addition to the Korean war, villagers were aware of tensions with the Nationalists on Taiwan and with the United States. Moreover, families were reluctant to let their sons join the army because it would result in reduced family income. Another concern was that village officials would "poach" their fiancées while they were away (see Neil J. Diamant, *Revolutionizing the Family: Politics, Love, and Divorce in Urban and Rural China, 1949–68* [Berkeley and Los Angeles: University of California Press, 2000], ch. 6).
6. See Jonathan Unger, "Introduction," in *Chinese Nationalism*, ed. Jonathan Unger (Armonk, N.Y.: M. E. Sharpe, 1996), xv; and James Townsend, "Chinese Nationalism," in ibid., 22.
7. *JGZFG*, 458.
8. Elizabeth Perry, oral communication.
9. Guangdong Province Local History Editorial Committee, ed., *Guangdong sheng zhi: minzheng zhi* (Guangzhou: Guangdong renmin chubanshe, 1993), 94.
10. Anhui Province Local History Editorial Committee, eds., *Anhui sheng zhi: minzheng zhi* (Hefei: Renmin chubanshe, 1993), 140.
11. Shanghai Municipal Archives (hereafter cited as SMA), B168-3-131, pp. 3–6. On the decision banning veterans organizations, see *Renmin ribao*, 26 January 1967; and *Hongqi*, 3 March 1967.
12. These "privileges," or "entitlements," were embedded in official state documents, but do not quite constitute "rights" in the way these are conceptualized in

liberal democracies. As Mirjan R. Damaska points out, in countries such as China claims "flowing from state decrees, even though routinely designated 'rights'" should not be "equated with personal entitlements" in states with long-standing democratic traditions. "All rights," Damaska notes, "are at least partially subject to qualification or denial" (see Mirjan R. Damaska, *The Faces of Justice and State Authority: A Comparative Approach to the Legal Process* [New Haven, Conn.: Yale University Press, 1986], 83).

13. On the plight of contract workers, see Elizabeth J. Perry, "The Shanghai Strike Wave of 1957," *China Quarterly*, no. 137 (March 1994): 1–27.

14. On the importance of procedural justice in state legitimacy, see Tom Tyler, *Why People Obey the Law* (New Haven, Conn.: Yale University Press, 1990).

15. A subject search in the online Bibliography of Asian Studies for "veterans" and "China" does not bring up a single entry.

16. Gerald N. Rosenberg, *The Hollow Hope: Can Courts Bring About Social Change?* (Chicago: University of Chicago Press), 32–36.

17. See Dorothy Solinger, *Contesting Citizenship in Urban China* (Berkeley: University of California Press, 1999); Tamara Jacka, "Working Sisters Answer Back: The Representation and Self-Representation of Women in China's Floating Population," *China Information* 13, no. 1 (1998): 43–75.

18. Solinger, *Contesting Citizenship in Urban China*, 2.

19. SMA, B168-1-607, p. 69.

20. SMA, B168-1-658, pp. 1–2.

21. SMA, B168-1-607, p. 49.

22. SMA, B168-1-607, p. 50.

23. SMA, B168-1-633, pp. 100–104.

24. On discrimination against these migrants in the pre-1949 period, see Emily Honig, *Creating Chinese Ethnicity: Subei People in Shanghai, 1850–1980* (New Haven, Conn.: Yale University Press, 1992).

25. "Guanyu mangmu lai hu de waiji fuyuan junren qingkuang yu chuli yijian de baogao," SMA, B168-1-633, p. 100; also Shanghai BCA to Ministry of Interior, SMA, B1-2-1519 (1954), pp. 1–3.

26. "Guanyu mangmu," SMA, B168-1-633, p. 102.

27. Ibid., pp. 100–101.

28. Ibid., p. 102.

29. Ibid., p. 102.

30. Ibid., p. 101; SMA, B168-1-611, p. 125.

31. "Guanyu mangmu," SMA, B168-1-633, p. 102.

32. SMA, B1-2-1519, p. 4.

33. "Guanyu mangmu," SMA, B168-1-633, pp. 103–4.

34. Elizabeth Perry, *Shanghai on Strike: The Politics of Chinese Labor* (Stanford, Calif.: Stanford University Press, 1992).

35. See "Guanyu anzhi fuyuan jianshe junren gongzuo de jueyi" (May 1955), *JGZFG*, 321–26.

36. SMA, B168-1-628, p. 30.

37. SMA, B168-1-517, p. 140.

38. SMA, B168-1-628, p. 99.
39. SMA, B168-1-628, p. 75.
40. SMA, B168-1-628, pp. 97–98.
41. SMA, B168-1-628, p. 75.
42. SMA, B168-1-628, pp. 140–56.
43. SMA, B127-1-358, p. 37.
44. SMA, B68-1-628, p. 31.
45. Guangdong Province Local History Editorial Committee, *Guangdong sheng zhi*, 94.
46. See Lynn White, *Policies of Chaos* (Princeton, N.J.: Princeton University Press, 1989); Andrew Walder, *Communist Neotraditionalism* (Berkeley: University of California Press, 1986); Judith Stacey, *Patriarchy and Socialist Revolution in China* (Berkeley: University of California Press, 1983).
47. SMA, A22-2-25 (March 1951), p. 54.
48. SMA, A22-2-25 (March 1951), p. 55.
49. SMA, A22-2-25 (March 1951), p. 55; SMA, C1-2-361, p. 33. Among educated elites, there were even greater suspicions about the war (see SMA C1-2-121, p. 22).
50. These documents were compiled by municipal and district "Resist America, Support Korea" committees, trade unions, the Women's Federation, and CYL. Space restrictions do not allow me to include more of these statements in this chapter.
51. SMA, B168-1-628, p. 91; SMA, B168-1-517, p. 139; Guangdong Province Local History Editorial Committee, *Guangdong sheng zhi*, 95.
52. Dongcheng District Archive [hereafter cited as DCA], 11-7-89, p. 151.
53. DCA, 11-7-96, p. 5.
54. Interior to Jiangxi Civil Affairs, SMA, B168-1-628, p. 166.
55. DCA, 11-7-89, pp. 151–52; DCA, 11-7-230.
56. SMA, B169-1-666, p. 4.
57. A comparison to post–World War I Great Britain is instructive here. There, disabled veterans received very little from the state; there was no law giving veterans preferential treatment in employment (unlike the situation in Germany after the war). Nevertheless, when British managers did not hire veterans, they often expressed great regret, and paid homage to their contributions. Epithets of the kind veterans experienced in China were extremely rare (for the treatment of disabled veterans in post–World War I Britain, see Deborah Cohen, *The War Come Home: Disabled Veterans in Britain and Germany, 1919–1939* [Berkeley and Los Angeles: University of California Press, 2001]).
58. SMA, B123-3-1442 (1956), p. 6.
59. SMA, B168-1-628, p. 98.
60. I am grateful to David Strand for bringing this point up. For an interesting perspective on the politics of "comparative sacrifice" in the U.S. context, see Gerald F. Linderman, *The World Within War: America's Combat Experience in World War II* (Cambridge, Mass.: Harvard University Press, 1997), 334–45; and Mark H. Leff, "The Politics of Sacrifice on the American Home Front in World War II," *Journal of American History* 77, no. 4 (March 1991): 1296–1318. The Daughters of the American Revolution (DAR) is another interesting example. To be admitted to the DAR, a

woman over the age of 18 has to "prove lineal, blood line descent from an ancestor who aided in achieving American independence." Under the list of "acceptable service" one finds clauses as specific as, "those who rendered material aid, in Spanish America, by supplying cattle for Galvez's forces after 24 December 1776," to "furnishing a substitute for military service" (see http://www.dar.org). In other words, the relative who paid someone *else* to serve in his stead "aided" independence as much as the lineal descendent who served in the Continental Army.

61. SMA, B168-1-628 (1957), p. 74.
62. Donald Lisio, "The United States: Bread and Butter Politics," in *The War Generation: Veterans of the First World War*, ed. James Diehl and Stephen Ward (Port Washington, N.Y.: Kennikat Press, 1975), 42.
63. SMA, B168-1-630, p. 11.
64. SMA, B168-1-628, p. 22.
65. JGZFG, 635.
66. SMA, B168-1-628, p. 31.
67. SMA, B168-1-630, p. 10.
68. SMA, B127-1-820, p. 27.
69. SMA, B1-2-1519, p. 29.
70. SMA, B127-1-820 (1956), pp. 27–28.
71. Paloma Aguilar, "Agents of Memory: Spanish War Veterans and Disabled Soldiers," in *War and Remembrance in the Twentieth Century*, ed. Jay Winter and Emmanuel Sivan (Cambridge: Cambridge University Press, 1999), 84–101.
72. A joint judiciary and BCA investigative team analyzed 135 criminal cases involving veterans and found that 51 percent of them (69 cases) involved either theft, corruption, or "swindling," with "counterrevolutionary" crimes coming up a close second at 25 percent. The next largest category of crimes (19 percent) were sex-related—rape, soliciting prostitutes, and illicit affairs (*luangao guanxi*) (see SMA, B168-1-628, p. 90).
73. SMA, B168-1-607, pp. 71, 73.
74. *Minzheng jianbao*, 15 August 1956, 5.
75. SMA, B168-1-619, p. 48.
76. SMA, B168-1-633 (1957), p. 80; SMA, B168-1-619, p. 70.
77. Qingpu District Archives [hereafter cited as QDA], 48-2-96, p. 50.
78. DCA, 11-7-89, pp. 128–29.
79. DCA, 11-7-306, p. 3.
80. QDA, 48-2-98, p. 112.
81. SMA, B168-1-628 (1956), p. 22.
82. SMA, B168-1-628 (1956), p. 22.
83. DCA, 11-7-74, p. 124.
84. DCA, 11-7-74 (1954), pp. 26–27.
85. SMA, B168-1-607, p. 69.
86. SMA, B168-1-619, p. 67.
87. DCA, 11-7-74, p. 1; DCA, 11-7-400, pp. 6–7.
88. DCA, 11-7-74, p. 1; DCA, 11-7-400, pp. 6–7.
89. DCA, 11-7-405, p. 2; *Minzheng jianbao*, 24 May 1956, 2.

90. DCA, 11-7-191, p. 23; QDA, 48-2-90 (1955), p. 26.

91. SMA, B168-1-168 (1955), pp. 54, 77; SMA, B168-1-619 (1955), p. 69. For a similar pattern among women in the 1950s, see Neil J. Diamant, *Revolutionizing the Family*, chs. 3, 6.

92. Kevin J. O'Brien, "Rightful Resistance," *World Politics* 49, no. 1 (October 1996): 31–55.

93. On the federal role in U.S. pensions, see Theda Skocpol, *Protecting Soldiers and Mothers: The Political Origins of Social Policy in the United States* (Cambridge, Mass.: Harvard University Press, 1992); and Megan McClintock, "Civil War Pensions and the Reconstruction of Union Families," *Journal of American History* 83, no. 2 (1996): 463. Wallace Davies writes, "An axiom of American history is that sooner or later the participants in all its wars have expected the government to grant them generous pensions." See *Patriotism on Parade: The Story of Veterans' and Hereditary Organizations in America, 1793–1900* (Cambridge, Mass.: Harvard University Press, 1955), 156.

94. Judith Sklar, *Ordinary Vices* (Cambridge, Mass.: Belknap Press of Harvard University Press, 1984). It was certainly the case that there was a "creaming effect" in the implementation of preferential policies in China, as is often the case with affirmative action programs. That is, those who were able to take advantage of preferential policies were those who needed them least, such as higher ranking officers, but had the skills and resources to make use of them. However, the fact that thousands of *officers* congregated in Beijing in 2002 (I do not know what rank they had) suggests that even those who were relatively well educated and had higher status experienced discrimination as well.

95. Steven Krasner, *Sovereignty: Organized Hypocrisy* (Princeton, N.J.: Princeton University Press, 1999).

96. This was the very similar rationale put forth by Green Raum, Commissioner of Pensions in the United States in the late nineteenth century (see Green Raum, "Pensions and Patriotism," *North American Review*, no. 153 [1891]: 206).

97. SMA, B168-1-628, p. 159.

98. I am not alone in thinking this. Several scholars at the Shanghai Academy of Social Sciences have proposed such legislation since veterans continue to experience discrimination in the urban workforce.

99. See Diamant, *Revolutionizing the Family*.

100. Charles Epp, *The Rights Revolution: Lawyers, Activists, and Supreme Courts in Comparative Perspective* (Chicago: University of Chicago Press, 1998).

PART III

Legal Institutions

ANDREW C. MERTHA 7

Shifting Legal and Administrative Goalposts
Chinese Bureaucracies, Foreign Actors, and the Evolution of China's Anti-Counterfeiting Enforcement Regime

> Fake and shoddy goods have greatly damaged the country's reputation and interest. We must launch a large-scale, solid campaign through joint cracking-down efforts to substantially improve our legal system.
>
> Zhu Rongji[1]

More than a dozen years after the first rounds of the U.S.–China bilateral negotiations over intellectual property rights (IPR) began, China remains saddled with an international reputation as a global manufacturing base and clearing house for counterfeit products. The perception that China is unable to afford protection for intellectual property, including trademarks, is a key deterrent to increased foreign direct investment to the PRC.[2] Chinese counterfeiting networks have become extremely sophisticated and decentralized over the past decade, and in most cases it is virtually impossible for consumers to distinguish genuine from fake goods at the retail level. Nike estimates one counterfeit produced for every legitimate Nike product made in China.[3] In certain retail markets, close to 90 percent of standard household products are counterfeit, while the Chinese government is on record as saying that the aggregate ratio of counterfeit goods to legitimate products is two to one.[4] Moreover, with China now a member of the World Trade Organization (WTO), not only are there concerns that China is unable to enforce its newly revised, WTO-compliant IPR laws, but fears have arisen that increased access to export markets will flood the world with Chinese-made counterfeit goods.[5]

Nevertheless, in contrast to the conventional wisdom that the Chinese government simply looks the other way as IPR violations continue unchallenged, there have been significant attempts to reverse this trend, albeit with more modest results. In the past three years, Beijing has ordered the centralization of several administrative enforcement bureaucracies in order to combat the "local protectionism" (*difang baohuzhuyi*) that shields local counterfeiters from the law.[6] Chinese consumers have also exerted pressure to rid the market of fake products, particularly medicines and foodstuffs that pose potential health hazards. Finally, the growing number of foreign commercial actors in China has shaped Chinese anti-counterfeiting enforcement activity in important ways.[7] In the pages to follow, I analyze this relationship between law and the growing foreign presence in Chinese society and how this relationship has helped form the trajectory of trademark protection and anti-counterfeiting enforcement in China.

Specifically, I argue that the growing numbers of foreign commercial actors in China have become active participants in Chinese society. With the arrival in China of a vigorous constituency in foreign commercial actors, some had hoped that trademark protection would be guaranteed by the courts under the civil Trademark Law. When it became clear that the courts were unwilling or unable to ensure trademark protection, many of these firms turned to China's administrative enforcement apparatus and met with greater success. However, administrative enforcement[8] could not establish a credible deterrent to would-be counterfeiters, and in recent years foreign trademark-intensive companies have attempted to work with national elites and local government officials to press for the prosecution of trademark violations under existing statutes in China's Criminal Law. A simple schematic for this evolution can be sketched as follows:

Civil Law (Judicial) → Civil Law (Administrative) → Criminal Law
To Mid-1990s   Mid-to-Late 1990s   Late 1990s to the Present

In this chapter, I examine the role of foreign actors in the mobilization of law enforcement in China through the lens of trademark protection and anti-counterfeiting. In doing so, I address two broad themes of this volume: how the legal process in China—and in particular, administrative enforcement—works in practice, and how law is mobilized in China.

Focusing on Administrative Enforcement of the Law in China

China's historical and cultural legacy regarding the law in general and intellectual property law in particular remains a rich topic for scholarly debate and academic analysis. Lubman argues that "law in China was not formally differentiated from other forms of state power, in striking contrast to the West."[9] The traditional function of law was as an often inelegant mechanism to buttress the existing normative order. Moreover, law was a less desirable option for the Confucianist elite than were other methods at their disposal. Recent scholarship has raised questions about the degree to which informal mediation eclipsed formal adjudication (or the resolution of disputes by magistrates and their superiors in the imperial hierarchy) during the premodern era,[10] and debate continues to evolve on the premodern antecedents of the contemporary legal process.

Alford provides a valuable contribution to this discussion with his analysis of the origins of intellectual property in the Chinese context. Although dynastic China was responsible for important scientific, artistic, and institutional innovations throughout its long history, it did not possess a Western-style legal—or even a normative—infrastructure to recognize, let alone protect, intellectual property. Rather than regarding invention as a private right to be protected, the diffusion of innovative activity and the careful examination and duplication of it was considered to be the proper way to manage creativity in traditional China. One can argue that the notion of "intellectual property" was a thoroughly alien concept in premodern China.[11]

Whatever legal institutions had existed in the Qing or under the Republic, Maoism effectively destroyed China's pre-1949 legal infrastructure. The legal process, like many other institutions at the time, was overwhelmed by the mass campaigns that dominated political life for the first twenty-five years of the People's Republic. Under reform, however, there has been a dramatic about-face. The establishment of a viable legal apparatus remained an important goal for the top leadership throughout the reform era. From 1978 to the end of the 1990s, China's National People's Congress enacted 327 laws and regulations, the State Council promulgated 750 administrative laws, and local governments approved 5,300 subnational decrees.[12] Yet, the swiftness in the development of this legal regime has not met with a corresponding appreciation for, or confidence in, legal-judicial conflict resolution on the part of many Chinese citizens.

Discontinuities between traditional China and the present day, and between the legacies of Maoism and the relative novelty of reform-era legal institutions, combine to mark Chinese legal practice today with a complicated amalgam of formal laws, informal norms, institutional incentives, and economic and political calculations, all of which have an important, albeit multifarious, impact on enforcement. Even while an increasing number of Chinese and foreign litigants go to the courts and the proliferation of learned Chinese lawyers and legal scholars reaches unprecedented levels, the contemporary Chinese judicial system is institutionally weak: it remains firmly under the control of the Chinese Communist Party, it suffers from a lack of social prestige and professional experience, and it is largely unable to enforce its own decisions.[13]

On the other hand, administrative enforcement, which involves the mediation and settlement of disputes and the enforcement of laws and regulations by administrative bureaucratic units as distinct from the courts, contin-

TABLE 7.1

Judicial vs. Administrative Cases of Anti-Counterfeiting Enforcement

	Cases taken to court	Administrative enforcement
1996	42	14,000
1887	45	32,027
1998	92	28,952
1999	65	32,298
2000	49	38,240

SOURCES: *Zhongguo gongshang xingzheng guanli nianjian, 1996–2000* [China Administration of Industry and Commerce Yearbook, 1996–2000] (Beijing: Gongshang chubanshe, 1997–2001); *Zhongguo zhishi chanquan nianjian, 2000* [China Intellectual Property Yearbook, 2000] (Beijing: Zhishi chanquan chubanshe, 2001).

ues to eclipse formal adjudication in China, as shown in Table 7.1.[14] Administrative enforcement is often more effective and less cumbersome than adjudication. This is underscored in the following passage describing a central component of administrative enforcement, the "enforcement action," or raid:

> Ordering a raid on a suspected IPR infringer by an administrative enforcement agency is so simple, and so immediately gratifying, it is little wonder such actions are by far the most popular method of dealing with IPR problems in China. . . . The procedure is straightforward. Once an infringement has been discovered, the rights holder presents evidence of piracy to the local office of the appropriate administrative authority. The authority will then decide whether the evidence is sufficient to merit a raid. As it is empowered by law to take these decisions without applying a judicial standard of proof, a positive decision from the administrative authority is almost assured. A team of officials from the local office will conduct the raid on their own, though in certain cases, if advisable, it may call a police escort. No warrant is required.[15]

Administrative enforcement offers three major benefits over the judicial process. First, it does not necessarily entail the formal and overt sparring between litigants that may occur in the courtroom. Second, the administrative process is much faster and often less expensive than the judicial process. Third, administrative agencies are better able than the courts to enforce their decisions. It should come as no surprise, therefore, that many in China consider administrative enforcement and not the judicial process the most effective route to pressing their legal claims, at least for the present. Nowhere is this more the case than with trademarks and anti-counterfeiting enforcement.

Foreign Actors as a Part of Chinese "Society"

This understanding of and appreciation for administrative enforcement, however, is not limited to Chinese actors. One of the most interesting developments in recent years is the growing importance of foreign actors within the context of China's legal development. From a broader perspective, this necessitates a rethinking of how to define "Chinese society" and what to include in such a conceptualization when discussing law and society in contemporary China.

In the latter half of the twentieth century, the state has been conceptualized either in terms of formal institutions or, in the case of the pluralists, in terms of the elements of society, and not the formal configuration of the state, to explain political outputs. In this latter view, the behavior of the state was seen as little more than the aggregation of societal preferences. In the early 1980s there was an important shift in focus, in which scholarship attempted to both disaggregate the state and identify the dynamics of, and the boundaries between, state and society, respectively.[16]

Statist scholars nevertheless often continue to analyze the state in largely undifferentiated terms, or simply view states as unitary actors. This is problematic. By "presenting [states] as holistic, some scholars have given the misleading impression that states, at key junctures in their histories, pull in single directions."[17] This has led to macro-level theorizing about "society" as well: "Scholars and journalists . . . have overemphasized the major battles among large-scale social forces (entire states, social classes, civil society and the like) operating on some grand level," while neglecting the day-to-day transformative experiences in state–society relations.[18] The dramatic events in the late 1980s and early 1990s in Eastern Europe (the fall of the Berlin Wall and the collapse of Communism) and in China (the Spring 1989 protests and subsequent crackdown in Tiananmen Square and in other parts of China) help reinforce scholarly focus on this level of analysis.

That focus, however, ignores the countless interactions between local agents of the state and Chinese society that make up the complex legal, political, and economic context of contemporary China. Recent scholarship underscores the importance of local political processes, specifically the dynamic interaction between elements of Chinese society and local agents of the state.[19] And although it would be overstating it to say that "all politics are local" in China, it would be equally problematic to limit our attention to elite interactions in Beijing when analyzing political developments in China more generally. Calls for analyzing the "anthropology of the state" thus require us to augment analyses from the "commanding heights" with those from the "trenches" of state–society interactions. Accordingly, this chapter focuses on dynamics cogently articulated by Migdal: "In . . . various settings is born the recursive relationship between state and society, the mutually transforming interactions between components of the state and other social forces."[20]

I argue here that in the arena on which this chapter is focused, the "society" making up state–society relations in China is becoming increasingly populated by non-Chinese actors. My focus is on the extensive, vigorous, ongoing interactions between foreign commercial actors and local Chinese administrative enforcement agencies in shaping the nature and course of anti-counterfeiting enforcement. Foreign actors bring new concerns, resources, and enforcement methods to the table, and this has had a tremendous effect on transforming the standard operating procedures of local Chinese enforcement agencies. Moreover, such interactions have helped some of these agencies increase and consolidate their power over other, competing bureaucratic units. These enforcement agencies, in turn, provide insights into how these foreign actors might realize their goals and manage their interests in a social, political, and cultural context often quite alien to their own. This endows these foreign actors with knowledge that can be converted into power and opportunities in their continuing interactions with Chinese state actors in this and other policy areas. The "foreign actors" discussed here are companies rather than individuals because my fieldwork to date suggests that these companies have a more direct impact on the evolution of China's anti-counterfeiting regime.

This stands in contrast to "civil society" theory, which suggests that insofar as foreign actors play a role in a given "society" they are often non-governmental organizations, not commercial actors.[21] Such theory usually looks at new domestic private businesses and/or commercial associations that offer individuals autonomy from state control, as has been the case in Hungary.[22] Foreign multinational corporations are rarely discussed in this context, perhaps because they might be regarded with suspicion either as "carpetbaggers" exploiting the fragile environment of political change or as supporters of the status quo, and considered obstacles to—and not agents of—change.[23]

Of course, I am not the first to make the claim that foreign actors can play a role in the political process in China. Liberthal and Oksenberg have argued that "foreigners may force an issue onto the agenda of the highest level leaders."[24] Gallagher has argued that foreign direct investment as a domestic force has opened up China's economy while helping thwart political reform.[25] My argument differs from Gallagher's because I make explicit claims about specific relationships and interactions between the Chinese state and foreign actors that are both direct and intimate. Unlike Lieberthal and Oksenberg, I focus on the sub-national level in an era in which the participation of foreign actors is far less regulated than it was in the mid-to-late 1980s.

Finally, I do not wish to deny the importance of Chinese actors or to inflate the importance of foreign actors in the analysis contained herein. It is almost universally acknowledged that the Chinese suffer more from intellectual property theft in China than do their foreign counterparts. Moreover, as I describe in the next section, Chinese actors do utilize resources against counterfeiters. However, what is often overlooked (and what some in China might find difficult to accept) is that in recent years foreign actors have also become important players in the process of shaping the patterns of Chinese law enforcement and therefore merit our attention.

The Shift to Administrative Enforcement

CHINESE ANTI-COUNTERFEITING ADMINISTRATIVE ENFORCEMENT AGENCIES

Starting around 1995, a number of Chinese and foreign private investigation agencies began to establish a presence in China. Although their services range from providing security for important company CEOs and celebrities to investigating corporate espionage, many of them found that the majority of their caseload was taken up with anti-counterfeiting work (up to 90 percent of their effort involves IPR enforcement, of which another nine-tenths is occupied with trademark / counterfeit issues).[26] These investigation companies, and their largely foreign clientele, soon realized that their short- and medium-term goals in combating counterfeiting in China would be best served by mobilizing the administrative apparatus, and not the courts.

The two principal administrative enforcement bureaucracies charged with anti-counterfeit enforcement power are the Administration for Industry and Commerce (AIC, or *gongshang xingzheng guanli ju*) and the Quality Technical Supervision Bureau (QTSB, or *zhiliang jishu jiandu ju*). These two bureaucracies share several characteristics. First, the AIC and the QTSB extend all the way down to the county level. The AIC, moreover, extends down to the village and township levels in the form of the generalist *gongshang suo*. Second, both bureaucracies are *zhifa bumen*, which means that they have enforcement arms that can levy fines and confiscate, destroy, and auction counterfeit goods. At the provincial level, these teams are christened the *zong dui*; at the district, prefecture, and municipal level, they are the *zhi dui*; at the county level, they are the *da dui*.[27] Third, after initially rebuffing outside pleas to redouble their anti-counterfeiting efforts, both bureaucracies quickly understood that such enforcement could provide an enormous amount of extrabudgetary income through "case handling fees" (*ban'an fei*), side-payments, and outright bribes. Moreover, before the recent system of *shouzhi liangtiao xian*, whereby fines, administrative fees, and service charges are placed in special bank accounts[28] managed by the finance bureaus before a portion of it is remitted back to the AIC or QTSB,[29] these offices could simply hold onto the money they collected and redistribute them in-house as they saw fit (*zishou zizhi*). Many still do.[30]

In other ways, the two bureaucracies are quite different. First, although there is considerable variation on this point, QTSB personnel have a reputation of being smarter, more professional, and less prone to corruption than their AIC counterparts. Part of this is because many of the early "foot soldiers" of the AIC (who have since risen in the ranks) were relatively less-educated People's Liberation Army troops demobilized in the mid-1980s. Second, and related to the above, the QTSB is a largely technical bureaucracy in which some level of higher education is necessary to undertake the inspection and analysis of product quality, measurement, and standards. Each enforcement agent in the QTSB must pass an examination before being admitted to the enforcement ranks.[31]

Third, the scope of responsibilities for the two bureaucracies is different. The AIC has enjoyed a long organizational history,[32] and although it had a somewhat secondary role during the planned economy under Mao Zedong, it nevertheless was able to amass a large number of responsibilities over time. These cover the range of administration, management, and regulation of China's growing market-oriented economy. Sometimes, these responsibilities are in conflict. For example, the AIC derives income from enterprise registration and continuing management fees (*guanli fei*), yet at the same time it is ordered to shut down enterprises found to be violating trademarks. Enterprise registration and market management directly or indirectly provide local AICs with a substantial amount of extrabudgetary income. Enterprise registration and market management are relatively straightforward tasks and rarely involve any real risk. Enforcing commercial laws and regulations, including those pertaining to trademarks, requires locating the violating factory, warehouse, or retail outlet and confiscating the offending merchandise, which are costly, time-consuming, and potentially dangerous undertakings. Taking the path of least resistance often meant that the AIC would allow counterfeiting to continue. This began to change when the AIC found a rival claimant to its enforcement portfolio, namely the Quality Technical Supervision Bureau.

The Technical Supervision Bureau (TSB) was established in December 1988 when the Bureau of Measurements and the Bureau of Standards were abolished and the product quality responsibilities of the State Economics

Commission were transferred to the TSB (since 1998, it has been renamed the Quality Technical Examination Supervision and Quarantine General Bureau—*Guojia zhiliang jishu jiandu jianyan jianyi zongju*—at the national level, and the Quality Technical Supervision Bureau at the provincial level and below). The broad responsibilities of the QTSB include regulating the formulation and implementation of national and regional standards and measurements and protecting consumers through the supervision of national and local product quality standards.[33] The QTSB responsibilities most relevant to this analysis have to do with product quality and consumer protection from substandard or dangerous goods. Insofar as counterfeit merchandise is of inferior quality relative to its legitimate counterpart, and as the unknowing purchase of counterfeit products harms the consumer, the QTSB can target the manufacture and sales of such offending merchandise. In and around 1994 the TSB began to interpret its role quite liberally to include directly and aggressively combating the production and sales of counterfeit goods, intruding upon what had essentially been the exclusive domain of the AIC.[34]

The foregoing suggests a degree of competition between the two bureaucracies.[35] Some years ago, in Sichuan, AIC–QTSB rivalry reportedly grew so intense that the provincial government and people's congress had to intervene. This case revolved around a Zhejiang color printing firm and forged letters of license. Both the AIC and the QTSB undertook investigations in very competitive fashion, and this competition hindered the government's ability to handle the case. The Sichuan provincial government was so incensed at this turn of events that the provincial people's congress called representatives from both the AIC and the QTSB to task and reportedly gave them a serious dressing-down.[36] The agencies' behavior in this matter was not an isolated phenomenon:

Rivalries have developed among the various government entities charged with the public enforcement against counterfeiting.... A number of these entities continue to upgrade their enforcement tools against counterfeiting in an effort to increase their capabilities vis-à-vis their bureaucratic competitors in order to corner the market on intellectual property enforcement. For example, in Guangdong Province the [Q]TSB recently had its power increased by local legislation leading to increased tensions with the AIC, which has primary authority over trademarks and believes that the [Q]TSB is encroaching upon its authority.[37]

Complicating enforcement even more is the fact that neither the AIC nor the QTSB is above actively participating in counterfeiting operations themselves. The AIC, in particular, continues to have a stake in deriving income from counterfeiting operations, either through enterprise registration, retail rental income, or through outright collusion and kickbacks. One need only travel to Yiwu Municipality in Zhejiang Province to witness firsthand the distribution and sales of an estimated annual two billion dollars' worth of product (one-fifth to one-third of which is estimated to be counterfeit[38]) under the regulatory eye of the AIC. Nevertheless, the competitive dynamics discussed above have shifted AIC behavior to be, on balance, more favorably disposed toward anti-counterfeiting enforcement than it was before. This shift, in turn, has been accelerated and deepened by the growing number of foreign commercial actors on Chinese soil.

THE TACTICS OF CHINESE FIRMS AS AN EXAMPLE TO FOREIGN ACTORS

When the number of foreign firms in China began to grow rapidly in the early 1990s, representatives of many of these companies might have hoped that China's courts, while far from perfect, would nevertheless provide the most appropriate forum to settle commercial disputes encountered in China, including those relating to intellectual property. Even if the process was less than completely objective, some representatives from larger companies reasoned that they could benefit from favoritism because of what they perceived as their role in providing much-needed foreign investment to China.[39] These expectations and assumptions often proved to be wrong. These same firms were confronted with the hard reality of an enforcement rate that dipped as low as 20 percent,[40] often in favor of the violators—not the rightholders—of intellectual property..

At the same time, Chinese companies were developing strategies that made virtue out of necessity in an environment where the prospects for trademark protection seemed remote, if not impossible. The following example is representative:

A well-known Chongqing company producing specialized trademark-protected ink found itself the target of counterfeiting from competitors as well as from its own licensees in Sichuan, Guizhou, and Yunnan provinces. These problems were exacerbated by the propensity of county-level governments in these provinces to extract money from these branch factories. In response, the company mobilized its sales staff as the front line in the fight to protect its trademark. In addition to their normal functions, these salespeople were responsible for locating counterfeit goods in the marketplace. They could undertake market investigations less obtrusively than the local police. The salesman would send suspected product to the company's technical department, which would then analyze it and follow up with further inspections or request action by administrative agencies such as the AIC and the QTSB, which are discussed immediately above. This "entrepreneurial" form of monitoring, and the tendency to employ administrative organs as opposed to the courts, reflected the company managers' preference for handling things administratively, and for precisely the reasons discussed above: simplicity, speed, and a lower burden of proof. A company representative said that the only way to truly reverse the trend of counterfeiting would be to use the revised Criminal Law to provide a suitable deterrent against future counterfeiting activity.[41]

This case is illuminating because it represents what many other Chinese companies are doing. What is particularly striking, however, is that this company's actions provide a de facto blueprint for the strategies many foreign companies adopted in the latter half of the 1990s: the mobilization of salespeople as investigators, the use of administrative channels to improve enforcement, and a long-term desire to transform counterfeiting into a criminal offense.

Foreign Actors and Enforcement

The majority of the clientele of both foreign and Chinese investigation agencies have tended to be foreign companies. This is partly because they usually have more money to spend on enforcement, which in the past may have cost up to $8,000 USD per raid. It is also partly because many Chinese companies either do not see the value in spending money on such enforcement activity or prefer that foreign companies carry the burden of providing the "quasi-public good" of anti-counterfeiting enforcement.

Foreign commercial actors in China have shaped enforcement patterns in at least three significant ways.[42] First, they play a vital role in raising the stakes and thus shaping the incentive structure so that these two bureaucracies find it increasingly in their interests to intensify their anti-counterfeiting enforcement activities.[43] A draft report of the China Anti-Counterfeiting Coalition provides a particularly good summary of this exchange:

[Anti-counterfeiting enforcement provides] many perks that authorities get from companies in the form of trips to conferences in the PRC and abroad, expensive post-raid dinners, lunches and other entertainment. Raids are also revenue-generating activities because authorities confiscate cash, goods, machinery and equipment, including cars and will then sell confiscated goods at public auctions. Fines imposed upon counterfeiters enrich government coffers and some administrative agencies give cash bonuses to personnel who participate in successful raids. Government authorities also routinely ask companies to reimburse the cost of lodging where travel is required, the cost of hiring trucks to load and move confiscated goods, and the cost of storing the goods if a private warehouse needs to be rented. Some government authorities will also ask companies to pay case handling fees. One local AIC has even established a special association, with a membership fee, for companies interested in around the clock twenty four [sic] enforcement services. Budget limitations are the reasons most commonly given for these fees and the reimbursement of costs, but increases in budgets and resources do not appear to change these practices.

After years of these practices, a culture seems to have developed that companies should subsidize enforcement activities.[44]

Side-payments are not always remunerative. From a political or organizational standpoint, one type of side-payment is to provide "face" to the enforcement agency through expressions of gratitude in newspaper and trade journal advertisements. Although this payment of "political capital" should not be exaggerated, neither should it be completely overlooked: in a country that puts a premium on political symbols, it is an effective way of providing positive exposure to bureaucracies such as the QTSB or the AIC. Such non-remunerative side-payments can be as mundane as helping enforcement agencies fulfill their monthly quota of raids by enlisting them in enforcement activity. The AIC often "lobbies" the investigation companies to provide such work, particularly during "lean" spells of enforcement activity.[45]

Second, while it would be an overstatement to say that these foreign actors play the AIC and the QTSB off against one another, they adeptly fan the flames of this inter-bureaucratic competition to their advantage. Individual company representatives and even investigation firms, whether Chinese or foreign, cannot undertake enforcement actions by themselves. They must secure the cooperation of the local enforcement authorities, most often the AIC or the QTSB. After identifying the least corrupt and most helpful and effective of these agencies, they begin to develop and nurture a relationship with the agency, although it can take up to eighteen months before the relationship becomes "productive."[46]

Finally, foreign companies and the investigation agencies in their employ have found that if they are willing to undertake the groundwork and if they are able to help disentangle the potential jurisdictional disputes that may arise, Chinese enforcement agencies are far more willing to work on their behalf. In the colorful language of the trade, foreign actors undertake the "grunt work" and the Chinese administrative enforcement agencies act as the "white knights" in this transnational "division of labor." The following cases illustrate these dynamics.

Case One: Participant Observation in an AIC Enforcement Action

In 1999 I was invited to observe an enforcement action. I made my arrangements from Hong Kong with a private investigation firm working on behalf of a U.S. company operating in China (it was the latter which allowed me to participate). One day in early June, I was instructed to meet my interlocutors in the bar of a Guangdong hotel the following day. Upon my arrival at the hotel at two o'clock the next afternoon, they introduced themselves as the representatives of the investigation firm. The five men were led by a forty-eight-year-old gentleman I will call Liu. Like many private investigators, Mr. Liu had formerly been with the Hong Kong police force but had moved into the private sector in anticipation of changes after Hong Kong's reversion to Chinese sovereignty in 1997. It did not matter much that he was not a mainlander; what was important was that he was ethnically Chinese, that he "blend in" (foreigners are often involved throughout the entire process, but rarely take part in the actual raids). Liu briefed me on the day's activities and we went to the local AIC office, the official Chinese agency that was undertaking the raid.

At the AIC building I was introduced to the division chief (*chuzhang*) of the AIC economic investigation division (*jingji jiancha chu*). While I waited, Liu and the AIC agents pored over handwritten maps that marked the locations of the target market stalls. It was only at this time that Liu informed the AIC of the actual targets (this was done in order to prevent leaks). Before we left, an AIC agent casually "deputized" Liu by giving him an AIC ID to wear (backward, so that nobody could tell that somebody else's picture was on the front). Once the group of seventeen assembled, we went downstairs and into three unmarked black minivans. En route, I asked about AIC–QTSB rivalry. An AIC official responded by saying that such a rivalry existed and was often quite intense under the surface, but that it has to remain understated or else it would invite "third-party mediation" from above that could result in the curtailment of the AIC's (or the QTSB's) jurisdiction, an outcome that neither party would welcome.

When we reached the market, the enforcement team of private investigators and AIC agents walked into the arcade and stopped at the first target stall, just inside the entranceway. As soon as the enforcers descended on the first stall, a man ran to the second stall and started to pack away some of the goods he had been selling there. A moment after that, the enforcers came over to his stall, cornered the man, and began questioning him. The next thirty minutes or so were spent interrogating the retailers and confiscating merchandise. The goods were catalogued and placed in boxes before being loaded onto a Jeep and taken away. We returned to the AIC office where the officials made photocopies of the sales receipts in order to calculate punishments and to use them to try to locate the middlemen (warehouses, wholesalers, and producers) involved in the production chain. Liu said that it was the policy of his client, the foreign company, to destroy all confiscated goods. This is no small issue. Destruction is expensive, and the local enforcement offices (whether the AIC or QTSB) are loath to expend scarce resources to destroy merchandise if another, cheaper solution is available (i.e., taking off the violating mark and selling the goods as "generic"). These costs are often borne by the trademark holder, not by the enforcement agency.

After this stage, as it neared 6:00 P.M., we went to a dinner for the AIC that was underwritten by the U.S. company via the investigation agency. Only male AIC members who had participated in the raid attended (the two women in the group went home). We were later joined by the AIC bureau chief (*juzhang*) and his assistant, neither of whom had taken part in the raid. The dinner was a typical Chinese banquet, during which Liu continued to ingratiate himself with the AIC people (he had been doing this nonstop all day, telling jokes, exchanging "war stories," and telling the AIC how important their work is). For his part, the *juzhang* did a masterful job at making himself appear not too eager to be enjoying himself. He seemed to be far less interested in trademark protection than in the fact that AICs in other regions of China had comparatively more power and were able to bear arms. There was some discussion among the higher-ranking cadres as to how to get rid of the lower-status officials, and they eventually settled on the line that the rest of us were "going to play mah-jongg." This was code for "karaoke," and the rest of us were put into taxis and went to a somewhat dodgy-looking karaoke parlor, where there was no shortage of alcohol, food, and hostesses. Indeed, when I finally turned to leave at one-thirty in the morning and wanted to express my thanks to the *juzhang*, I was (finally) told that he was upstairs "getting a massage" and could not be disturbed.

This extended anecdote is important for several reasons. First, although no two enforcement actions are exactly alike, it confirms a general pattern in the relationships between private investigators and Chinese administrative agencies in terms of functional divisions of labor: the former lay the groundwork and absorb the costs, the latter provide the official authority (i.e., legitimacy, legality) and take the credit. Second, it underscores another crucial pattern in such cooperation between external actors and Chinese administrative agencies: this enforcement action and others like it would not have taken place were it not for the expectation of some sort of side-payment, either in the form of direct monetary transfers (which I did not observe directly in this case), payments in kind (dinner, karaoke, "massages"), or some other sort of direct benefit (face-giving on the part of the investigation agency representatives, especially Mr. Liu). It should also be noted that this investigation firm, like many others, undertakes several enforcement actions like this on a typical day. Finally, although some might argue that this is simply "business as usual," in the sense that this is the way that the Chinese have often conducted government–business relations, what is suggested here is that foreigners are becoming increasingly proficient in these formerly "uniquely Chinese" interactions.

Case Two: Overcoming Local Protectionism in Guangdong's "Battery Villages"

This second case illustrates the problems encountered in transcending various administrative layers and spheres of "local protectionism" in order to undertake an enforcement action in the first place. It also underscores the active efforts of foreign actors that are so often necessary to secure Chinese enforcement.

A consortium of foreign battery manufacturers (hereafter, "the consortium") sponsored a major enforcement action in late April 1999 against a counterfeit battery-manufacturing center in Shantou, Guangdong Province. This was a network of over thirty battery manufacturers, printing houses, and assembly operations, located in two villages, the economies of which were based on the illegal production and sales of these counterfeit batteries, earning them the appellation, the "battery villages" (*dianchi cun*). Individual members of the consortium had undertaken raids against this target in the past, but without substantial effect. Finally, in the spring of 1999, the consortium collectively hired twelve private investigators to case the area and collect detailed information on the illegal activity (this included drawing up maps; the investigators had to give names to various streets that lacked discernible names of their own). Such groundwork-cum-information was critical in securing the help of a government enforcement agency, the next critical step taken by the consortium.

Because the Shantou AIC had a reputation as a lax enforcement agency, and because local protectionism was particularly severe in Shantou more generally, the consortium decided to appeal to the national-level QTSB. The QTSB was responsive to the consortium's argument that this was a problem for the Chinese government, not simply one faced by foreign manufacturers. The consortium also suggested that the case provided a high-profile opportunity to showcase the QTSB's utilization of the Product Quality Law in trademark enforcement. Moreover, the central government had already earmarked Guangdong, Zhejiang, and a few other provinces as "model areas" in which the enforcement of the Product Quality Law should be implemented. The QTSB agreed to (indeed, actively sought) a large amount of media exposure, and China Central Television, the *People's Daily*, the *Yancheng Evening News*, and Guangdong Asia TV were invited to cover the event.

The national QTSB sent an internal document to the Guangdong provincial QTSB stating that illegal battery production in Shantou was hurting other, legitimate battery-producing joint ventures in other parts of Guangdong and that something needed to be done. This internal document was for the Guangdong provincial QTSB *juzhang*'s eyes only. An investigation date was fixed, but first adequate personnel had to be organized to accomplish an enforcement action of this size (estimated as requiring more than 100 agents), since the Guangdong provincial QTSB could manage 20 agents at most. A central government official flew in from Beijing and the deputy mayor of Shantou was called up to the provincial capital, Guangzhou, where he met with this official and with other, provincial officials to discuss the matter.[47] The deputy mayor returned to Shantou late Sunday afternoon. However, because of the fear of possible leaks, the consortium and the investigation team pushed the date of the raid up to early Monday morning, April 26, 1999 (the original date was Thursday, April 29).

The raid, which began in the early morning hours, uncovered an enormous cache of counterfeit batteries destined for the domestic and export markets, including such brands as Duracell, Energizer, Panasonic, Sony, and Kodak. In one printing house, agents found more than a hundred negative films for several sizes and brands of batteries. The estimate of the production capacity in the village was staggering, at close to 100 percent of all the counterfeit batteries produced in China for export and "no less than" 40 percent of all the counterfeit batteries for the entire Chinese domestic market. The confiscated product was equally immense: 1.6 million cells of Duracell (finished); close to a million cells each of Energizer, Toshiba, and Panasonic; and four million "unfinished" cells (i.e., without the labels). Much of this product was assembled by migrant workers from Sichuan Province hired illegally (by undertaking this work in their homes, they did not need to register with the local AIC), who used personal hair dryers to shrink-wrap the labels onto the counterfeit batteries.[48]

As in the AIC case above, this enforcement action would have been inconceivable without the active involvement of foreign companies and private investigation agencies working closely and intensively with Chinese administrative enforcement agencies.

Administrative Enforcement Outcomes

This increased aggressiveness of the AIC and the QTSB helps explain why anti-counterfeit enforcement has remained largely within the administrative enforcement system in China: nothing succeeds like success. There have been three principal outcomes: better enforcement (as noted), centralization, and a clarification of the AIC–QTSB division of labor. Although only the first of these is directly germane to the argument of this chapter, the others are noteworthy and have also contributed to improved anti-counterfeiting enforcement, albeit more modestly.

Statistics showing improvements in AIC and QTSB performance over time are unavailable because such data would imply that these enforcement agencies had been somewhat lax in the past. Nevertheless, foreign investigators who have been in the field for several years all confirm a significant change in the effectiveness of anti-counterfeiting enforcement. All this may not necessarily mean that there is less counterfeiting in absolute terms, as the pirates have become more sophisticated, so the baseline for comparison is not stationary. However, the AIC and the QTSB have improved dramatically in their enforcement performance, often demonstrating less corrupt behavior and a greater inclination toward a "partnership" with the foreign investigation companies and their clients, compared to their behavior when the revised Trademark Law and the Unfair Competition Law came into effect in 1993.

The second outcome has been a shift toward centralized management (*chuizhi guanli*).[49] In large part due to the recognition that these enforcement agencies provide the front line against local protectionism, the relationships of these agencies with local governments have been dramatically restructured.[50] Under China's reform program, decentralization was an essential first step in raising sensitivity to local market conditions. Local governments' power over their functional bureaucracies was enhanced: local governments and not these functional units' administrative superiors monopolized power to issue binding orders (*kuaishang lingdao*) and to provide personnel, budgetary revenue, and properties necessary for the functioning of these bureaucracies (*rencaiwu*).[51] More recent recentralization has placed such binding orders and *rencaiwu* allocations firmly within these agencies, with minimal interference by their local government hosts (*tiaoshang lingdao*). Although foreign investigators have found, at most, only a modest change in behavior among the newly centralized AIC and QTSB, the potential power of these agencies vis-à-vis local governments has been significantly enhanced.

There has also been an attempt in 2001 to clarify the division of labor between the AIC and the QTSB: the QTSB is in charge of anti-counterfeiting before the product goes to the retail market (production and wholesale), while the AIC is in charge of anti-counterfeiting at the retail level.[52] By 2003, several local officials repeated to me the mantra that "the AIC investigates markets, while the QTSB investigates factories and warehouses," albeit without much conviction.[53] It remains to be seen what effect, if any, such a clear delineation of responsibilities is likely to have on inter-bureaucratic competition, and by extension, the effectiveness of anti-counterfeiting administrative enforcement.

The Push Toward Criminalization of Counterfeiting

Although these latter two developments may be significant in theory, they are less effective in practice. One investigator noted that even if a company underwrites hundreds of enforcement actions a year, counterfeiting activity will continue.⁵⁴ This is due in part to the diffuse and decentralized nature of the production and distribution channels for counterfeit goods. The case of a simple counterfeit Dunhill shirt sold at the infamous Huating (now relocated and renamed "Xiangyang") market in Shanghai is instructive. Counterfeiters purchase legitimate, "generic" shirts in Guangdong Province and "sell" them to peasants, who sew on the Dunhill logos in their homes and receive a supplemental monthly income, or "profit," of 400 RMB when they "re-sell" the shirts back to the counterfeiters. Then the shirts are boxed, but only just before they are sent, a few dozen at a time, to the market. It is virtually impossible to go after the "manufacturers" of these shirts because the factory that makes them is legitimate, and undertaking raids on people's homes (where the sewing of the counterfeit logos take place) is very difficult. Moreover, the shirts are perfectly legal before the offending mark is affixed to them. The shirt itself is made in Chaoyang, while the counterfeit logos are sewn in Shantou, the "Dunhill" buttons manufactured outside Shenzhen (all in Guangdong Province), and the labels and the boxes are made outside of Wenzhou (in southern Zhejiang Province).⁵⁵

Because of this diffusion in the manufacturing and distribution stages of the production line, the fines that *are* meted out tend to be quite small (the merchandise on hand is always kept in limited quantities in order to ensure that fines are minor if the sellers are caught) and can simply be factored into the costs of doing business. Out of the twenty-three raids from March to September 1995 in Beijing and Guangzhou targeting counterfeit Nintendo products, in only ten instances were fines levied. In these ten cases, the average fine was 8,230 RMB, or $990 USD. There were only two cases where business licenses were invalidated, and in such cases, the business is often simply re-registered under the name of another family member or business associate.⁵⁶

In other cases, the entire economic well-being of a locality may depend on counterfeiting, as was the case in Zengcheng, Guangdong Province:

According to Chinese press and television reports, Guangzhou's "Counterfeit Crackdown Office" was formally notified by a Hong Kong clothing company that seven factories in the nearby town of Zengcheng were mass-producing jeans and shirts with the Hong Kong company's trademark. This came as no surprise to the Guangzhou authorities: they had already issued several requests to the Zengcheng city government to deal with the problem. But local officials had no interest in cracking down. Realising this, the Guangzhou authorities organised their own raiding party, which set out for Zengcheng on the morning of November 7th. On the way they rang Zengcheng's Counterfeit Crackdown Office and asked for support; they were flatly refused. At 9 A.M. the inspection team (which included several reporters) arrived in Zengcheng and split into six groups, each responsible for a single factory. No sooner had the team entered the factories and started confiscating piles of pirated jeans than they were attacked by mobs of local residents. The rioters beat the inspectors with clubs and stones, overturned their cars, and seized videotapes taken by the television reporters. The mobs then blocked off the main streets of the town with tractors and surrounded the team's vehicles so they could not leave.[57]

Although somewhat dramatic, this case illustrates the general dynamics of local protectionism and how they can contribute to the counterfeiting problem. Insofar as counterfeiting provides employment and thus economic and social stability, local protectionism is especially difficult to resolve because it nestles such economic calculations within a political context. Many foreign (and Chinese) commercial actors have concluded that it is impossible to address this problem effectively simply by increasing the number of enforcement actions. In their view, something more stringent is necessary.

Deterrence

For policy to be implemented systematically and successfully, it is necessary but not sufficient to have a viable enforcement arm. Policing the police (in this case, the AIC and the QTSB) while trying to cope with the diffuse nature of the counterfeiting activity suggested above renders the costs of such enforcement prohibitively high. What is needed, according to many Chinese and foreigners, is "deterrence," which, according to Peterson and Bailey,

> rests upon the premise that individuals weigh the costs and rewards associated with alternative actions, and choose behaviors that yield the greatest gain at the least cost. Thus, crime occurs when illegal actions are perceived either as more profitable (rewarding) or less costly (painful) than conventional alternatives. . . . To achieve maximum deterrence, sanctions must be severe enough to outweigh the benefits derived from crime, administered with certainty, administered promptly, and made known to would-be offenders.[58]

Without such a "fear factor," an increasing number of trademark owners operating in China believe, there is simply too much of a positive economic incentive to continue the illicit activity.[59] As a result, there has been a steady effort by foreign companies and the investigation firms in their employ to revisit what has been a seemingly distant but sought-after goal for the past half-decade, by placing anti-counterfeiting enforcement squarely within the arena of criminal prosecution.

The 1997 revised Criminal Law has specific provisions for intellectual property offenses. Section 7 provides for sentences of up to three years in prison or hard labor and a fine for IPR-related offenses. If the value or the quantities involved are deemed particularly "huge" (*judade*), the sentence is between three and seven years and a fine. The baseline appears to be if the product sold on the market is valued at 50,000 RMB ($6,000 USD) or more (although this appears in the "economic crimes" section of the Criminal Law and not the "intellectual property" section). Sentences of more than seven years, even the death penalty, can be invoked if the economic crimes (i.e., counterfeit production and sales) in question involve serious injury to or the death of the consumer, and the stipulations regarding pharmaceuticals and foodstuffs are particularly severe. According to one source, "three-time losers," recidivists who have been found guilty of three counterfeiting offenses, can be automatically turned over to the Public Security Bureau (PSB).[60]

Although the number of cases that end in criminal prosecutions is still very low, the cases that do result in prosecutions often carry sentences that are quite severe. One foreign company reported that it was able to secure thirty-four criminal prosecutions, with an average jail sentence of three years. Although three years seems modest, incarceration in prison or in a labor camp for any amount of time can act as a powerful deterrent. It is not simply that conditions can be terrible, but there is a tremendous social stigma attached with having gone to prison. A prison sentence often means losing one's livelihood, one's family, and any prospects for a decent job in the future. This is true all over Asia, but it is particularly true in China. Moreover, in China it is impossible to "trade in" one's jail time for monetary compensation, as was the case in Taiwan.

Indeed, one private investigator expressed some concern that current attempts toward increased criminalization of counterfeiting could become a tool for repression. Moreover, he implied that some foreign trademark owners were indifferent to such an outcome or to the possible negative impact on the fundamental rights of Chinese citizens.[61] Investigation agencies acknowledge a rising trend in which their clients are pressuring them to conduct raids so that the 50,000 RMB threshold is met and the case can be brought to criminal court. But this could backfire: if various individuals along the enforcement chain feel that the criminal penalties are too high, and if they have enough discretion, they may simply drop the case or knock it down to a lesser offense. Nevertheless, at present, this concern appears to be the exception and not the rule as momentum for the criminalization of counterfeiting continues to grow, as it has over the past five years.

The China Anti-Counterfeiting Coalition / Quality Brands Protection Committee

In mid-1998, the last officials at the U.S. Embassy in Beijing directly involved in the Special 301-led Sino–U.S. IPR negotiations (the last of which were concluded in June 1996) were being rotated to posts outside of China. One of these officials noted that trademark issues had not been adequately addressed in the formal Sino–U.S. IPR negotiations. To remedy this, he began to assemble an informal coalition of businesses willing to address the issue of trademark counterfeiting in China. The CACC was formed on May 14, 1998,[62] and one of its principal aims was to push for the increased criminalization of counterfeiting in order to deter would-be counterfeiters in the future.

Very quickly, an internal schism emerged within the CACC over the tone and substance of the coalition's approach to the Chinese government. On the one hand, the "radicals" wanted to maintain an aggressive, confrontational approach and a "zero tolerance" rubric to abuses in enforcement. On the other side were the "gradualists," who believed that they would only be able to reach their medium- and long-term goals by working with, and not against, the Chinese government.[63] Their philosophy is captured in a comment by a representative of one of the CACC member companies: "[The U.S. Trade Representative approach of] confrontational bilateral IPR negotiations can be termed, 'the nuclear bomb approach'—it is an effective strategy if you do not have any troops on the ground."[64]

In fact, even though the CACC membership was comprised overwhelmingly of huge multinational corporations, this fact alone did not guarantee a sympathetic ear from China's top leadership or the leverage necessary to compel the leadership to act. Having these "big guns" on board in the QBPC was a necessary, but not a sufficient condition to get China's leaders to take the group seriously. It was also necessary to develop a strategy that was modeled less on confrontation, and that could simultaneously draw upon and reinforce an evolving constructive and consultative relationship with political elites in Beijing.

Over the course of the next two years, the cooler heads of the "gradualists" prevailed. As a result, the approach of the CACC changed, even as its ultimate goal—the default criminalization of counterfeiting—did not. First, the CACC jettisoned its initial approach, one that was confrontational in the style of the U.S. Trade Representative, for one of cooperation with the Chinese authorities. Second, on the "advice" of the Ministry of Foreign Trade and Economic Cooperation (MOFTEC, now renamed the Ministry of Commerce, or MOFCOM), which quickly became a sponsor, it changed its name to the more benign-sounding Quality Brands Protection Committee (QBPC) in March 2000.[65] It was also placed under the China Association of Enterprises with Foreign Investment (CAEFI, or *Zhongguo waishang touzi qiye xiehui*.)[66] Although traditionally a few foreign companies have joined CAEFI, according to Pearson, "the vast majority of members have been Chinese, and the association is geared heavily toward their participation."[67] This is significant because it makes the QBPC a sub-association of foreign companies *within a largely Chinese governmental association*, CAEFI. It is also noteworthy that in July 2001, MOFTEC Minister Shi Guangsheng became the Chair of CAEFI, which, according to one source, is the first time that an incumbent ministry-level official has served simultaneously as the chair of an association.[68]

In 2000, the QBPC first got its foot in the door when it issued a study of the economic impact of counterfeiting which reported that the annual value of counterfeit goods in the Chinese market represented a 132 billion RMB loss (including, pointedly, 25 billion RMB in taxes) to the Chinese government. This report made it to the desk of Liu Huaqiu, the head of the Foreign Affairs Office of the Chinese Communist Party Central Committee, who then passed it on to Premier Zhu Rongji himself.[69] Zhu was supposedly so outraged at the laxity of middle-level officials that during a meeting with QBPC representatives, he turned to these officials and said: "Look at how much you have shamed me."[70]

One QBPC representative struck up a friendship, quite by accident, with the same Liu Huaqiu, unaware of Liu's important gatekeeping function vis-à-vis the top leadership. Liu, initially professing no knowledge about the scope of the counterfeiting problem, reportedly became increasingly incensed as he learned more about it (and the QBPC was more than happy to supply him with this information). In mid-2001 he told the QBPC to write another report on counterfeiting, which he then distributed among the top leadership. These two "breaks" put the QBPC squarely on the radar of the top leadership.[71]

Since then, the QBPC has also been actively involved in preparing suggestions to the Chinese government on changes to other relevant laws, such as the Product Quality Law, with varied amounts of success.[72] The QBPC has also worked closely with central and local officials, including then vice-premier (now chairman of the National People's Congress, NPC) Wu Bangguo, former NPC standing committee vice-chairman Wang Guangying, and MOFCOM vice-minister Ma Xiuhong, to educate them on the negative impact of counterfeiting on the Chinese economy, to provide advice and expertise to the Chinese government in its development of laws and regulations, and to press for more prosecutions of counterfeiters. The vice-director of the NPC legislative affairs commission even came to Shanghai to consult with two QBPC representatives on how to strengthen anti-counterfeiting legislation.[73] At the same time, the QBPC has expanded its membership roster to include eighty companies united in their goal of making criminal prosecutions the default dispute settlement mechanism for counterfeiting in China.

Continuing Problems

While the QBPC has become the "good cop" in the shift toward increased criminal prosecutions, many other individual companies have taken up the goal of aggressively pursuing criminal prosecutions on the ground.[74] After a great deal of reluctance on the part of the Public Security Bureau (PSB) and the People's Procuracy to intervene, the numbers have begun to increase slowly, but steadily. One investigator said that in the four years he had been in Shanghai, he has participated in three thousand enforcement actions. In the thirteen years he lived in Taiwan, he had participated in just over half that number. The big difference is that, in Taiwan, they were all prosecuted as criminal offenses. In 1996, .025 percent of all trademark-violating cases were being prosecuted under China's revised Criminal Law. Today, the number is between 2 and 2.5 percent. Although this number is still small, it does represent a five- to tenfold increase in five years.[75] One U.S. company was able to secure only one criminal prosecution in 1999. The following year, the number went up to three. In 2001 the number jumped to twelve and doubled in 2002. At the same time, this same company undertook between five and six hundred enforcement actions in 2001 alone. Half of them were prosecutable under the Criminal Law, but only a dozen were actually prosecuted.[76] Another knowledgeable source indicated that 90 percent of cases with which he was familiar could have been prosecuted in the criminal court but instead were handled administratively.[77]

The main reason why these numbers remain low is that resistance to the invocation of the criminal law for anti-counterfeiting offenses comes from several directions, the first of which is illustrated in the following:

A recent example of this problem involved a company in Guangdong province that produced large amounts of oil lubricants and similar products under the names of Mobil, Esso, Shell and STP, as well as various local brands. The local AIC fined the company RMB 4 [million], one of the largest fines ever imposed in a Chinese trademark case. China's chief prosecuting agency, the Supreme People's Procuracy, ordered Guangdong prosecutors to pursue a criminal case but the AIC refused to release its files to prosecutors. The AIC said its policy was not to release such files until at least two-thirds of assessed fines had been paid. In this case, the AIC had received only 10% of the assessed fine. The prosecutors, meanwhile, said they would not pursue the case until they received the AIC's files.[78]

This anecdote underscores the enormous disincentive on the part of the administrative enforcement agencies to hand over their cases for criminal prosecution. AIC and QTSB units, in particular, have realized over time that the "really big money" was not in exacting case fees and bribes from foreign clients but from using the fines levied against the counterfeiters to enhance their own official and unofficial operating budgets.[79]

After working for years to establish relations with foreign companies and their private investigation agencies, and amassing significant financial and other benefits in doing so, the AIC and the QTSB are loath to give these up. First, a criminal conviction means that the counterfeiter will not only go to jail, he will be put out of business. Thus, the AIC loses both a source of revenue through enterprise registration and the regular management fees it collects, while more corrupt AICs also lose the opportunity to skim money off the fines that they levy on the counterfeiter.[80] Second, handing cases over to the PSB leaves the AIC and the QTSB with no records to indicate that they have undertaken the initial investigation of the case, and their activities do not make it onto their own enforcement quota reports. And if the cases get "bounced" back to the AIC or QTSB, there is a good chance that they have already gone cold and will be next to impossible to pursue with any expectation of success.[81] Third, it diminishes the notion that the AIC and the QTSB are effective enforcement agencies in the eyes of superiors within the government, a reputation these two bureaucracies have painstakingly nurtured over several years. One investigator said that in his two years in Shanghai, he has never seen one case of the AIC or the QTSB voluntarily passing off a case to the PSB.[82] Oftentimes, the AIC or QTSB will increase the fine (with the acquiescence of the investigator or company) in exchange for being able to hold onto the case.[83]

However, this does not mean that the PSB has been aggressively taking cases away from the AIC and the QTSB. In fact, it has taken an enormous amount of coaxing to get the PSB to take on IPR cases in the first place. Anti-counterfeiting work is regarded by the PSB as a swelling of responsibilities without a corresponding increase in budgetary revenues. Moreover, there has been a perception that IPR cases are "civil" in nature and that they do not have the gravitas of "standard" criminal offenses. It was only about three to four years after promulgation of the revised Criminal Law that the PSB started to take an interest in IPR cases. PSB attention to the issue is gradually increasing; there is even a shadowy figure within the Shanghai PSB known as the "IPR Czar," as well as a special PSB intellectual property enforcement unit known simply—and ominously—as "803," after its street address.[84] But even though the PSB is somewhat more willing than before to bring counterfeiters to justice, it will not send cases to the prosecutor unless chances for a successful conviction, in the opinion of one investigator, are 95 percent or higher.[85] Sending a case back to the AIC or to the QTSB gives the PSB the equivalent of a "black eye" and negatively affects its case record file (*po'an lu*).

Moreover, the prosecutors, like the PSB, will only take a case if they are almost certain to get a conviction. Once the PSB hands a case over to the prosecutors, the latter group must decide whether to go ahead and prosecute. In the past, the conviction rate was very high, and prosecutors are resistant to the idea of diluting their success rate with cases that might not end in a conviction. If they decide not to take the case, they hand it back to the PSB, which then passes it off to the AIC or the QTSB, something that PSB does not like to do, for reasons mentioned above.[86] This overly cautious approach to prosecutions is changing, but very slowly.

It also appears that counterfeiters from other locales (*waidi ren*) make up the majority of convictions. It is still very tricky to prosecute "local boys." It is also difficult to establish recidivism, as there is no national database, and demonstrating a pattern of counterfeiting often requires coordination among several different bureaucracies at different levels of the vertical administrative hierarchy across several provinces, an almost impossibly complex undertaking.[87]

Finally, in several instances the laws themselves remain vague in critical areas. What demonstrates "huge" or "serious" (*yanzhongde*) remains unclear. Moreover, even the seemingly clear and objective criminal threshold of 50,000 RMB is also open to interpretation.[88] Valuation is tricky when the merchandise itself is a fake. If the methodology for calculating the value of the goods only takes into account real production costs and ignores the value of the intellectual property being violated (the preferred method of the enforcement authorities because calculating intellectual property losses is difficult and disputable), this depresses the price and makes it more difficult to establish the 50,000 RMB threshold.[89] And until the recent promulgation of the Judicial Interpretation on the Handling of the Crime of Manufacturing and Selling Inferior and Shoddy Goods, on April 10, 2001, a significant loophole existed that manufacturers could use to assert that they were involved in manufacturing, not selling, goods and that the 50,000 RMB threshold for *sales* did not apply to them. In some cases, local authorities have been slow to adopt the new interpretation, if they are even aware of it at all.[90]

More ominously for the preceding discussion, however, is the possibility that deterrence will ultimately fail. Although deterrence is a powerful and intuitive idea, the literature on deterring criminal activity in the United States suggests caution in oversubscribing to this concept. Much of the literature on capital punishment does not find support for the death penalty as a successful deterrent to capital offenses.[91] Other treatments of deterrence in the criminal process, particularly studies on the "economy of deterrence," tend to find support for the deterrence hypothesis but not without some qualification.[92] And if this mixed picture is not enough, there is also a normative dimension that should not be overlooked. As noted earlier, the more discretion there is throughout the enforcement chain and the greater the perception that the penalty is needlessly severe, the more difficult it is likely to be to gain convictions. In other words, even if all the key elements are in place, deterrence may not have the anticipated effect on counterfeiting that these foreign and Chinese actors believe it will.

Conclusion

This analysis provides some examples of what Migdal has termed "closely viewed crucial instances"[93] in the evolution of China's anti-counterfeiting enforcement regime. From a broader conceptual law-and-society perspective, the story behind this shift from civil litigation to administrative enforcement to criminal prosecution reminds us that not only is the Chinese state apparatus becoming disaggregated, but so too is Chinese society, which is rapidly becoming far more heterogeneous than at any other time in its history. Specifically, this process tells us something about the newly emerging role of foreign actors within the increasingly diversified Chinese state. It is no longer accurate to assume that foreign actors are only peripheral to the political process in China. They are no longer simply restricted to formal interactions with officials in Beijing, and they are no longer dependent upon a state-controlled modern-day comprador class.

Increasingly, foreign actors in the arena that has been studied here have moved closer into the nexus of domestic governance in China and have established informal yet direct partnerships with state actors. Moreover, as I have argued, these interactions are occurring at all levels of the state, from consultations with members of the Politburo Standing Committee to continuous interactions with officials at the county level and below. Foreign actors have resources and goals they bring to existing authority relationships, shaping local interests in China. By skillfully utilizing the resources at their disposal, these foreign actors have been able to help change the incentives of national and local state agents and bring them closer in line with their own.

However, state actors, such as the enforcement agencies discussed above, also have their own interests that may not be evolving along the same lines as the goals of the commercial actors with whom they have been interacting. Forward movement on these policy fronts requires both sets of actors to maintain ongoing relationships and to secure the compromises necessary for all interested parties to work together. The evolution of China's anti-counterfeiting enforcement regime, then, is marked by changing interests of local state actors and foreigners, and recurring episodes of conflict and resolution.

Notes

I wish to thank the Grimm Fellowship Committee and the Weidenbaum Center on the Economy, Government, and Public Policy at Washington University for providing funding that made fieldwork in China in 2002 and 2003 possible. This builds on earlier research in 1998 and 1999 which greatly benefited from a Fulbright-Hays Fellowship and from the National Bureau of Asian Research project, "Advancing Intellectual Property Rights in China." I have also profited enormously from comments on earlier drafts by William Alford, Jerome Cohen, Neil Diamant, Frances Foster, John Haley, William Jones, Stanley Lubman, Kevin O'Brien, and from two anonymous reviewers. Any remaining errors are mine.

1. As quoted by then vice-premier Wu Bangguo in a speech at the national "Crack Down on Fakes [*dajia*]" United Movement Tele-Meeting, 26 October 2000, cited in CAEFI Quality Brands Protection Committee [QBPC] pamphlet.

2. For example, because of diminished sales volume due to counterfeiting and smuggling, Unilever suspended its joint-venture plans in Shanghai, causing layoffs and a loss of over 30 million RMB (*China Business Times*, 2 June 2000, quoted in QBPC pamphlet).

3. *South China Morning Post*, 4 March 2000, quoted in QBPC pamphlet.

4. QBPC position paper, quoted in QBPC pamphlet.

5. Interview 02SH05, 27 June 2002; Interview 02SH10, 2 July 2002. Because this chapter relies in large part on extensive fieldwork with sources that wish to remain anonymous, I indicate interviews by number. The first two digits indicate the year, the middle two letters indicate the location ("BJ" for Beijing, "CD" for Chengdu, "CQ" for Chongqing, "GY" for Guiyang, "GZ" for Guangzhou, "KM" for Kunming, "SH" for Shanghai, "XJ" for an anonymous county in Sichuan Province, and "US" for the United States). The last two digits place the interview in the overall interview sequence in a given locale. Finally, if there was a sequence of interviews with a particular interviewee, the number of interviews is indicated by the letters A, B, C, etc., at the end of the interview number.

6. Interview 02CD03, 12 July 2002.

7. To cite just one example, until a few years ago, most provincial-level patent bureaus were at the lowest administrative rank of provincial level offices (*xian ji ju*). A handful of these offices were positioned at the higher *er ji ju* level. Only one in the entire country was placed the highest of the three ranks (the *yi ji ju*), that of Sichuan. The Sichuan Patent Bureau had a personnel allocation and corresponding budgetary outlays that were almost ten times those of *xian ji ju*–level patent bureaus. However, Sichuan Province had no comparative advantage in patent applications, as it is situated in the relatively underdeveloped Southwest (especially after the industrial center of Chongqing secured its independence from Sichuan by becoming a provincial-level municipality in May 1997). Rather, this ranking had to do with the provincial government's goal of attracting foreign investment. In this case, even unrealized potential future foreign investment could profoundly shape the organization and rank ordering of Sichuan's Patent Bureau (Interview 99CD01, 28 June 1999).

8. This should not be confused with China's Administrative Litigation Law (*xingzheng susong fa*), which empowers citizens to address grievances against Chinese administrative units by bringing suit in the law courts.

9. Stanley B. Lubman, *Bird in a Cage: Legal Reform in China after Mao* (Stanford, Calif.: Stanford University Press, 1999), 23.

10. See, e.g., Kathryn Bernhardt and Philip C. C. Huang, eds., *Civil Law in Qing and Republican China* (Stanford, Calif.: Stanford University Press, 1994); and Matthew H. Sommer, *Sex, Law, and Society in Late Imperial China* (Stanford, Calif.: Stanford University Press, 2000).

11. William P. Alford, *To Steal a Book Is an Elegant Offense: Intellectual Property Law in Chinese Civilization* (Stanford, Calif.: Stanford University Press, 1995).

12. Li Rongxia, "Outstanding Results in Building a Legal System," *Beijing Review*, 16 August 1999, 16.

13. Lubman, *Bird in a Cage*; Interview 98SH17, 28 May 1998; and Interview 98SH21, 31 May 1998.

14. Of course, one should be skeptical of official Chinese statistics. Nevertheless, there is no compelling reason why China would want to underreport cases of formal adjudication.

15. Economist Intelligence Unit, "China Hand," October 1998, 10.

16. On this evolution of the state, see Theda Skocpol, "Bringing the State Back In: Strategies of Analysis in Current Research," in *Bringing the State Back In*, ed. Peter B. Evans, Dietrich Rueschemeyer, and Theda Skocpol (New York: Cambridge University Press, 1985), 4–5.

17. Joel S. Migdal, "The State in Society: An Approach to Struggles for Domination," in *State Power and Social Forces: Domination and Transformation in the Third World*, ed. Joel S. Migdal, Atul Kohli, and Vivienne Shue (New York: Cambridge University Press, 1994), 8.

18. Ibid., 9.

19. See, e.g., Elizabeth J. Perry and Mark Selden, eds., *Chinese Society: Change, Conflict, and Resistance* (London: Routledge, 2000).

20. Migdal, "The State in Society," 9.

21. See, e.g., Alexander Cooley and James Ron, "The NGO Scramble: Organizational Insecurity and the Political Economy of Transnational Action," *International Security* 27, no. 1 (Summer 2002): 5–39.

22. Norman A. Graham, "Globalization and Civil Society in Hungary and the Czech Republic," in *The Revival of Civil Society: Global and Comparative Perspectives*, ed. Michael G. Schechter (New York: St. Martin's Press, 1999), 135–58.

23. On civil/state and society in China, see, inter alia, Gu Xin, "A Civil Society and Public Sphere in Post-Mao China? An Overview of Western Publications," *China Information* 8, no. 3 (Winter 1993–94): 1–14; and Timothy Cheek, "From Market to Democracy in China: Gaps in the Civil Society Model," in *Market Economics and Political Change: Comparing China and Mexico*, ed. Juan D. Lindau and Timothy Cheek (Oxford: Rowman and Littlefield, 1998), 219–54.

24. Kenneth Lieberthal and Michel Oksenberg, *Policy Making in China: Leaders, Structures, and Processes* (Princeton, N.J.: Princeton University Press, 1988), 31.

25. Mary E. Gallagher, "'Reform and Openness': Why China's Economic Reforms Have Delayed Democracy," *World Politics* 54, no. 3 (April 2002): 338–72.

26. Interview 98SH03A/D, 19 March 1998 and 7 July 1998, respectively; and Interview 99BJ38, 5 August 1999.

27. In the case of the AIC, this same enforcement system also goes by the name

of the Fair Trade Enforcement bureaucracy (*gongping jiaoyi xitong*). Oftentimes, it is the same group of people (*yitao ren liangkuai paizi*), with an internal division of labor in which some focus on counterfeiting issues and others spend more time on broader issues of unfair competition (Interview 02CD08, 18 July 2002).

28. These accounts are usually within the Industrial and Commercial Bank of China, although the Shanghai AIC also has an account in the China Construction Bank (Interview 02SH04, 25 June 2002).

29. Interview 02GY02, 24 July 2002; Interview 02GY03, 25 July 2002.

30. Interview 02GZ01, 25 July 2002.

31. Interview 98CD04, 17 June 1998; Interview 98KM04, 1 September 1998; Interview 02SH12, 5 July 2002.

32. *Zhonghua renmin gongheguo zhengfu jigou wushinian* [Government organizations of the People's Republic of China over fifty years] (Beijing: Dangjian duwu chubanshe, 2000), 152–55.

33. *Zhonghua renmin gongheguo zhongyang zhengfu jigou, 1949–1990* [Central government organs of the People's Republic of China] (Beijing: Jingji kexue chubanshe, 1993), 203–8.

34. See *Zhonghua renmin gongheguo zhiliang jishu jiandu fagui huibian: Chanpin zhiliang fence, 1982–98* [The People's Republic of China quality technical supervision laws and regulations handbook: Product quality sub-volume] (Beijing: Zhongguo jiliang chubanshe, 1998).

35. I analyze these dynamics in detail elsewhere; see Andrew C. Mertha, "'Policy Enforcement Markets': How Bureaucratic Redundancy Contributes to Effective IPR Policy Implementation in China" (article under review).

36. Interview 02CD10, 19 July 2002; "Jiajiang County Loses Final Judgment," *Sichuan Daily*, 2 July 1996; "The Anti-Counterfeiters Win, the Counterfeiters Lose," *Sichuan Daily*, 9 April 1996; "Inside and Outside the Court," *Chengdu Commercial News*, 9 April 1996.

37. China Anti-Counterfeiting Coalition, "Report on Counterfeiting in the People's Republic of China" (draft), 25 February 1999, 20–21.

38. Interview 99SH06B, 18 May 1999.

39. Interview 99SH01, 5 April 1999.

40. Peter Howard Corne, *Foreign Investment in China: The Administrative Legal System* (Hong Kong: Hong Kong University Press, 1997), 189–90.

41. Interview 98CQ07, 8 April 1998.

42. Interview 02GZ01, 25 July 2002; Interview 02SH02, 21 June 2002.

43. Interview 99BJ06, 15 March 1999; Interview 99BJ36, 3 August 1999.

44. China Anti-Counterfeiting Coalition, "Report on Counterfeiting in the People's Republic of China" (draft), 25 February 1999, 20–21.

45. Interview 02GZ01, 25 July 2002.

46. Ibid.

47. There was debate about whether to leak to this official that the target was the Shantou battery manufacturers or whether to deceive him temporarily by saying that they were going after cigarette counterfeiters. The decision was made that he should be told the truth because to do otherwise would be an indication that he

could not be trusted, causing him to lose face and possibly lead to his refusal to cooperate (Interview 99HK02, 2 June 1999).

48. Gillette and Panasonic were the original sponsors of the raid, but once the extent of the counterfeiting became clear, Eveready and Toshiba also chipped in to help defray the costs of the raid (ibid.).

49. See "Wu Yi Guowuweiyuan zai gongshang xingzheng guanli tizhi gaige ji gongzuo huiyi" [Speech by State Councilor Wu Yi at the National Administration of Industry and Commerce Structural Reform Work Conference], *Gongshang xingzheng guanli* 1, no. 2 (10 January 1999): 4–7; Li Yafei, "Gongshang xingzheng guanli chuizhi lingdao tizhi queli hou zhifa lidu he nandu yanjiu (1–3)" [Research into the establishment, execution, and difficulties encountered by the centralized leadership of the Administration for Industry and Commerce System], *Zhongguo gongshang guanli yanjiu* (September–November 2001); and Hunan Province, Chenzhou Municipality, Commercial Institute Task Force, "Chuiguan hou gongshang ban'an de zhang'ai yi duice" [Obstacles and countermeasures to the AIC's handling of cases after centralized management], *Zhongguo gongshang guanli yanjiu* (June 2001): 56–58.

50. Interview 02CD03, July 12, 2002. For more on the nature and scope of this administrative centralization, see Andrew C. Mertha, "'Vertical Reality': Growing Pains in China's Shift towards Greater Administrative Centralization, 1998–2003" (article under review).

51. See Lieberthal and Oksenberg, *Policy Making in China*, 148–49.

52. Interview 02CD03, 12 July 2002; Interview 02CD07, 18 July 2002; Interview 02CD08, 18 July 2002; Interview 02GZ01, 25 July 2002.

53. Interview 03CD01, 14 July 2003; Interview 03XJ01/2, 17 July 2003; Interview 03GY01, 19 July 2003.

54. Interview 02GZ01, 25 July 2002.

55. Interview 98SH03C, 29 May 1998.

56. Nintendo Special 301 Submission, 20 February 1996, on file in the USTR Reading Room, Office of the United States Trade Representative, Washington, D.C.

57. Economist Intelligence Unit, "China Hand," October 1998, 11.

58. William C. Bailey and Ruth C. Peterson, "Murder, Capital Punishment, and Deterrence: A Review of the Evidence and an Examination of Police Killings," *Journal of Social Issues* 50, no. 2 (1994): 54.

59. Interview 02GZ01, 25 July 2002.

60. Interview 02SH02, 21 June 2002.

61. Ibid. This opinion is echoed in Michel Oksenberg, Pitman B. Potter, and William B. Abnett, "Advancing Intellectual Property Rights: Information Technologies and the Course of Economic Development in China," *National Bureau of Asian Research: NBR Analysis* 7, no. 4 (November 1996): 31.

62. Interview 98BJ01, 13 June 1998. Some place the origins of the CACC earlier, as an outgrowth of informal meetings among trademark-intensive firms that shared information and discussed possible strategies with one another, which also stipulated that such information should be shared with the Chinese government and that there

should be "some" U.S. government involvement. The CACC received a major boost when the U.S. embassy made attempts to institutionalize it and when the representative from Procter and Gamble took the helm (Interview 99SH01, 5 April 1999).

63. Interview 99SH06B, 18 May 1999.
64. Interview 99SH02, 27 April 1999.
65. According to one QBPC representative, Chinese government officials in Beijing were becoming nervous that the QBPC—an independent association with foreign roots—was growing so rapidly and made it clear that it was to be co-opted within the relevant Chinese government associations (Interview 02BJ09, 9 August 2002).
66. QBPC pamphlet. There is some confusion regarding the acronym. It is generally written as "CAEFI," but in QBPC publications it is written as "CAFEI." Both refer to the China Association of Enterprises with Foreign Investment.
67. Margaret M. Pearson, *China's New Business Elite: The Political Consequences of Economic Reform* (Berkeley: University of California Press, 1997), 123.
68. Interview 02SH09, 2 July 2002.
69. There were two versions of this report that arose from information provided by the QBPC—an "open" (*gongkai*) and an internal (*neibu*) version. The *neibu* version gave a much more serious assessment of the counterfeiting problem and made it all the way up to Jiang Zemin for review (Interview 02BJ09, 9 August 2002).
70. In fact, these QBPC representatives had some fence-mending to do after this meeting, as these middle-level officials were so bruised by Zhu's comments that—immediately following the meeting—they were reluctant to work with the QBPC, lest they receive another tongue-lashing (Interview 02BJ09, 9 August 2002). This, of course, raises the question of how "rehearsed" Zhu's response may have been and whether it was largely for effect. None of the actors discussed here—local officials, national leaders, and foreign IPR holders—are above manipulating the IPR issue toward other goals or, alternatively, ignoring other rights in their pursuit of greater IPR protection. As noted above, the AIC is often involved in the actual counterfeiting it is supposed to be eradicating, while foreign IPR holders are often all too happy to subsume citizens' fundamental rights to protecting intellectual property.
71. Interview 02BJ09, 9 August 2002.
72. For example, the QBPC was unable to secure an opportunity to advise the Chinese government in the Prosecutorial Guidelines (promulgated 18 April 2002) and the Case Transfer Regulations (promulgated 9 July 2001) (Interview 02SH09, 2 July 2002).
73. Interview 02SH09, 2 July 2002.
74. Interview 02GZ01, 25 July 2002.
75. Interview 02SH02, 21 June 2002.
76. Interview 02GZ01, 25 July 2002.
77. Interview 02SH10, 2 July 2002.
78. Economist Intelligence Unit, "China Hand," October 1997, 35.
79. Interview 02SH02, 21 June 2002.
80. Interview 02SH01, 20 June 2002; Interview 02GZ01, 25 July 2002.
81. Interview 02SH05, 27 June 2002.

82. Ibid. The foregoing trend is also the case regarding the General Administration of Customs, and for the same reasons; one source indicated that he is not aware of a single case in which Customs voluntarily transferred a case to the PSB (Interview 02SH10, 2 July 2002).

83. Interview 02SH01, 20 June 2002.

84. Ibid.

85. Interview 02GZ01, 25 July 2002.

86. Interview 02SH05, 27 June 2002.

87. Interview 02SH02, 21 June 2002.

88. Interview 02SH10, 2 July 2002.

89. Interview 02SH05, 27 June 2002.

90. Interview 02SH09, 2 July 2002.

91. See, e.g., Ruth D. Peterson and William C. Bailey, "Felony Murder and Capital Punishment: An Examination of the Deterrence Question," *Criminology* 29, no. 3 (1991): 367–95; William C. Bailey and Ruth D. Peterson, "Murder, Capital Punishment, and Deterrence: A Review of the Literature," in *The Death Penalty in America: Current Controversies*, ed. Hugo Adam Bedau (New York: Oxford University Press, 1997); and Jon Sorensen, Robert Wrinkle, Victoria Brewer, and James Marquart, "Capital Punishment and Deterrence: Examining the Effect of Executions on Murder in Texas," *Crime and Delinquency* 45, no. 4 (October 1999): 481–93.

92. Isaac Ehrlich, "Crime, Punishment, and the Market for Offenses," *Journal of Economic Perspectives* 10, no. 1 (Winter 1996): 43–67.

93. Migdal, "The State in Society," 8.

MURRAY SCOT TANNER 8

Rethinking Law Enforcement and Society
Changing Police Analyses of Social Unrest

Introduction: Law, Society, and the Policing of Protest

Most of the chapters in this volume examine China's changing law–society relationship by inquiring how effectively social actors can use China's fledgling legal system to advance their political interests. They inquire why social actors succeed or fail in manipulating the system as it is, or in trying to change the system, or—in the tradition of McCann[1]—they ask how the very action of using the legal system might create inadvertent "spin-off" organizational and other advantages in advancing these citizens' demands.

This chapter, by contrast, argues that we should also search deep within the state legal system for the sources of change in the state–law–society relationship, even among the unlikeliest of actors—the state's law enforcement professionals. Studies of the political role of Chinese legal professionals focus overwhelmingly on lawyers or judges. This chapter, instead, examines some striking and unexpected efforts by China's police analysts and professionals to rethink a highly sensitive legal issue: the policing of protest.

Few actions symbolize the relationship among state, law, and society more starkly than the way in which law enforcement authorities police protest. Major changes in how police perceive and handle unrest can reforge the hard frame of what social movement theorists genteelly call the "political opportunity structure" of mass movements.[2] Changes in protest policing often foreshadow more significant changes in regimes, and can involve wrenching dilemmas for the state.[3] As South Korea demonstrated in the 1980s, authoritarian regimes that permit persistent, moderate levels of social protest may be signaling that they are willing to enter into—or are unable to resist—a long-term political renegotiation with society over fundamental issues of policy and power. Recent studies of reform and coercion underscore that the institutional attitudes of law enforcement bodies toward mass unrest can play a pivotal role in shaping the outcome of the "game" of reform and liberalization.[4]

Historically, the institutional norms and attitudes of China's police toward social control have often been fundamentally shaped and reshaped through security crises, which are then followed by bitter political struggles over the proper "institutional lessons" to be drawn from those crises.[5] A pitched internal debate of this type flared within China's Ministry of Public Security (MPS) in the wake of the 1989 Tiananmen protests and massacre. The protests had been an unmitigated institutional disaster for China's police, whose inability to contain the unrest led hard-line leaders to feel they had to call in the People's Liberation Army. This debate resulted in the imposition of some rigidly ideological institutional lessons about social unrest.

Over the past several years, however, senior analysts and officials within China's public security system have launched a debate to rethink these basic institutional views about social protest—its origins, political character, and potential danger; its relationship to the legal system; and the legal and political strategies the police should adopt in response. In some respects, these arguments revive and extend attitudes toward social protest that were just emerging on the eve of Tiananmen. In the process of this debate, however, many authors have unleashed frank criticisms of the social problems and political failings of the regime's reform policies and the inadequate institutional channels for citizens to peacefully voice discontent. This debate also opened up more fundamental discussions over the proper relationship among the state, its law enforcement organs, and society.

In analyzing these internal debates aimed at reshaping post-Tiananmen police institutional attitudes toward social unrest, I will argue that the debate defies any simple "bottom-up" or "top-down" explanation, and instead has been brought about by a mixture of social order problems, police–society interactions, police institutional interests, and even the influence of foreign ideas.[6] Fundamentally, these debates represent a reaction by a key portion of the party-state—members of its legal–coercive sector—who feel uncomfortably sandwiched between the Party leadership and an increasingly restive society. In response, these law enforcement professionals are responding by seeking a less passive, and less purely repressive, role in maintaining social control.

The Institutional Lessons of 1989

There is significant evidence that by late 1988–early 1989 a number of ranking police officials and analysts were promoting new institutional lessons about the effective handling of dissent. Leading security officials, including

Politburo member Qiao Shi and Vice Minister of Public Security Yu Lei, were stressing that lower levels should largely treat unrest as a sign of "non-antagonistic" contradictions; they should use less repressive tactics, and rely on "democracy and the legal system . . . and the methods of dialogue."[7]

One impetus for this rethinking stemmed from the violent mishandling of several protest incidents during the late 1980s—crude tactics that exacerbated popular anger in some towns and were at odds with the broader policy efforts to "professionalize" policing. Police experts cited a May 1988 Sichuan soccer disturbance as an early object lesson in how excessive police violence can exacerbate unrest. Police in Nanchong beat several students while suppressing the incident, touching off a major student protest.[8] Vice Minister Yu criticized local authorities for an even more prominent mishandled incident—the December 1988 student protests in Nanjing, during which many public security personnel and paramilitary People's Armed Police personnel were injured.[9]

A second catalyst for rethinking the policing of protest was the effort in 1988–early 1989 to draft a law on demonstrations and public assemblies. Like many reform-oriented pieces of legislation at the time, the Demonstration Law's drafting reflected what Judy Polumbaum refers to as a debate over whether to "protect or restrict" an emerging political or economic right.[10] In such cases, multiple competing drafts of such legislation often circulated, some clearly calibrated to enshrine a limited right in Chinese law, and another designed to restrict such a right—or at least to provide local party-state authorities with such broad administrative discretion as to effectively deny the right in reality. The Party leadership took the then bold and unusual step of publishing the draft Demonstrations Law in national newspapers to encourage public debate.

It appears that the calls by the more reformist Ministry of Public Security officials for more restrained, professional handling of unrest contributed to the relatively restrained, largely nonviolent tactics Beijing police and People's Armed Police employed in the early stages of the 1989 student protests. There is also evidence of significant sympathy for student protestors both within the street-level police and even among some MPS leaders.[11]

The June 1989 crisis, however, temporarily crushed efforts within the police system to develop more restrained, professional strategies for containing social unrest. The official verdict on the demonstrations—"turmoil" and "a counterrevolutionary riot"—imposed a diametrically contrary set of institutional lessons on the police system for nearly a decade. Interpretations of the origins of demonstrations were almost exclusively conspiratorial, stressing the role of foreign and domestic class enemies as instigators and manipulators. Protests did not just "happen" in response to socio-economic change or policy errors—they were caused. Leaders, organizers, or active participants in protests were portrayed as either conscious conspirators or, at best, ideologically misled. Protest was not seen as a normal and manageable feature of a changing society. Rather, owing to the implacability of the Party's enemies, even small-scale demonstrations were treated as something that could easily spin badly out of control. Protests were officially labeled as dangerously unstable, "suddenly occurring social order incidents" (*turan fasheng shehui zhi'an shijian*, or *tufa shijian* for short) and were rarely described as having a "mass" character or as reflecting contradictions "among the people." Internal police analyses of the 1989 demonstrations—such as the official report prepared by Gu Linfang, vice-minister of public security in charge of "political security work"—railed against the recent weakening of ideological vigilance and enumerated presumably nefarious contacts among Chinese officials and Western or Taiwanese institutions.[12] Hard-line police and military analysts of a Leninist or neo-Maoist bent excoriated excessively "soft-handed" police and PAP for naively underestimating domestic and foreign class enemies and for allowing demonstrations to get out of control. For most of these analysts, a zero-tolerance policy toward protest was required, and demonstrations needed to be suppressed quickly and in many cases quite harshly. Throughout the early 1990s, the available public security literature, open-source as well as internal, was virtually devoid of any serious empirical or theoretical analysis of the social, economic, or political origins of unrest.

Reflecting these fears and official interpretations of unrest, the draft Law on Assemblies, Marches, and Demonstrations was quickly revised, finalized, and passed in late 1989 in a version clearly designed to permit easy criminalization of protest. Despite arguments by some delegates within the National People's Congress that the law should do more to affirm the right to demonstrate, the final draft granted local police and government officials maximum administrative discretion to make virtually any form of social protest illegal by requiring would-be protesters to apply for permission in advance. The law permitted local officials to deny such applications for any number of reasons, with no effective avenues for legal appeal.[13]

Recent Police Reinterpretations of Unrest

Only around the time that Deng Xiaoping's 1992 Southern Tour reinvigorated support for reform did some less rigid public security officials cautiously begin to suggest a reconsideration of this exaggerated conspiratorial interpretation.[15] Within a few more years, by the mid-to-late 1990s, it was increasingly clear that the post-Tiananmen institutional diagnosis of unrest and how to deal with it was failing. Even official Party and police sources began admitting that the number of protests was growing rapidly. Internal Ministry of Public Security statistics revealed that between 1993 and 1996 the number of mass protests had risen nationwide from about 8,700 to 13,000—a nearly 60 percent increase. This rise in protests accelerated dramatically as economic growth slowed beginning in 1997.[16] In late spring 2001 a widely publicized Party Organization Department report spotlighted this rapid rise in protests.[17] Both national and provincial public security reports reveal that the protests have not only increased in number, but also in average size, social scope, and degree of organization.

This increase in protest is sparking an important reconceptualization within China's law enforcement system about the nature and social origins of unrest. This reassessment, moreover, is not limited to public security scholars (whom we might be tempted to dismiss as fringe elements). It has also been embraced in the writings of some senior police officials.

Conceptually, most police analysts now once again portray the vast majority of incidents of unrest as the result of "non-antagonistic" contradictions or "contradictions among the people."[18] This appears to be the official verdict of both the Ministry of Public Security and the Party Center. This change in verdict has sparked some debate over the proper terminology to use in labeling incidents of protest. Within the mainstream public security literature, most analysts refuse to characterize China's current wave of unrest with the sort of pejorative labels, such as "turmoil," that were officially attached to the 1989 student and Tibetan protests. Even the more vaguely negative terms that became common in police and military journals during the early 1990s—even "suddenly occurring social order incidents"—are being jettisoned in favor of designations that clearly and actively affirm the current "mass nature" of protest. While most analysts have executed this change quietly and without explanation, one police analyst from Ningxia has boldly defended the shift to more sympathetic terminology. Attacking many of the terms police analysts have employed until recently in describing unrest, he claims that such characterizations ignore the "key objective factor" that mass groups protest because they feel their "interests" have been hurt or ignored.[19] He therefore defends the now-standard official characterization—"incidents of a mass group nature" or "mass group incidents" (*quntixing shijian*). Since at least 1999 publications by MPS think tanks and the People's Public Security University have almost uniformly employed "mass group incidents"—a designation with obvious and powerful positive associations—as their standard term in analyzing protests. Judiciously, these analysts have undertaken sympathetic terminological shifts without suggesting that the Party should rethink its official verdict that the 1989 protests were a "counterrevolutionary riot . . . aimed at negating the leading role of the Communist Party."

Still, nearly all available recent police analyses greatly downplay the role of enemy instigators. Once officially a central factor, foreign and domestic conspiracies are now largely relegated to the position of a very secondary catalyst among many more fundamental explanatory forces. One influential police textbook on social order, for example, still lists "international enemy forces" prominently among a long list of sources of unrest, and repeats official warnings that class enemies "have never ceased pushing for overthrow and destruction in our country" through "infiltration" and "peaceful evolution."[20] But more typical is a recent analysis by Fujian Provincial Public Security Chief Fu Yongkun which cites a long list of political, social, and economic explanations for the dramatic increase in unrest in his province in recent years, but barely mentions conscious instigation by hostile forces.[21] Yet another recent article by Hunan Provincial Deputy Chief of Public Security Yang Hongguang has an even lower assessment of the role of "enemy forces," noting that "in our province, there have only been a few sprouts or inclinations of these, though we cannot permit ourselves to overlook them."[22]

Uniquely anti-Chinese conspiratorial explanations have increasingly been supplanted by the same sort of standard structural, socio-economic, and state–society interpretations favored by non-Chinese social scientists who study political instability in other developing countries. Only after positing the central importance of such factors do most analysts note that such circumstances provide an opportunity for "enemy elements and those with ulterior motives" to exacerbate preexisting social discontent.

Several recent police analyses go so far as to contend that *all* social protest is ultimately traceable to economic interests and change.[23] Popular anger generated by unemployment and layoffs and by improperly withheld wages, pensions, and healthcare payments now figure as prominently in police analyses as they do in Western analyses of Chinese unrest. Police experts from Sichuan and Zhejiang estimate that anywhere from 80 percent to 95 percent of recent mass protests in their provinces were due to readjustments in the structure of economic interests and dissatisfaction with the effects of reform. Some analysts interpret popular dissatisfaction in terms relatively charitable to the state's reform project—as a failure of citizens' "psychological acceptance capacity" to keep up with the rapid economic changes in which they find themselves caught. But many police scholars demonstrate a keen understanding and sympathy for the pain suffered by these workers and pensioners, coupled with a lack of sympathy for the entrepreneurs and managers who laid these workers off.[24]

Some of the most widely accepted economic explanations for unrest relate to China's increasingly unequal income distribution. Several analysts draw on their understanding of cross-national statistical studies of development to claim that China's suddenly exploding Gini index places it in a zone of genuine danger for instability.[25] As one analyst frankly admits, the growing income gap "inevitably causes gaps in social status and the political rights that people enjoy."[26] These analyses are liberally laced with judgmental language. A recent report by the Fujian Public Security Bureau is typical of many that freely suggest that rising inequality contributes to unrest primarily because impoverished working-class citizens have taken note of how many of China's new wealthy got that way through exploitative, shady, or downright illegal means.[27]

Few of the economic interpretations of unrest attribute these troubles to globalization or the pressures of WTO accession. Many public security analysts, however, are well aware that the pressures of globalization are likely to exacerbate unrest in the near future. While one might anticipate efforts to demonize foreign influence for causing instability, in general these analysts primarily blame domestic economic changes without much reference to their international connections.

Growing numbers of police analysts explicitly subscribe to the thesis that moderate levels of social protest, though potentially dangerous, are nonetheless an inevitable and manageable side effect of development and reform. A municipal police analyst from Sichuan, for example, argues that "in modern societies, contradictions and conflicts of interest among multiple principals cannot be avoided; and mass incidents which result from a sharpening of social contradiction are something that cannot be completely stopped."[28]

Another increasingly common argument is that even though socio-economic changes may be generating the underlying "non-antagonistic" contradictions, government failures are most often responsible for turning these disputes into dangerous "antagonistic" contradictions. When there is a major loss of control, the pivotal catalyst is usually government mishandling of contradictions, bureaucratic indifference, authoritarian attitudes, exploitative policies, judicial corruption, and injustice.[29] Police analysts routinely lambaste basic-level Party and government officials for unfair or illegal administrative tactics or increasing tax and fee burdens on the masses (the so-called "three arbitrary exactions"), or for twisting the law to their benefit, among other charges.[30]

The stress on socio-economic explanations has also yielded a related critique of China's badly underdeveloped legal institutions: many analysts freely blame the lack of adequate legal protections for the economically disadvantaged for heightening resentment. Several analysts have attacked the lack of timely, strong legal punishments for those who take advantage of China's ill-regulated capitalism, in particular, firms that illegally delay or withhold social insurance or pension payments, or squander and misuse enterprise funds that should go to workers.[31] These critiques of bureaucratic abuses yield some of the most explicit expressions of police sympathy for the "justified" motivations for public unrest.

A few analysts are wrestling to explain why official abuses (hardly a new phenomenon in China) have begun encountering tougher popular resistance. Some have turned to explanations rooted in Western studies of the impact of development on political culture. In language that almost echoes Almond or Lipset, these police scholars contend that twenty years of economic development and political opening has resulted in a much more "open" and "developed" political culture. Hunan's deputy chief of police argues that a widening gap has emerged between the "citizens' legal consciousness," which is strengthening, and a lagging, corrupt, and unfair bureaucracy.[32] A key manifestation of this change is an emerging new "logic" of protest, as growing numbers of citizens have apparently put their post-Tiananmen fear of the consequences of protest behind them and increasingly believe that only "the squeaky wheel gets the grease."[33]

The highly malleable regulations on demonstration passed in the wake of 1989 were clearly intended to discourage protest by granting local officials virtually unlimited discretion to criminalize organized dissent. With the recent reassessment of the character and motivations of protest, these undefined legal regulations may be starting to play a different role. Many recent police analyses of protest treat the illegal status of most protests—once treated as proof of evil intent and antagonistic contradiction—as a far less important factor in assessing the character of unrest. The fact that most protests are technically illegal, although noted, is now sometimes treated as a fact of marginal significance. Rather than implying that all illegal or criminal protest activities should automatically be equated with "antagonistic" contradictions, these authors argue that public security organs should learn to clearly distinguish between genuinely violent and much less serious threats to social order.[34] One provincial analyst rather freely concedes the illegality of most of the incidents he has studied, but argues that most were also "reasonable" and non-antagonistic, and that protesters took great care to ensure that social order was maintained in the general vicinity of their protests.[35]

At least some analysts have even chosen to deliberately blur distinctions of legality, contending that disgruntled citizens choose from among a broad array of actions to voice their discontent. Rather than categorize these actions as dichotomously legal or illegal, they portray them as moving along a single, seamless continuum ranging from the clearly peaceful, safe, and legal to the highly violent, dangerous, and clearly illegal.[36] Such efforts to back away from earlier black-and-white legal formulations underscore a desire by police to find less confrontational approaches for dealing with unrest that do not automatically equate protesters—even clear lawbreakers—with "class enemies."[37] Such efforts to ratchet down the tension in dealing with unrest clearly benefit from China's flexible Demonstrations Law.

At the same time, most police analysts still seem comfortable with the largely unfettered administrative authority they enjoy to declare unrest "criminal," if need be. Although many police analysts express clear sympathy for protesters, not one of the essays consulted for this project actually advocates revising the Demonstrations Law. There appears to be little support for more clearly affirming the public's legal right to protest, clarifying the conditions under which a protest should be considered "legal," or strengthening the public's avenues for appealing a police decision to ban a protest. Thus, while recent public security debates clearly do not represent a move toward legalization of social protest, there may be some police advocates for a tacit, partial decriminalization of protest. Under such circumstances, the deliberately broad administrative discretion in the Demonstrations Law could permit some localities to shift the law's function—from facilitating the criminalization and suppression of nearly all protests to facilitating a more permissive approach. Police can still rely upon their explicit, latent authority to "act decisively according to law" to encourage protesters to restrain themselves.

Dilemmas of More Moderate Tactics

Despite this emerging reevaluation of the political character and origins of protest, neither China's leaders nor police authorities are prepared to permit large-scale protest that might spin out of control. But clearly, the more sympathetic reevaluation by public security analysts increases the pressure on police to professionalize their tactics in ways that would enable them to forecast, prevent, or contain protests without excessive violence. Several analysts suggest "raising the bar" for police use of repression and limiting violence to cases that risk degenerating into mob attacks, the storming of Party and government buildings, and "beating, smashing, burning, and looting."

These analysts are fully aware of the dangerous and potentially paralyzing dilemmas that moderate strategies can produce. They note that the national leadership has ordered police units to observe the "three cautions" in policing protests—cautious use of police power, weapons, and coercive measures. At the same time, some police leaders stress that using these powers cautiously does not mean not using them at all, and they warn local police not to transform the "three cautions" into the "three fears"—fear that they will be held responsible if incidents are mishandled, fear that the masses will surround and injure them, and fear that they will face official punishment or popular revenge. Many fear that police forces will increasingly find themselves paralyzed and trapped between Central leaders' official calls for restraint, local Party leaders' demands for repression, and crowds enraged by violent police tactics.

Police analysts have begun debating the risks and rewards of the government trying to "buy off" protesters—an increasingly common government strategy. One Shanghai police official endorses the practice, arguing that in his area certain types of protest declined in the late 1990s after the local government enacted greater guarantees for workers' health care and pensions. He contends that Party Committees at all levels should focus on "resolving mass problems"—including material concessions—as this helps keep contradictions from spawning mass protests and enables the police to avoid resorting to repressive tactics. But a Henan security official counters that when local governments use material concessions to resolve problems the contribution to social order is more apparent than real. Such responses, he argues, simply encourage the "mistaken view" among the masses that "launching great disturbances" is the most effective way to win concessions from the government, and workers in other regions will be encouraged to adopt similar tactics.[38]

Preventing Protest by Strengthening Institutional Channels

Notwithstanding these debates over tactics, a dominant theme in recent analyses is that any successful strategy for dealing with social protest should not—indeed cannot—rely exclusively on the state's legal–coercive organs, no matter how professional and effective they may be. Unless coercion is combined with broader legal-democratic reforms that permit the state to respond more effectively to popular demands, successful containment of protest will be impossible. Although political norms prevent police leaders from explicitly proposing reforms outside the legal system, and these analyses strenuously avoid politically laden terms such as "political structural reform," still, the implicit recommendation is unmistakable.

Several analysts buttress this reform motif with a theoretical framework for unrest that draws clearly from Western comparative political development theory. In this view, social protest arises when economic, social, and political development produces new demands but socialist democratic and legal institutions fail to keep up with this change. Frustration spills over into the streets when citizens either have not yet learned how to effectively use the legal tools and avenues available to them to voice their demands (e.g., they do not yet fully understand their legal rights[39]) or the institutional avenues for voicing demands are "underdeveloped" or "clogged." The obvious influence of early Western political development theory, in particular Samuel P. Huntington's 1968 classic, *Political Order in Changing Societies*, is not at all accidental.

Zhang Shengqian, who explicitly notes Huntington as an influence, contends that as society and the economy develop and basic needs are satisfied, more and more members of society will desire to participate in politics and express their interests. But "imperfect political structures" often thwart this desire. Lacking "proper channels" to press their demands, citizens "will often express them through improper channels . . . such as illegal assemblies, marches, and demonstrations." To legitimize his argument with a source more politically appropriate than Huntington, Zhang cites apposite quotes from the *Selected Works of Deng Xiaoping* about the "reasonableness" of the demands of many petitioners.[40]

Zhang is hardly alone. Other public security analysts argue frankly that the Party cannot expect to contain, channel, and defuse social unrest until it cracks down on corrupt local officials and greatly strengthens legal and other institutional avenues of participation available to citizens.[41] One Hunan municipal official criticizes not only Public Security departments, but also local Communist Party officials for attempting to rely exclusively upon police and People's Armed Police suppression in dealing with local unrest. Since mass incidents are politically and socially complex, exclusive reliance upon large-scale shows of police power will only sharpen mass anger rather than containing and defusing it. When protests are motivated by economic interests or problems between the party-state and the people, these can only be handled effectively through compromise solutions between the protesters and the concerned political and economic units.[42]

These analysts further develop an earlier concern, widespread among security officials, that police units handling demonstrations risk being caught between enraged protesters and intransigent government officials or enterprise managers. Many police officials have decried the severe damage such situations cause to the police's reputation and police–mass relations.[43] These officials concede that when there is trouble the police must loyally carry out the orders of local Party leaders. But they also contend that the police must simultaneously maintain a sense of "proportion" and "appropriateness" in handling unrest, so that they do not lose popular trust. Some analysts argue that public security units should try to avoid getting stuck in a "passive position" by playing a more active role as intermediaries—strengthening their ties with social groups, work units, enterprises, and government units and urging them to negotiate over the sources of popular dissatisfaction.

A Hunan municipal security official, Zhou Yehe, has argued with particular force that the police are uniquely suited to play this special role as intermediaries when "proper" legal-democratic avenues between the party-state and society are weak or clogged. Their location on the frontlines between state and society allows them to serve as a "link" or "bridge" between government units and frustrated citizens. They should also act as social order "staff officers," drawing on their detailed knowledge of social problems to provide local Party and government officials with frank analyses of how failed government policies might lead to unrest.

Some police analysts have argued that the police should play an even more assertive role—one seemingly bordering on autonomous—as state-society intermediaries helping to forestall mass protests. This reconceived, expanded role is captured in a new metaphor—"clearing [or dredging] channels" (*shudao*). Again, this seems to posit a Huntington-style explanation of social unrest. Advocates envision the police acting as "social guides" who can assist Party, government, and economic unit leaders through mediation with disgruntled citizens. By assisting them in finding "channels" to voice their demands, and presumably persuading or pressuring government and economic leaders to deal with these demands, the police could avert illegal protests.[44]

"Clearing channels" involves police employing political, ideological, and legal persuasion to turn prospective protesters toward more "legal" channels. Advocates stress the importance of this as a means of foreseeing and "curing" social problems "early and completely," while they are still manageable. It places great stress on the police rebuilding and strengthening their badly eroded social contacts and intelligence networks, to allow them to foresee and investigate the roots of social contradictions. Advocates believe the police should intervene very early as sympathetic social balancers, well versed in assisting people in finding "legal" avenues to seek redress to prevent social unrest.[45] Other analysts interpret *shudao* as the police acting as legal-political intermediaries who can alert government and economic units about the depth of social dissatisfaction within their units and persuade them to undertake the actions necessary to resolve these underlying social problems.

Explaining Changes in Institutional Attitudes

How do we explain the changing attitudes of these law enforcement analysts and officials? We have available to us fairly detailed expositions of their viewpoints, but we still lack the kind of evidence that would allow us to go much beyond speculation about the sources of this effort to reforge the post-1989 institutional lessons of handling unrest. Certainly, one place to start would be a better understanding of the historical debates—in particular, the efforts by some reformist senior security officials to reconsider the non-antagonistic nature of protest that began shortly before Tiananmen.

The sense of crisis touched off after 1993–94 by the failure to stem the widespread increase in protests seems to have opened a window to reconsider official verdicts on the origins and political character of social protest.

The actual timing of the debate—which really took off in 1999—strongly suggests that the 1997–98 economic downturn and subsequent acceleration in unrest were pivotal in undermining the "official" lessons of 1989 and encouraging new discussion.

Interaction between police and protesters may also provide a partial explanation. Several of the analysts cited here describe protests in language that appears to have been influenced by the self-restrained, legalistic protest repertoires adopted by many protesters in the early-to-mid 1990s. They maintain this same tone even though most of them insist that demonstrators' activities are now becoming far more organized and widespread than the sort of practices that Kevin O'Brien labeled "rightful resistance."[46] These authors' arguments may have contributed to police judgments that demonstrations are overwhelmingly "non-antagonistic" and to their greater optimism that basic social order can survive amid moderate levels of public protest than was the case after 1989.

Common "recruitment pools" may also have much to do with the palpable sympathy for demonstrators. Many of the protesters discussed in these analyses—in particular, state factory workers and senior citizen pensioners—draw from a similar pool as many police officers. The sometimes tough characterizations made by analysts and officials of heartless, selfish entrepreneurs making tainted profits and throwing good people out of work very possibly reflects a class of state officials who feel that they—like the unemployed—are likely to be among the victims of reform. Unquestionably, some of these authors identify far more viscerally with the economically marginalized. And, indeed, police newspapers since the late 1990s have been full of articles discussing the burdens borne by officers now forced to support numerous laid-off relatives on meager official police salaries.

Foreign ideas about the origins of social unrest and proper police handling of protests are having an impact among police analysts. Western analysts must, of course, be very cautious in attributing any reforming impact on China's police to outside intellectual influences. Still, these analyses do seem to reflect the influence of the foreign police forces' anti-riot training that is being taught extensively in Chinese police colleges, as well as the active effort by some Ministry of Public Security-affiliated think tanks and staff colleges to study foreign police writings and practices. The effect of this intellectual borrowing by law enforcement professionals merits more attention by Western analysts.

Finally, institutional/bureaucratic imperatives and fears are also clearly driving the effort by this portion of the party-state to shape a new role for itself. Several authors give voice to fears that their own public security units will get caught in the middle between the Center, their local Party bosses, and the protesters they must see every day. This desire to avoid playing the "heavy" clearly propels their search for preventative solutions and improved political institutions.

This institutional quest for a less passive position can help Western analysts understand the otherwise puzzling calls for police officials to actively "clear channels." Such a romanticized neo-Maoist dream of forging the police into benevolent semiautonomous "social guides" or legal intermediaries severely stretches credulity—especially when we measure it against the current reality of a police corps that is tightly controlled by local Party officials, badly underpaid, sorely lacking professional training and education, and awash in cases of corruption, abuse, and torture. Clearly, the current police corps is completely ill-equipped to assume a role as a trusted, activist state–society intermediary or ombudsman that can head off unrest. These calls for police to "clear channels" do not so much reflect realistic conceptions of future policing policy. Rather, they appear to represent the efforts of police leaders—tired of being caught between despot and mob—to grasp for some way to forge a less reactive role they can play. They may also reflect the depth of dissatisfaction many reformist senior police professionals feel about the shortcomings of the current political system that leaves countless legitimately aggrieved citizens with few choices but to engage in illegal protest—and the police with few choices but to invite social scorn for containing and suppressing them.

Social Protest and the "Brazilianization" of Chinese Law Enforcement?

Such frank contentions that mass protests result primarily from the social pain and injustice caused by reform and exacerbated by official indifference or mismanagement raise serious questions about the morale of the public security forces charged with demonstration control.[47] For Western analysts it becomes pivotal to ask how many of China's police are coming to view aggrieved citizens much more sympathetically than either the party-state officials they are assigned to defend or the managers and entrepreneurs against whom protests are mounted? Some of these analyses—laden with attacks on selfish enterprise owners, entrepreneurs, and their corrupt protectors within the party-state—hardly constitute a ringing vote of confidence in Jiang Zemin's "three represents" strategy of recruiting the emerging wealthy classes into the Party leadership. Of course, overt criticism of "the Three Represents" and its change in Party recruitment is not possible among the police. But we cannot help but wonder whether some police analysts suspect that the Chinese state's legal-coercive relationship with society is undergoing increasing "Brazilianization"—that is, the often brutal, extralegal use of police forces as defenders of the wealthier segments of a highly inegalitarian developing society, accompanied by the demonization, criminalization, and suppression of disgruntled social groups that see themselves as losers in this process.[48] At a minimum, some police analysts and officials betray a growing discomfort with being ordered to defend China's recent socio-economic changes with force in the streets.[49]

A final, crucial "unknowable" is the degree to which these represent the views of working police officials. To the extent that they do, they tempt us to speculate about how such views might shape or restrict the legal-coercive strategies available to senior Chinese state leaders. As these authors continually note, police officials are under the absolute leadership of their local Party and government leaders. But might a police leadership surrounded by coercive officials subscribing to "inevitability" and "management" theses, or uncomfortable with the social realities they must defend, eventually feel more inclined to treat sustained protest as a process of "negotiation" among the state, law enforcement, and society over fundamental issues of policy and even some forms of state power?

Notes

For helpful comments on this paper, the author wishes to thank the organizers and participants of the conference, especially Neil Diamant, Stanley Lubman, Kevin O'Brien, Mary Gallagher, Andrew Mertha, and also Dorothy Solinger.

1. Michael W. McCann, *Rights at Work: Pay Equity Reform and the Politics of Legal Mobilization* (Chicago: University of Chicago Press, 1994).

2. Doug McAdam, Sidney Tarrow, and Charles Tilly, "Toward an Integrated Perspective on Social Movements and Revolution," in *Comparative Politics: Rationality, Culture, and Structure*, ed. Mark Irving Lichbach and Alan S. Zuckerman (Cambridge: Cambridge University Press, 1997), esp. 152–53.

3. I have discussed these dilemmas of change in authoritarian protest policing in Murray Scot Tanner, "Will the State Bring You Back In? Policing and Democratization," *Comparative Politics* 33, no. 1 (October 2000): 101–24. For a discussion of the evolution of protest policing and political change in democratic systems, see Donatella Della Porta and Herbert Reiter, eds., *Policing Protest: The Control of Mass Demonstrations in Western Democracies* (Minneapolis: University of Minnesota Press, 1998); and Peter J. Katzenstein, *Cultural Norms and National Security: Police and Military in Postwar Japan* (Ithaca, N.Y.: Cornell University Press, 1996).

4. Although this essay does not employ a rational-choice analysis, some analysts have used strategically oriented or rational-choice analyses to clarify these dilemmas of liberalization and coercion. See, e.g., Tanner, "Will the State Bring You Back In?" Much of that analysis is inspired by Adam Przeworski, "The Games of Transition," in *Issues in Democratic Consolidation: The New South American Democracies in Compara-*

tive Perspective, ed. Scott Mainwaring, Guillermo O'Donnell, and J. Samuel Valenzuela (Notre Dame, Ind.: University of Notre Dame Press, 1992), 105–52; Douglas A. Chalmers and Craig H. Robinson, "Why Power Contenders Choose Liberalization," *International Studies Quarterly* 26, no. 1 (March 1982): 3–36; and Christopher Young, "The Strategy of Political Liberalization: A Comparative View of Gorbachev's Reforms," *World Politics* 45, no. 1 (1992): 47–65.

5. On the role of crisis in forging police institutional norms, see Murray Scot Tanner, *Who Wields the Knife? An Institutional History of Chinese Communist Police and Intelligence Organs, 1927 to 1950* (Berkeley: University of California Center for Chinese Studies China Monographs Series, forthcoming).

6. To be clear, the analysis in this essay, though largely focused on the battles of state institutions to redefine their relationship to society, is sympathetic to theoretical arguments for a more "disaggregated" view of the state and a more interactive model of state–society relations. On the former, see Elizabeth J. Perry, "Trends in the Study of Chinese Politics: State-Society Relations," *China Quarterly*, no. 139 (September 1994): 704–13; on the latter, see Joel S. Migdal, Atul Kohli, and Vivienne Shue, eds., *State Power and Social Forces: Domination and Transformation in the Third World* (Cambridge: Cambridge: University Press, 1994).

7. See Qiao's speech excerpted in Chinese Communist Party, Fujian Provincial Committee, Political-Legal Committee, ed., *Shehui Zhi'an Zonghe Zhili Zhengce Fagui Huibian* [Collected laws and regulations on comprehensive management of social order] (Beijing: Qunzhong Chubanshe, 1992), 60–61.

8. The Nanchong incident is still taught as an object lesson in Chinese social-order-management texts (Zhang Shengqian, *Zhi'an Shijian Chuzhi* [Handling social order incidents] [Beijing: Zhongguo Renmin Gongan Daxue Chubanshe, 2001], 78–79).

9. Yu said that this was "originally just a college security matter that was very easy to resolve, if it had been handled properly." He suggested that a combination of restraint by security forces and arrests of the key guilty parties was more effective in preventing such demonstrations from spreading out of control (*Renmin Ribao*, cited by Reuters, 24 January 1989).

10. Judy Polumbaum, "To Protect or Restrict? Points of Contention in China's Draft Press Law," in *Domestic Law Reforms in Post-Mao China*, ed. Pitman B. Potter (Armonk, N.Y.: M. E. Sharpe, 1994), 247–69; also, Judy Polumbaum, "In the Name of Stability: Restrictions on the Right of Assembly in the People's Republic of China," *Australian Journal of Chinese Affairs*, no. 26 (July 1991): 43–64. These types of "protect or restrict" legislative battles are discussed in Murray Scot Tanner, *The Politics of Lawmaking in China: Institutions, Processes, and Democratic Prospects* (Oxford: Oxford University Press, 1998), 214.

11. This is based on the author's own conversations with police officers in 1989, as well as the rather sympathetic internal speech given by Minister of Public Security Wang Fang in May 1989 ("Wang Fang Tongzhi zai Gonganbu Jiguan bufen Juji yishang Ganbu Huiyi shang de Jianghua" [Comrade Wang Fang's speech at a meeting of some cadres from Ministry of Public Security organs above the bureau level, 22 May 1989], *Renmin Gongan* 7, July 1989, 9–10).

12. See Vice-Minister Gu Linfang's Fall 1989 report to five central departments, "Looking at Class Struggle in the Initial Stage of Socialism from the Turmoil and Riot" (*Renmin Gongan*, 5 October 1989, 3–9, and continued in the subsequent issue of the magazine).

13. Judy Polumbaum, "In the Name of Stability," 43–64.

15. This section is a greatly abbreviated version of my article, "China Rethinks Unrest," *Washington Quarterly* 27, no. 2 (Summer 2004): 137–56. Noteworthy with respect to this new support for reform are the late 1991–early 1992 speeches and articles by Qiao Shi and MPS senior adviser Mu Fengyun. The author has provided more detailed analyses of these internal police and PAP debates over protest in "Ideological Struggle over Police Reform, 1988–93," in *Transition from Communism in China: Institutional and Comparative Analyses*, ed. Edwin A. Winckler (Boulder, Colo.: Lynne Rienner, 1999), esp. 125–27; see also, Murray Scot Tanner, "The Institutional Lessons of Disaster: Reorganizing China's People's Armed Police After Tiananmen," in *The People's Liberation Army as Organization*, ed. James Mulvenon (Washington, D.C.: RAND Corporation, 2002); and Murray Scot Tanner, "Cracks in the Wall: China's Eroding Coercive State," *Current History*, September 2001, 243–49.

16. Zhang Shengqian, *Zhi'an Shijian Chuzhi* [Handling social order incidents] (Beijing: People's Public Security University Press, 2001), 24, 25.

17. *2000–2001 Zhongguo Diaocha Baogao: Xin Xingshi xia Renmin Neibu Maodun Yanjiu* [China investigation report 2000–2001: Studies of contradictions among the people under new conditions] (Beijing: Central Compilation and Translation Press, 2001), esp. 62–69.

18. For examples of those who characterize these incidents as overwhelmingly "among the people," see Zhou Yehe, "Gongan jiguan chuzhi quntixing shijian ying zouchu si da wuqu, zengqiang sizhong yishi" [In handling mass incidents, public security organs should avoid four great mistakes and strengthen their consciousness in four ways], in *Quntixing Shijian* [Collected research essays on mass incidents], ed. Li Zhongxin (Beijing: Chinese People's Public Security University Press, 2001), 69–71; and Yang Hongguang, "Dui Dangqian Quntixing Shijian de Jidian Renshi" [A few views on mass incidents at the present time], *Gongan Yanjiu*, no. 7 (2002): 15.

19. Han Jingui, "Qiantan Quntixing Shijian de Gainian, Tezheng, Xingzhi ji Chuzhi Fanglue" [A superficial discussion of mass incidents: Their conception, characteristics, nature, and strategies for handling them], in *Quntixing Shijian* (see note 18), 22–30.

20. Zhang Shengqian, *Zhi'an Shijian Chuzhi*, esp. 21–23. Note, however, that even though Zhang lists enemy forces near the front, they are but one of several "political" factors underlying unrest, and Zhang devotes far more space to a variety of more standard social and economic factors.

21. Fu Yongkun, "Jiji Yufang, Tuoshan Chuzhi Quntixing Shijian Quanli Weihu Shehui Wending" [Actively prevent and appropriately handle mass incidents: Powerfully protect social stability], *Gongan Yanjiu*, no. 12 (2001): 44–46.

22. Yang Hongguang, "Dui Dangqian Quntixing Shijian de Jidian Renshi," 14. Yang argues that former criminals who were previously punished by the police were far more likely than "enemy forces" to cause trouble during demonstrations.

23. Zhou Guangyang, "Sichuan," in *Quntixing Shijian*, (see note 18), 14.

24. Bao Zhaoyong, "Qianxi Shichang Jingji Tiaojian xia Quntixing Zhian Shijian de Tedian, Chengyin ji Chuzhi Duice" [A superficial analysis of the characteristics, causes, and counterstrategies for handling mass social order incidents under the conditions of a market economy], in *Quntixing Shijian* (see note 18), 57; also Zhou Guangyang, "Lun Quntixing Zhian Shijian" [On mass social order incidents], in *Quntixing Shijian* (see note 18), 12–21.

25. Zhang Shengqian (*Zhi'an Shijian Chuzhi*, 36–37), for example, claims that in the twenty years of reform China's Gini index has grown from 0.18 to 0.467, producing an "unfair distribution" of income and "an imbalance in values."

26. Bao Zhaoyong, "Zhejiang," in *Quntixing Shijian*, (see note 18), 58. Clearly, such criticism of how mishandling of contradictions by the party-state can transform their nature draws upon Mao's "On the Proper Handling of Contradictions among the People."

27. Fujian Provincial Public Security Bureau, "Lun Quntixing Shijian ji qi Chuzhi" [On mass incidents and their handling], in *Quntixing Shijian* (see note 18), 2–3.

28. Zhou Guangyang, "Lun Quntixing Zhian Shijian," in *Quntixing Shijian* (see note 18), 19.

29. Bao Zhaoyong, "Qianxi Shichang Jingji Tiaojian xia Quntixing Shijian . . . ," in *Quntixing Shijian* (see note 18), 58.

30. Zhou Guangyang, "Lun Quntixing Zhian Shijian," in *Quntixing Shijian* (see note 18), 16–17.

31. Zhou Guangyang, "Lun Quntixing Zhian Shijian," in *Quntixing Shijian* (see note 18), 14–17; Wang Chunwang, "Dui Dangqian Quntixing Shijian de Yanjiu yu Sikao" [Research and reflections on contemporary mass incidents], in *Quntixing Shijian* (see note 18), 76–77; Yang Hongguang, "Dui Dangqian Quntixing Shijian de Jidian Renshi," 13–16; and Zhang Shengqian, *Zhi'an Shijian Chuzhi*.

32. Yang Hongguang, "Dui Dangqian Quntixing Shijian de Jidian Renshi," 14.

33. This changing logic of protest is noted by many, including Bao Zhaoyong, "Qianxi Shichang Jingji Tiaojian xia Quntixing Shijian . . . ," in *Quntixing Shijian* (see note 18), 58; Wang Chunwang, "Dui Dangqian Quntixing Shijian de Yanjiu yu Sikao" [Research and reflections on contemporary mass incidents], in *Quntixing Shijian* (see note 18), 76–77; and Yang Hongguang, "Dui Dangqian Quntixing Shijian de Jidian Renshi," 13.

34. For example, although police analysts Wu Dan and Zhang Baorui clearly list several legal clauses under which illegal demonstrators can be prosecuted, they nonetheless argue that such legal and coercive measures should only be used in very serious or violent cases (see Wu Dan and Zhang Baorui, "Quntixing Zhi'an Shijian ji ge Redian Wenti Yanjiu" [Research on several hot topics concerning mass social order incidents], in *Xinshiqi Gongan Gongzuo Lilun yu Tansuo* [Theory and investigation into public security work in the new period], ed. Shang Jiping et al. [Beijing: Zhongguo Renmin Gongan Daxue Chubanshe, 2001], 118–23).

35. Han Jingui, "Qiantan Quntixing Shijian de Gainian, Tezheng, Xingzhi ji Chuzhi Fanglue" [A superficial discussion of mass incidents: Their conception, char-

acteristics, nature, and strategies for handling them], in *Quntixing Shijian* (see note 18), 22–24.

36. Ibid., 22–30.
37. This point is discussed in Tanner, "Ideological Struggle over Police Reform," 118–21.
38. Wang Chunwang, "Dui Dangqian Quntixing Shijian de Yanjiu yu Sikao" [Research and reflections on contemporary mass incidents], in *Quntixing Shijian* (see note 18), 76–77.
39. Zhou Guangyang, "Lun Quntixing Zhian Shijian," in *Quntixing Shijian* (see note 18), 14–17.
40. Zhang Shengqian, *Zhi'an Shijian Chuzhi*, 24. In a discussion of the relationship between income inequality and unrest, Zhang quotes what appears to be a 1989 Chinese translation of *Political Order in Changing Societies* (ibid., 36).
41. See also, e.g., Zhou Guangyang, "Lun Quntixing Zhian Shijian," in *Quntixing Shijian* (see note 18), 20.
42. Zhou Yehe, "Gongan jiguan chuzhi quntixing shijian ying zouchu si da wuqu, zengqiang sizhong yishi" [In handling mass incidents, public security organs should avoid four great mistakes and strengthen their consciousness in four ways], in *Quntixing Shijian* (see note 18), 69–71.
43. Ibid., 69–71. See also Zhou Guangyang, "Lun Quntixing Zhian Shijian," in *Quntixing Shijian* (see note 18), 17–18; and Bao Zhaoyong, "Qianxi Shichang Jingji Tiaojian xia Quntixing Shijian . . . ," in ibid., 58–60.
44. Wang Chunwang, "Dui Dangqian Quntixing Shijian de Yanjiu yu Sikao" [Research and reflections on contemporary mass incidents], in *Quntixing Shijian* (see note 18), 76–77.
45. Ibid.
46. For insightful analyses of self-restrained protest styles in China, see Kevin O'Brien, "Rightful Resistance," *World Politics* 49 (October 1996): 31–55. See also Elizabeth Perry and Mark Selden, eds., *Chinese Society: Change, Conflict, and Resistance* (London: Routledge, 2000); and especially Ching Kwan Lee, "Pathways of Labor Insurgency," in that volume; as well as the essays by Pei Minxin ("Rights and Resistance: The Changing Contexts of the Dissident Movement"), David Zweig ("The 'Externalities of Development': Can New Political Institutions Manage Rural Conflict?"), and Tyrene White ("Domination, Resistance, and Accommodation in China's One-Child Campaign)." On recent protest in China more generally, see David Shambaugh, ed., *Is China Unstable?: Assessing the Factors* (Washington, D.C.: Gaston Sigur Center for Asian Studies, George Washington University, 1998); and Larry Wortzel, "Beijing Struggles to 'Ride the Tiger of Liberalisation,'" *Jane's Intelligence Review*, 1 January 2001.
47. For an example of the regime's concerns on this score, see the August 1, 1998 edition of *Renmin wujing bao* [People's Armed Police Daily], which devotes an entire page to articles that attempt to persuade PAP troops to embrace the party's enterprise reform policies despite the widespread pain created by unemployment, even to some police families.
48. The term "Brazilianization" of law enforcement is my own, but it draws di-

rectly on two excellent portrayals of the abusive use of police in highly inegalitarian systems: Paul Chevigny, *The Edge of the Knife: Police Violence in the Americas* (New York: The New Press, 1995); and Juan E. Mendez, Guillermo O'Donnell, and Paulo Sergio Pinheiro, eds., *The (Un)Rule of Law and the Underprivileged in Latin America* (Notre Dame, Ind.: Notre Dame University Press, 1999).

49. Zhou Guangyang, "Lun Quntixing Zhian Shijian," in *Quntixing Shijian* (see note 18), 18–19.

FU HUALING 9

Punishing for Profit

Profitability and Rehabilitation in
a *Laojiao* Institution

Introduction

There are two principal types of imprisonment in China: *laogai* and *laojiao*. *Laogai*, or *laodong gaizao* (reform through labor), is a punishment rendered by a court after trial according to provisions of the Criminal Law. It is a criminal punishment ranging from six months to twenty years. *Laojiao*, or *laodong jiaoyang* (reeducation though labor),[1] is an administrative punishment rendered by the police according to a series of Decisions of the Standing Committee of the National People's Congress, State Council Regulations, and Rules of the Ministry of Public Security. Legally, police use *laojiao* to punish "minor offences" summarily, but the maximum term that can be imposed by the police is incarceration for three years. *Laojiao* is subject to limited judicial review.

This chapter is a case study of the penal economy of a *laojiao* institution, the LB Laojiao Institution (the LB) in a Southern Chinese city (the City).[2] It examines the necessity of commercialization, the organization of production, and the motivation of guards and inmates in the LB. It further analyzes the tension between the imperative of production and profitability on the one hand, and the imperative of reform and rehabilitation of offenders on the other, as well as the impact of penal production on the management of penal institutions. The principal argument is that, due to the fiscal crisis facing China's penal institution, penal production has become the goal of reform in China's penal institutions, instead of the means to achieve it. As such, penal production marginalizes reform. Nevertheless, an improvement in the penal economy, coupled with increasing internal and external supervision of penal institutions, can improve the living standards of inmates, and commercialization serves to soften the harshness of punishment in China, making it relatively less brutal and less repressive.

This chapter has six sections. The first examines the status of penal economy in China and the fiscal crisis facing China's penal institutions. The second section introduces the LB Laojiao Institution, focusing on its financial arrangement. Section three describes the contracting mechanisms that have been commonly used in China's penal institutions. Section four analyzes the penal economy in the LB and the organization and division of labor. Section five explores the impact of the penal economy on the rights of inmates. The final section offers some concluding observations.

The Chinese Penal Economy

Penal labor and production are fundamental to China's penal institutions. There are three presumptions underlining Chinese orthodox penology.[3] First, labor transforms prisoners and thus is the means to achieve their reform and rehabilitation. Labor, especially collective and industrial labor, remolds the minds of inmates and re-socializes their behavior. "It is in the image of a factory," according to Dutton, "where education and production are joined as one, where life and labor are organized around the pole of productive collectivity, that *laogai* is set apart from the reformative schemes of the bourgeoisie."[4]

Second, penal production is planned and forms an integral part of the national economy. It is collective, large in scale, and designed to be educational and meaningful in transforming individuals. This orthodoxy also implies that the state not only plans the production and sale of products, but also, in line with Rusche and Kirchheimer's arguments,[5] determines the forms, severity, and magnitude of punishment and the supply of inmates in accordance with the prevailing economic conditions.

Third, the planned penal economy makes a significant contribution to the state economy. For many, this statement is an article of faith. A recent book coauthored by some of the leading researchers on Chinese *laogai* continued to confirm the "material wealth" created by the penal economy and *laogai*'s contributions in reducing the state's burden and in supporting the country's economic development.[6] Since the early 1990s, after Chinese prison labor became an important issue in Sino–U.S. relations,[7] the Chinese government has become cautious in claiming the profitability of its penal economy, but many critics of Sino–U.S. relations continue to make such claims. For them, *laogai* and *laojiao* are as politically repressive as they are financially lucrative.[8]

More recent assessments, by *laogai* and *laojiao* administrators in particular, have shown much less confidence in penal labor and its transforming power. While the administrators continue to acknowledge that collective labor only provides the means for rehabilitation, they nevertheless focus on the lack of central funding to finance penal institutions and the necessity of the penal economy to subsidize the operation of its institutions. Penal labor primarily benefits government institutions by alleviating a financial crisis. Penal labor could be harsh, menial, lacking in any educational value or otherwise meaningless, but it is necessary given the current economic development in China.[9]

No statistics are available on the profitability of the *laojiao* economic system as a whole. According to government researchers, the *laojiao* economy has developed quickly since 1989, with annual output increasing at a rate of 18 percent per year, investment in fixed assets increasing by 25 percent per year, and business profits increasing by 25 percent per year. By the end of 1998, *laojiao* assets amounted to 5.5 billion RMB, including 2.4 billion RMB in fixed assets and 3.9 billion RMB in bank loans.[10]

While it is difficult to quantify the *laojiao* economy, the economic performance in *laogai* is more straightforward. It has been said that "fixed assets in the industrial enterprises in Chinese prisons grew from 3.4 billion RMB in 1984 to 11.16 billion RMB in 1994, and the industrial output doubled since 1980."[11] But more than 80 percent of the so-called growth is loans taken from state banks.[12] As of 2000, assets in the penal enterprises of five provinces were insufficient to meet their liability.[13] By the end of 1997 the penal economies in nineteen of China's thirty-one provinces and regions showed a total deficit of 431 million RMB. Although the total loss had been reduced to 182 million RMB by the end of 1998, the penal economies in fourteen provinces continued to lose money.[14]

Until the mid-1990s, the shrinking profits in the penal economy had been accompanied by declining government budgets for penal institutions. Since the 1980s, the move toward a socialist market economy in China has seriously exposed the inadequacies of China's old revenue regime and has driven the government into a financial crisis. In the wake of economic liberalization, the government's share of gross-domestic-product (GDP) expenditure has noticeably decreased. By 1994, budgetary expenditures by the government accounted for only 14 percent of GDP, a sharp decline from the 39 percent of GDP in 1978.[15]

Because of the relative decline of the government budget, *laogai* and *laojiao* institutions have suffered declining funding, which has proven to be insufficient to cover their expenditures. In the post-revolutionary society, where economic development prevails over other considerations, criminal justice institutions have become a secondary priority in government funding. The fiscal crisis simply drives penal institutions to the market, and cadre police are forced to rely on extrabudgetary funds to sustain their operation.

Another important reason for the government's refusal to provide full funding is the fact that *laogai* and *laojiao* are thought to have the income-generating capacity to become self-financing. As a *laogai* cadre from Shanxi Province complained, the government regards *laogai* enterprises as "a piece of fat meat." It imposes production quotas on *laogai* institutions and scrutinizes them according to their productivity and profitability. It requires *laogai* enterprises to generate profits through the free labor of inmates.[16] Indeed, the financing arrangement of penal institutions is not unique. The government has also forced the police and judiciary to become partially self-financed.[17]

By the end of 1998, there were 284 *laojiao* institutions (*yuan* or *suo*), including 209 industrial institutions and 75 farms. The *laojiao* institutions had established 364 enterprises, including 217 industrial enterprises and 147 agricultural enterprises. Among the enterprises, about 20 can be regarded as large or medium-sized. There are about 50,000 cadre police involved in *laojiao* enterprises, 46,000 civilian employees, and 250,000 inmates.[18] At the same time, there were about 700 *laogai* institutions, with 270,000 cadre police who were responsible for the custody of 1,450,000 inmates.[19]

As mentioned above, the state only provides a partial budget for both *laogai* and *laojiao*. Before 1993, when the central government decided to increase funding for penal institutions, a policy which was written into the 1994 Prison Law, the government gave only partial financial support to penal institutions. In extreme cases, government funding would cover only about 15 percent of expenditures. The government's contribution to the budget has increased over the subsequent years. According to one estimate, the minimum cost to sustain China's penal system was 10 billion RMB in 1998, of which the state provided about 68 percent, with the balance covered by the penal economy. But the actual cost to run the penal institutions amounts to 17 billion RMB.[20]

Financing the LB Laojiao Institution

Founded in the 1950s, the LB is the only *laojiao* institution established by the City government where it is located. It incarcerates male inmates sentenced by the police from within the City, and occasionally from nearby small cities. The LB today is headed by a director, who is assisted by a political commissar and a number of deputies. It is divided into the headquarters (*duibu*) and brigades (*dadui*). The headquarters is composed of eight sections (*ke*) devoted to administration, including production and sanitation, education, political work, and accounting, among others. Presently, there are four brigades. Different from the arrangement in the headquarters, a political director is in charge of each brigade, and the director is supported by a brigade head. There is also a deputy head, an accountant, and an office assistant. Each brigade is further divided into several squadrons (*zhongdui*). There are presently fourteen squadrons. While the headquarters administers the institution, the brigades and squadrons are responsible for production and the daily supervision of inmates.

Wardens in *laojiao* institutions are officially referred to as cadre police (*ganjing*), but are called cadres (*ganbu*) in less formal contexts, except for those who hold management positions and who are addressed according to their official titles. By the end of 2000, the established size of the LB called for 170 cadre police, but the actual size of the police contingent was 236, as there were 66 surplus officers who were not on the government's payroll. These extra officers were hired principally for the purpose of *guanxi*. These are the children of officials in the *laogai* or the *laojiao* system who cannot find other employment and so are allowed to work within the system, often at another *laogai* or *laojiao* institution where the parents do not work. There has been political and financial pressure to downsize *laogai* and *laojiao* institutions, and the LB has resolved the problem of too many employees by the forced early retirement of cadre police. By the middle of 2001, the established size of cadre police in the LB had been reduced to 154, of which 125 were male and 29 were female. Slightly more than half (81) of the cadre police worked in the brigades, while the others worked in the headquarters.

There are also a number of civilian workers, whose numbers have been decreasing. In 2000, there were fifteen civilian workers in the LB, seven of them working in the convenience store and the guesthouse run by the headquarters and the others working as gatekeepers. Civilian members are exclusively family members or relatives of cadre police in the LB. In a *laojiao* institution, cadre police serve as supervisors and managers, civilians serve as technicians, and inmates serve as free labor. The ratio of civilian workers to inmates is largely determined by the nature of the institution's products. More sophisticated products require more civilian technicians.

Inmates in *laojiao* are referred to "trainees" (*xueyuan*). At the end of 2001, there were 1,407 inmates on record in the LB, but only 1,379 were actually serving their terms there. The rest had been discharged to seek medical treatment, attend schools, or work.

A *laojiao* budget includes line items for both personnel and special projects. The personnel budget includes costs incurred in paying and supporting cadre police, retired cadre police, and inmates. Actual costs per cadre police and inmate are normally higher than budgeted costs. For example, the annual budget per officer in 2000 was 19,340 RMB, but the actual expenditure was 25,210 RMB; the budget per inmate was 1,600 RMB, but the actual expenditure was 3,010 RMB. Table 9.1 shows the total budget, actual costs, and the shortfall in operating the LB in 1999 and 2000. In total, for the year 2000, there was a budgetary shortfall of 3,975,000 RMB, which was covered by extrabudgetary income through the *laojiao* economy. Table 9.2 shows the

TABLE 9.1

Budget and Actual Costs in the LB, 1999–2000

	Budget (RMB)	Actual Costs (RMB)	Shortfall (RMB)
1999	6,252,000	9,476,000	3,224,000
2000	7,231,000	11,206,000	3,975,000

income generated in LB in 2000. Total profits from business ventures were 6,895,000 RMB. After allocating 3,975,000 RMB to cover the budget shortfall, the LB still had a net profit of 2,920,000 RMB at the end of 2000. There was also a 1,688,000 RMB profit carried over from the previous year. Any excess profits are spent on the cadre police and on those in senior positions or at the highest administrative levels in the LB. For example, the LB purchased more than ten vehicles from 1999 to 2001, mostly for leaders at the *ke* level for their personal use. It also built a new dormitory for the senior cadre police and covered their traveling expenses to Hong Kong and other domestic resorts.

The Responsibility System in China's Penal Institutions

The essential element of a responsibility system is management through the mechanism of a contract. Under the terms of the contract, institutions and individual officers are rewarded and punished according to their performance. Inspired by the success of the responsibility system in the agricultural and industrial sectors of the economy, this mechanism was initiated in penal institutions in the early 1980s as a way to make penal enterprises more profitable.

There is multiple contracting. First, the *laogai* or *laojiao* bureau of a government will negotiate and sign contracts with their own respective *laogai* or *laojiao* institutions. Then, the *laogai* or *laojiao* institution will negotiate and sign contracts with its own brigades. Finally, the brigades will sign contracts with their sub-units, which directly represent the interests of the cadre police. The contracting system is a bargaining process between the government, the institution, and the individual cadre police.

The contracting process often results in conflicts of interest, especially between the bureaus of justice and the penal enterprises. This particular relationship was described as one of "squabbling and bickering" and filled with "sharp conflicts." According to a *laogai* cadre from a Changsha prison, the parties spent a great deal of time bargaining about production quotas and

TABLE 9.2

Production Items and Income Generated in the LB, 2000

Production item	Income (RMB)
Pink bricks	3,300,000
Wooden walls	1,674,000
Automobile repair	1,470,000
Bookbinding	2,180,000
Printing	32,000
Labor services	842,000
Drug treatment fees from inmates	633,000
Driver training for inmates	109,000
Hairdressing	43,000
Notebooks	21,000
Footballs	72,000
Formica	42,000
Decoration lights	463,000
Special dishes for inmates	483,000
Vegetables	457,000
Pork	87,000
Other Income	1,140,000
Total	13,200,000

profit-sharing formulas, with the government making excessive demands on the institutions. Of course, the Bureau of Justice is not the only institution that may be guilty of imposing an unreasonable quota. Under pressure to expand profits, penal institutions often impose similar requirements on their sub-units. In the 1980s, for example, the Ministry of Justice imposed a 6 percent annual growth rate for the penal economy, which grew to about 10 percent at the provincial-level Department of Justice. But in the internal contracts between the headquarters unit and the prison's sub-units, the required quota was increased to more than 20 percent.[21] The formula differs from one province to another, and sometimes from one institution to another, largely depending on local expectations of profitability and institutional necessity. But a common complaint has been that the government "whips the buffalo that moves faster"—that is, that it takes more profit from those who make more.²² In general, the contracting system encourages quick profitability and short-term economic planning. While authorities at the higher levels want to reap as much profit as possible by imposing excessive quotas and dismissing noncompliant managers, the subordinate units often falsify accounts to hide profits so that they can keep as much as possible within the institution and line their own pockets.

Contracts specify the targets to be reached for the duration of the contract, normally one year to three years. The contract has two major components: economic production and prisoner rehabilitation. The cadre police within each brigade have the double responsibility of achieving these targets.

Although the production component of a contract can be broken down into numerous items, it is the annual net profits generated by a brigade that are taken into account. As mentioned above, under this item the parties agree to a base production figure and the amount of profit that will be turned over by one (subordinate) party to the other (superior) party. The subordinate party is allowed to keep any surplus and is also required to compensate any losses.²³

The second component of the contract is inmate rehabilitation. This aspect of the contract has a narrow focus and includes a few key indices, principally the institution's escape-and-capture rate, the crime rate in an institution and its clearance rate, and the percentage of inmates who obtain educational or vocational certificates. In the literature on the contract system, rehabilitation is not clearly distinguished from security, and obviously, the concern for security prevails. More detailed contracts also include items such as the number of times a cadre police officer has had a personal discussion with inmates under his control or the behavior of inmates.

Under the contracting system, there are three models for organizing rehabilitation within the *laogai* and *laojiao* economy. The first model encompasses the double responsibilities of rehabilitation and production. This mechanism was created in 1980 in response to the drastic change in China's economic policy. Its principal characteristic is that the same authority in a penal institution or a sub-unit is responsible for both production and inmate rehabilitation and is rewarded or penalized according to the terms of the contract. Thus, the director of a penal institution is also the general manager of its enterprises, and cadre police perform the dual functions of production and rehabilitation. The main problem associated with this model is that although the same group of people is responsible for both tasks, they tend to prioritize. Not surprisingly, profit-making is prioritized and inmate rehabilitation becomes marginalized.

The second model is called the two-track model, in which cadre police are separated into two groups: one group is responsible for production, the other for re-education. Although responsibility is divided, the benefits from production are shared between the two groups. This mechanism was created in the early 1990s in response to the problem inherent in the first model. In this model, production and rehabilitation are said to be equally important and should be given equal weight. But because of the operational difficulties in dividing cadre police and profits and the inherent conflict between production and rehabilitation,[24] only a few *laojiao* institutions currently adhere to this model.

The third model was developed from the second model and is sometimes referred to as "One Institution, Two Systems." In this model, the production component is structurally separated from the *laojiao* institution and becomes an independent corporate entity—that is, ownership is separated from management. Cadre police are not involved in production, and their entire salaries are paid by the government. The penal economy is either run by civilian members or contracted out to private businesses.

It is here that we can see the privatization of prison labor in China very clearly. In Hunan Province, for example, a cement factory owned by the prison became de facto insolvent because of corruption on the part of the prison director, putting the prison in debt in the amount of 40 million RMB (the director was sentenced to thirteen years in prison). Since the prison was incapable of running the cement factory, it had to contract the plant out to a private businessman. Under the new contract, the prison received a fixed amount in fees each year and also rented out inmates to the factory.

The introduction of the contracting system has made the penal economy the principal goal of penal institutions. In 1989 one *laogai* cadre claimed that for a long period of time "production prevails over reform and reform is secondary to production," and that the requirement of profitability had "created a huge burden on *laogai* institutions, which can hardly breathe now."[25] There is no doubt that since the 1980s, inmate production has become a priority of all *laogai* and *laojiao* institutions in China.[26] One of the principal tasks of the person in charge of a penal institution is to develop a harmonious relationship with business partners and to coordinate with related government authorities, such as taxation authorities, industrial and commercial administrators, banks, and authorities in charge of water or electricity.[27]

The reform programs within penal institutions are geared to the creation of business opportunities and the enhancement of profitability. Cadre police are evaluated mainly according to their economic performance. If income increases, it is said, every other requirement will have been satisfied. Increasingly, directors in penal institutions are chosen because of their business skills, capable officers are diverted into production management and the time allocated for inmate study is used for production instead. Rehabilitation has become a "soft responsibility" which is easily marginalized or even overlooked, and education is at best a mere formality. As one cadre police officer wrote: "The double contract system is satisfied if there are no escapes, no deaths, and the production quota is achieved."[28] There has been a qualitative and quantitative shift of resources, then, from rehabilitation to production.[29]

There are limits, however, to the production imperative in the LB. For example, incarcerated Falun Gong members are not required to work, or at least not as hard as others. They only "study." There are also rules which require *laojiao* inmates to study two hours a day, and authorities from the City and the province have occasionally organized political and literacy examinations for inmates. But penal institutions have their own ways of handling those non-production requirements. The LB, for example, organizes study sessions only when there is less work to do, and study is actually used to control the idle inmates. To reduce the time that is necessary for examinations, the LB is able to obtain examination questions in advance and prepare answers for inmates. That explains why, beginning in the year 2000, the passing rate for inmates in the LB has always been close to 100 percent.

Most inmates prefer to participate in production, even though they may not want to work very hard. Political indoctrination and education serve as a form of punishment for inmates who have violated prison rules or who refuse to be hard-working. As one LB cadre police officer noted: "It must be very hard to sit on the floor to sing revolutionary songs and recite prison rules all day long."

Profitability and the Rights of Inmates

Economic change has led to a subtle shift in the relationship between inmates and cadre police. The commercialization of *laogai* and *laojiao* has depoliticized punishment, diluted the rhetoric of class struggle, and softened the harshness of the dictatorship that is expected of a penal institution in China.[30] As a result, the cadre police, under existing policies at least, have become de facto managers and inmates have become workers in function if not in name. Rather than representing political and moral authority, the cadre police now depend on inmates' labor for their salaries.

The primary task for cadre police is no longer punishment or rehabilitation. Rather, it is to produce a proper environment conducive to production and the maximization of profit. The pragmatic concern for monthly output outweighs the moral concern of rehabilitation, and production prevails over re-education. The managerial model is preoccupied with risk prevention and management, cost savings, and rationalizing and compromising with inmates so as to achieve the best economic results. Although rehabilitation and re-education of inmates are still part of the institution's goals, they now have a different substance and priority. Instead of turning inmates into new persons, prison administrators are satisfied if there are no escapes, no abnormal deaths, no serious crimes, and no major industrial accidents.[31] The penal economy has to replicate the real-world working environment as much as possible, and that demands new thinking about the objectives of the *laogai* and *laojiao*. Cadre police have been well aware of the "economic law." As a *laogai* official from Jiangsu Province noted: "Every producer of a commodity is equal in front of the judge of the commodity economy. There's no exception. *Laogai* enterprises would be penalized by this law if they didn't become fully aware of this point and voluntarily follow and use the law of the commodity economy."[32]

The economic rationale in the *laogai* and *laojiao* context rules against repression, which is regarded as counterproductive, in the literal sense of the word. A tortured laborer is a wasted laborer, increasing the cost of production and narrowing the profit margin. Inmates are first and foremost workers, and they need to be treated as such. Moreover, the cadre police may also become subject to investigation and punishment. Under the contract system, random violence by individual cadre police is brought under control, and power in relation to reward and punishment is centralized within the institution and is exercised rationally according to the needs of production.

The direct participation in production has blurred the line between cadre police, managers, and inmates. While cadre police work side by side with inmates, capable inmates are allowed unlimited freedom and are even utilized as salesmen for *laogai* or *laojiao* enterprises. Cadre police are well aware of their peculiar relationship with the inmates and have thus readjusted their attitudes toward and the treatment of inmates. Sophisticated sentence-reduction schemes, improvements in living standards, and a variety of other services are all part of this readjustment. As one *laogai* officer noted, the contract system has tied the interests of cadres and inmates together. Guided by the principle of doing whatever is necessary to make money, cadres follow the motto that "family scandals cannot be publicized" to protect the interests of small groups and individuals. "They cover up and tolerate wrongs committed by inmates to avoid any negative effect on the points gained by the squadrons," one officer noted.[33] At the same time, cadre police have to use whatever means they have at their disposal to motivate inmates. The officer continued: "Cadres are afraid that the production quota will not be completed if inmates refuse to work hard, so they dare not control inmates strictly. On the contrary, they either put in a good word for inmates, . . . offer some material benefits, or promise to reduce their sentence."[34] In general, cadre police and inmates collude to advance their common interests.[35]

At the individual level, cadre police and inmates are not adversaries either. From partners in the penal economy, they have even became "brothers" and "friends," and they openly address each other as such. In the LB, officers have lent their mobile phones and uniforms to inmates who were on duty outside the institution. In other places, officers brought food and alcohol from the outside to reward their hard-working inmates, both in flagrant violation of the rules. There have been widespread complaints, particularly in the late 1980s, about the lack of discipline in the penal institutions, that "inmates are not treated as inmates (*qiufan buqiu*)."[36] As one officer noted succinctly when I asked him "Do you beat up (*da*) inmates?": "Women dacheng yipian" (We become one with them).

An increase in profits in penal institutions will have a positive impact on the living standard of inmates, especially when the institution is confident that its profitability can be sustained. There are no standard living condition requirements for *laojiao* inmates. What inmates receive totally depends on the financial condition of the relevant institution. As a general requirement, inmates need to bring with them clothing, quilts, and other daily necessities. They need to purchase all daily necessities, such as toilet paper and toothpaste.[37] Until recently, a *laojiao* institution, including the LB, would charge a fee of a few RMB per day for room and board. Whatever income an inmate might have earned during his incarceration would be deducted for room and board. At the end of his sentence, he would normally have owed the institution some money. An inmate would have had to rely on family and friends to pay the debt. If the payment was late, his release would be delayed.

In the LB, until the mid-1990s, the diet and living conditions of the inmates had been deplorable. The main staples were rice (which was full of sand) and boiled cabbage. There might be one meal per week which was served with some pork, while good food routinely found its way to the dining table of cadre police. There was neither a heating nor air-ventilation system in the inmates' dormitories. In the summer, life was particularly harsh, with twelve men being squeezed into a small room infested with mosquitoes. Since the mid-1990s, however, inmates have enough to eat and the quality of the food has been tolerable. The LB claims that each inmate is provided with 45 jin of rice, 2 jin of pork, 4 jin of fish, and 2 jin of cooking oil. There may even be additional food on the day when the LB is inspected by one of the supervisory bodies, such as deputies from the people's congress in the City.[38] Fourteen out of the fifteen inmates whom I interviewed expressed general satisfaction with the quantity and quality of the meals.

It is difficult to determine the exact amount of money spent on inmates. First, the daily food rations for inmates may find their way to the dining table of the cadre police. It has happened before, and without any effective control system no one can guarantee that money allocated for food for inmates will be spent on inmates. This is exactly what is happening now in the case of medical expenses for inmates. The headquarters buys medicine at the LB clinic for inmates. But it is common practice for cadre police to ask for such medicines for free. Moreover, only simple medicines for simple diseases are free for inmates, and the LB doctors can decide when to charge them a fee, although destitute inmates may receive free services upon application. The same can also be said about miscellaneous expenses. Newspapers and periodicals are purchased from this fund, but inmates have no access to them.[39]

Second, the spending allocation is also problematic. There is, for example, a small pig farm in the LB and it has been contracted out to the head of the production section. The farm returns 23,500 RMB per year to the LB as the contract fee, but is entitled to use the cheap labor of inmates and, more importantly, to sell the pork to the canteens in the LB at market price. Many suspect that corruption may be at work, given the position of the contractor in the LB.

Conclusion

The LB is not a representative institution. Most of the *laojiao* institutions in China are not as successful as the LB in exploring business opportunities and in generating profits. But its experience is illustrative of the nature of the penal economy in China and the difficulties involved in the ongoing reform of China's penal institutions.

This chapter has argued that China's penal practice is deeply embedded in larger political and economic policies. Changes in national policies are directly felt in penal institutions. Macroeconomic policies in China affect the livelihood of ordinary citizens as well as the living conditions in penal institutions. In the early 1960s a disastrous economic policy caused starvation inside penal institutions just as it did among ordinary citizens. In much the same way, the "open door" policy and the introduction of a contract system in the early 1980s has had a direct impact on the penal economy. Penal institutions are well aware of their identity and consciously change their management structure in accordance with changing national economic policies. The dual responsibilities of the contracting system mimic the prevailing management structure in China's agricultural and industrial sectors. The "plunging into the sea" of commerce by penal institutions and the shifting from agriculture to light industry and commerce were also direct responses to changing economic policies in the early 1990s.

A penal institution has its own interests, however, and it is largely autonomous in organizing penal production and in negotiating with the government to advance its economic interest. There is little central planning, and each institution has to improvise to generate income. Facing a structural shortage of government funding, penal institutions in China are forced to generate extrabudgetary funds and to become semi-self-financed by turning to the free labor of inmates and organizing them into profitable production units. Penal production depends on, and indeed demands, the continuous induction of people into penal institutions.

There are inherent limits in a penal economy. As we have seen in the case of the LB, the work is often seasonal, mostly simple, menial, individualized, and does not contribute in any meaningful sense to inmate rehabilitation. It is difficult to have long-term economic planning if cadre police are always on the lookout for new business opportunities. Penal enterprises tend to compete among themselves for labor-intensive, low-skilled manufacturing and processing businesses. This is a particularly serious issue for *laojiao*, where inmates are poorly educated and the term of incarceration is short. *Laojiao* inmates are suitable only for work which requires little or no skill and, from the vantage point of an institution, it is not cost effective to properly train them so that they can support themselves with their labor upon their release.

Penal production under the contract system endangers security and marginalizes rehabilitation. Nevertheless, the profits it generates can enrich the institution, increase the salaries of cadre police, and collaterally, improve the living conditions of inmates. More importantly, commercialization, while bringing about contradictory results, can in general soften the harsh edge of dictatorship as practiced in Chinese penal institutions. The common goal among inmates and cadre police of profit-making depoliticizes an otherwise rigid hierarchical relationship. To a degree, convict exploitation has alleviated political repression, and the reliance on inmate labor for the salaries and welfare of cadre police necessitates better and more decent treatment of inmates. An improvement of penal economy may not by itself bring about the enhancement of inmates' living standard, but it is a necessary condition for any positive change in China's penal institutions.

Notes

The author would like to thank Richard Cullen, Randall Peerenboom, Sophia Woodman, Andrea Wooden, and the editors of this volume for their valuable comments.

1. For studies on *laojiao*, see Chu Huaizhi, Chen Xinliang, and Zhang Shaoyan, eds., *Lixing yu zhixu: Zhongguo laodong jiaoyang zhidu yanjiu* [Rationality and order: Research on the *laojiao* system in China] (Beijing: Law Press, 2002); Zou Keyuan, "The 'Re-education Through Labor' System in China's Legal Reform," *Criminal Law Forum* 12, no. 4 (2001): 459; Veron Mei-ying Hung, "Improving Human Rights in China: Should Re-education through Labor be Abolished?" *Columbia Journal of Transnational Law* 41 (2003): 307.

2. In addition to internal and publicized periodicals on *laogai* and *laojiao*, this essay also relies on documents and statistics from the LB, as well as extensive interviews with four existing and former cadre police and civilian workers from the LB, four

cadre police from three other *laogai* and *laojiao* institutions, and fourteen inmates currently serving their terms in the LB.

3. Yang Diansheng and Zhang Jinsang, eds., *Zhongguo tese jianyu zhidu yanjiu* [Research on the prison system with Chinese characteristics] (Beijing: Law Press, 1999).

4. Michael Dutton, *Policing and Punishment in China: From Patriarchy to "the People"* (Hong Kong: Cambridge University Press, 1992), 5; also Harold Tanner, "China's 'Gulag' Reconsidered: Labor Reform in the 1980s and 1990s," *China Information*, no. 9 (1994–95): 40.

5. Georg Rusche and Otto Kirchheimer, *Punishment and Social Structure* (New York: Columbia University Press, 1939); also, David Garland, *Punishment and Modern Society: A Study in Social Theory* (Chicago: University of Chicago Press, 1990).

6. Yang and Zhang, *Zhongguo tese jianyu zhidu yanjiu*, ch. 6. Ironically, the only statistics that the authors cite are from 1953 and 1958.

7. Information Office of the State Council of the People's Republic of China, *Criminal Reform in China* (Beijing, 1992), available at the website of China Internet Information Centre, http://www.china.org.cn. The government claims that "the annual output value of prison labor in the reform-through-Labor system for 1990 was only 2.5 billion RMB, which is about 0.08 per cent of the nation's total industrial and agricultural production output value for the year." Seymour and Anderson's study of penal institutions in Qinghai, Gansu, and Xinjiang clearly demonstrated the small and diminishing role of the penal economy in China's national economy (James D. Seymour and Richard Anderson, *New Ghosts and Old Ghosts: Prisons and Labor Reform Camps in China* [Armonk, N.Y.: M. E. Sharpe, 1998]). See also Jonathan M. Cowen, "One Nation's 'Gulag' Is Another Nation's 'Factory Within a Fence,'" *UCLA Pacific Basin Law Journal* 12 (Fall 1993): 190.

8. Harry Wu, *Troublemaker: One Man's Crusade Against China's Cruelty* (London: Chatto and Windus, 1996); Harry Wu, "The Struggle for Human Rights," *Hofstra Labor and Employment Law Journal* 17 (Spring 2000): 351; Harry Wu and Carolyn Wakeman, *Bitter Winds: A Memoir of My Years in China's Gulag* (New York: John Wiley and Sons, 1994). See also Melissa Pearson Fruge, "The *Laogai* and Violations of International Human Rights Law: A Mandate for the *Laogai* Charter," *Santa Clara Law Review* 38, no. 2 (1998): 473.

9. See Du Jun, ed., *Zhongguo jianyu jingji tanxi* [Analysis of China's prison economy] (Kunming: Yunnan University Press, 1997); Xia Zongsu, ed., *Laodong jiaoyang zhidu gaige wenti yanjiu* [Research on reform of re-education through labor system] (Beijing: Law Press, 2001); and Feng Jiancang, ed., *Jianyufa de chongshe yu wanshan* [Completion and perfection of the prison law] (Beijing: China Procuracy Press, 2000). See also Seymour and Anderson, *New Ghosts and Old Ghosts*, 7.

10. Xia Zongsu, *Laodong jiaoyang zhidu gaige wenti yanjiu*, 275.

11. Cao Bingyan, "Review of Prison Economic Development in China in the Past 50 Years and the Prospect," in *Zhongwai jianyu zhidu bijiao yanjiu wenji* [Collection of theses concerning the comparative studies of the prison systems], ed. Xia Zongsu and Zhu Jiming (Beijing: Law Press, 2001), 86.

12. Penal institutions in Henan Province paid about 100 million yuan in interest a year (Wang Youren, "On the Dependence of Prisons on Prison Economy," *Fanzui yu gaizao yanjiu* [Studies of Crimes and Reform] 142, no. 7 [2001]: 30).

13. Wang Mingdi, "Discussion on Prison Economic Work," *Fanzui yu gaizao yanjiu* [Studies of Crimes and Reform] 126, no. 2 (2000): 3.

14. Nan Xin and Li Xiaoqing, "Research on the Historical Development of Prison Economy in New China," in *Zhongwai jianyu zhidu bijiao yanjiu wenji* (see note 11), 92–93.

15. Richard Cullen and Hualing Fu, "Fiscal Reform in China: Implications for Hong Kong," *Loyola of Los Angles International and Comparative Law Journal* 19 (1997): 389.

16. Li Chengyun, Zhang Wenjun, and Feng Laiyong, "Preliminary Discussion on the Management System of Factories Run by Prisons," *Laogai laojiao lilun yanjiu* [Theoretical Studies on Reform and Reeducation through Labor] 21, no.2 (1989): 48.

17. H. L. Fu and Pinky Choy, "Policing for Profit: Fiscal Crisis and Institutionalized Corruption of Chinese Police," in *Policing, Security, and Corruption*, ed. Stanley Einstein (Chicago: Office of International Criminal Justice, University of Illinois at Chicago, forthcoming).

18. Xia Zongsu, *Laodong jiaoyang zhidu gaige wenti yanjiu*, 275–76.

19. Wang Mingdi and Guo Jianan, *Suiyue minji* [History remembers: 50 years of prison work in New China, 1949–99] (Beijing: Law Press, 2000), 23; and Feng Jiancang, *Jianyufa de chongshe yu wanshan*, 206.

20. Zhang Jingshan et al., *Suiyue minji*, 23.

21. Lin Xiaoling, "'Short Term Behaviors' in the Economic Work of *Laogai* Enterprises and Their Resolution," *Laogai laojiao faxue yanjiu* [Studies of the Law of Reform and Reeducation through Labor] 10, no.3 (1989): 30.

22. The Ministry of Justice has been encouraging long-term planning in the penal economy. One of its investigative teams reported, approvingly, that in Yunnan Province, the percentage of profits handed to the government depended on both the profitability and the necessity of reinvestment in the institution. A prison coal mine which produced a net profit of 30 million RMB (the most profitable in the province) was required to return 12 million RMB to the government. The Provincial Nos. 1 and 2 Prisons and Kunming Truck Factory each produced several million RMB in net profit. Because they all needed technological upgrading and facility expansion, the government allowed them to keep all the profits from 1985 to an unspecified date for upgrading and expansion (see Yunnan Investigative Group, Ministry of Justice *Laogai* Bureau, "Turning a Difficult Period to a Period of Construction and a Period of Development," *Fanzui yu gaizao yanjiu* [Studies of Crimes and Reform], no. 6 [1987]: 47).

23. He Shengtang, "Making an Accounting Unit Smaller and Improving the Vitality of *Laogai* Enterprises," *Laogai laojiao lilun yanjiu* [Theoretical Studies on Reform and Reeducation through Labor] 18, no.5 (1988): 30.

24. Xue Xiaoping, Ren Guangbo, and Tian Dong, "On the Appropriate Separation between Prisons and Enterprises," *Zhongguo jianyu xuekan* [Chinese Prison Journal] 89, no.4 (2000): 50.

25. Li Chenyung et al., "Preliminary Discussion on the Management System of Factories Run by Prisons," 16.

26. Seymour and Anderson, *New Ghosts and Old Ghosts*, 209.
27. Feng Jiancang, *Jianyufa de chongshe yu wanshan*, 204.
28. Cited in Editing and Writing Group, *Zhongguo laogai xue yanjiu* [Research on reform through labor in China] (Beijing: Social Science Literature Press, 1992), 551.
29. Wang Youren, "On the Dependence of Prisons on Prison Economy," 12.
30. Tanner, "China's 'Gulag' Reconsidered," 45.
31. This is the so-called "Four No's" requirement as imposed by the Ministry of Justice.
32. Chen Taihua, "*Laogai* Enterprises Must Adopt the Requirements of Commodity Economy," *Laogai laojiao lilun yanjiu* [Theoretical Studies on Reform and Reeducation through Labor] 18, no. 5 (1988): 41.
33. Editing and Writing Group, *Zhongguo laogai xue yanjiu*, 544–45. See also Tanner, "China's 'Gulag' Reconsidered," 4.
34. Editing and Writing Group, *Zhongguo laogai xue yanjiu*, 544–45.
35. Zhao Minghui, "Investigation of Three Consecutive Cases of Intentional Injury in a *Laogai zi dui*," *Laogai laojiao faxue yanjiu* [Studies of the Law of Reform and Reeducation through Labor] 10, no. 3 (1989): 40; and Zhang Juqing, "My Comments on Clean Government in the Basic-Level Laogai Institutions," *Laogai laojiao faxue yanjiu* [Studies of the Law of Reform through Labor and Reeducation through Labor], no. 3 (1989): 4.
36. Jiang Zhongxian, "Reflections after Bleeding," *Laogai laojiao faxue yanjiu* [Studies of the Law of Reform and Reeducation through Labor], no. 3 (1988): 32.
37. Wang Zongliang, "The Person Who Chooses the Green Color," *Zhongguo sifa* [Judicature of China], no. 3 (2000): 20.
38. The dormitory conditions have also been improved. A fan is installed in every room, and measures have been taken to prevent the rooms from being infected with mosquitoes.
39. Money allocated to inmates may be used for other purposes. It was reported in 1987 that the central government allocated 27 million RMB to penal institutions in Yunnan Province as fees for newly arrived inmates. But the authorities in Yunnan decided not to spend all the money on inmates and used the money on production so as to generate more profits (Yunnan Investigative Group, Ministry of Justice *Laogai* Bureau, "Turning a Difficult Period to a Period of Construction and a Period of Development," 51).

Contributors

Neil J. Diamant is Associate Professor of Asian Law and Culture at Dickinson College. He is the author of *Revolutionizing the Family: Politics, Love, and Divorce in Urban and Rural China, 1949–1968* (University of California Press, 2000), as well as articles on conflict resolution, state–minority relations, and the politics of marriage registration. His current research is on the politics of rights in China, focusing on veterans and family members of revolutionary martyrs and soldiers.

Mark W. Frazier is Assistant Professor of Government and the Henry Luce Assistant Professor of East Asian Political Economy at Lawrence University. He is the author of *The Making of the Chinese Industrial Workplace: State, Revolution, and Labor Management* (Cambridge University Press, 2002). His current research examines domestic and international influences on China's pension reform.

Hualing Fu is Associate Professor in the Faculty of Law at the University of Hong Kong. He has published widely on criminal justice, cross-border legal relations between Hong Kong and mainland China, and human rights in China.

Mary E. Gallagher is Assistant Professor of Political Science and Faculty Associate of the Center for Chinese Studies at the University of Michigan. Her research interests include comparative politics, especially of developing and post-communist countries, law and social change, and labor politics. She is the author of *Contagious Capitalism: Globalization and the Politics of Labor in China* (Princeton University Press, forthcoming), as well as articles in *World Politics* and other edited volumes.

Hua Linshan is an Associate Researcher in History at the Centre d'Etudes sur la Chine Moderne et Contemporaine in Paris. Among his publications is a French-language book co-authored with Isabelle Thireau, *A Sociological Investigation on China, 1911–1949* (1996) and a paper entitled "The Sense of Fairness in China: Looking for New Labor Rights" in *Annales HSS* (2001).

Lianjiang Li is Associate Professor of Political Science at Hong Kong Baptist University. His work focuses on village elections and collective action in rural China. His articles have appeared recently in *China Quarterly, China Information, Asian Survey, Journal of Contemporary China,* and *Comparative Politics.*

Stanley B. Lubman has specialized in Chinese law as a scholar and practicing attorney for forty years. He is Lecturer at the School of Law and Visiting Scholar at the Center for the Study of Law and Society at the University of California at Berkeley, and consultant to The Asia Foundation on legal projects in China. He is the author of *Bird in a Cage: Legal Reform in China After Mao* (Stanford University Press, 1999)

Andrew C. Mertha is Assistant Professor of Political Science and the Earle H. and Suzanne S. Harbison Faculty Fellow at Washington University in St. Louis. His research interests include bureaucratic politics and institutional development in China, trade policy, and intellectual property. He is currently revising a book on the politics of intellectual property in reform-era China.

Kevin J. O'Brien is Professor of Political Science at the University of California at Berkeley. His research focuses on theories of contentious politics and popular protest in the Chinese countryside. Some of his recent articles have appeared in *Mobilization, China Journal, China Quarterly, Modern China,* and *Comparative Politics.*

Murray Scot Tanner is a Senior Political Scientist at RAND Corporation. Dr. Tanner has published widely on Chinese politics, in particular on leadership politics, the dilemmas of legal reform, social control and internal stability, policing, lawmaking politics, and human rights issues. His articles have appeared in such journals as *Comparative Politics, China Quarterly, China Journal, Problems of Post-Communism,* and *Current History.* He is the author of *The Politics of Lawmaking in Post-Mao China: Institutions, Processes, and Democratic Prospects* (Oxford University Press, 1998), and editor and contributor to *China's Think Tanks: Windows on a Changing China* (2001).

Isabelle Thireau is a sociologist and Director of Research at the French National Center for Scientific Research. She recently edited (with Wang Hansheng) *Disputes in Chinese Villages: Forms of Fairness and Local Reconfiguration of Normative Spaces* (2001), and she also edited a special issue of the journal *Etudes Rurales* on the return of the merchant in rural China (2002).

Index

ACFTU (All-China Federation of Trade Unions), 57, 121
Administration for Industry and Commerce (AIC), *see* intellectual property disputes, foreign actors in
administrative enforcement of intellectual property issues, *see* intellectual property disputes, foreign actors in
Administrative Litigation Law (ALL), 31–53; acceptance of case by court, 33–36; appeals to higher courts, 38; charges common under, 31–33; collective action, 36, 39–40, 43, 52n83; connections (*guanxi*), 38; dictation of verdicts, 37; disposition, number of suits by, 1990–2001, 31, 32, 45n2; failure of government parties to appear in court, 37–38; favorable verdicts, problems with enforcement of, 41–42; higher-level officials, intervention by, 40–41; implications of, 43–45; information blockades, 33–35; legal culture and legal consciousness, 33–36, 42–43, 44; mobilization processes, 9, 11, 13, 14; outcomes, significance of, 42–43; perjury by government parties, 38; procrastination and delays, 37, 41; restrictions on who may be sued and scope of litigation, 35–36, 38; retaliation, 41–42; right to sue, questions regarding, 36; rights and rights consciousness, 42–43, 44; settlement or withdrawal of case, attempts to ensure, 36–37, 48–49n33; support structures and advocacy groups, 38–41
administrative punishment via reeducation through labor camps, *see* reeducation through labor camps
Aguilar, Paloma, 146

AIC (Administration for Industry and Commerce), *see* intellectual property disputes, foreign actors in
Alford, William P., 21, 163
ALL, *see* Administrative Litigation Law (ALL)
All-China Federation of Trade Unions (ACFTU), 57, 121
Allee, Mark, 4
anti-counterfeiting enforcement, *see* intellectual property disputes, foreign actors in
appeals, judicial: ALL, 38; labor disputes, 59, 73–74; letters and visits offices vs. appeal of capital cases during Qing dynasty, 88
arbitration of labor disputes, 70–72; arbitrated mediation and arbitral judgment, 58, 70–71; cost of, 59; dissatisfaction with legal implementation and enforcement, rising arbitration rates as sign of, 76; judicial appeals of, 72–74; LAC (Labor Arbitration Committee), conducted by, 58; pension cases, 121–24; percentage of disputes resolved by, 72. *See also* expressions of injustice in arbitration committees and letters and visits offices

Bankruptcy Law of 1988, 123
Bernhardt, Kathryn, 4
birth control cases, reluctance of courts to accept ALL suits involving, 35, 47–48n23–24
Black, Donald, 7, 8
bourgeois rights, 16
"Brazilianization" of police force, 206–7
Bureau of Civil Affairs (BCA), veteran assistance provided by, 147, 149–50

China Anti-Counterfeiting Coalition (CACC), 171, 180–82, 190–91n62

234　Index

China Association of Enterprises with Foreign Investment (CAEFI), 181–82
Chinese Communist Party (CCP): intellectual property disputes, attention paid to, 182; judicial system under control of, 163; labor disputes, 54, 57, 60, 69, 75; veteran membership in, 137, 144
Chow, Nelson, 109
citizenship practices, emergence of, 14–15, 75–76
Civil Trademark Law, 162
Clarke, Donald, 111–12
class difference in China, 16–17
Communist Youth League (CYL), veteran membership in, 137, 144
Confucianism: desirability of law as option, 162; humanity/inhumanity, complaints emphasizing in letters and visits offices,, 101; mobilization processes, 6, 8, 12; spread and penetration of Confucian norms, 15–16
connections (*guanxi*): ALL suits, 38; labor complaints to arbitration committees and letters and visits offices, 89; mobilization processes, 13; reeducation through labor camps, 217
Constitutional pension provisions, 114–15
contracts: labor-contract system (LCS), 60–66; responsibility system, reeducation through labor camps, 218
Cottereau, Alain, 84
counter-mobilization by officials, 12–13; ALL suits, *see* Administrative Litigation Law (ALL); labor disputes, concern regarding, 74; veterans, 135, 144–46
counterfeiting, *see* intellectual property disputes, foreign actors in
court cases, *see* litigation
Criminal law use in intellectual property disputes, 162, 170, 177–80, 183–85
criminal punishment via reform through labor camps, *see* reform through labor camps
Cultural Revolution, 3, 25n42, 132–33, 140, 149, 151

dagongzai, *see* migrant workers
Damaka, 18
Damaska, Mirjan R., 154–55n12
Deng Xiaoping, 196, 203
difang lifa (local pension legislation), 118
disaggregation of state, 17–20; ALL, 44; intellectual property disputes, foreign actors in, 165; social unrest and protest, analysis of, 208n6; veterans, 134–35
disputing pyramid and disputing trajectories, 7–8, 12, 21
Dutton, Michael, 214

economic issues: social unrest and protest, explanations for, 198–99; veterans, economic backwardness and employment problems of, 135, 137, 139–40, 146–47, 149–50. *See also* reeducation through labor camps
enterprise-level mediation used to settle labor disputes, 58, 67–70, 71, 86
Epp, Charles, 5, 9–10, 90, 154
Épreuves de justice (tests of justice), 84–85. *See also* expressions of injustice in arbitration committees and letters and visits offices
Esherick, Joseph, 16
ethical norms, *see* moral and ethical norms
Ewick, Patrick, 4, 5, 9
expressions of injustice in arbitration committees and letters and visits offices, 84–107; administrative response to complaints, 93–95; means of resolving labor disputes, 85–86; mobilization of Labor Law, 95–102; persons registering complaints, analysis of, 89–95; reasons for complaints, 91–92; spaces for expression, need for, 84–85, 102–3
—arbitration committees, 86–87; administrative response to complaints registered with, 93–94; mobilization of Labor Law in complaints to, 95–97; particularization of facts presented to, 92; reasons for complaints registered with, 91–92; skilled employees predominating in complaints registered with, 85, 90; tabled comparison to letters and visits offices, 95
—letters and visits offices, 87–89; administrative response to complaints registered with, 94–95; generalization and collectivization of complaints registered with, 92–93; humanity/inhumanity and moral issues, emphasis on, 101–2, 103; impoverished and migrant workers predominating in complaints registered with, 85, 90–91; mobilization of Labor Law in complaints to, 98–102; reasons for complaints registered with, 91–92; tabled comparison to arbitration committees, 95

Index 235

Falun Gong, 18, 131, 222
fazhihua (legalization), 3, 6, 17-8
FDI (foreign direct investment), labor disputes affected by liberalization of, 67, 166
fieldwork, role of in law and society research, 5, 19
firm-level mediation used to settle labor disputes, 58, 67–70, 71, 86
foreign actors in intellectual property disputes, *see* intellectual property disputes, foreign actors in
foreign and Western concepts of social unrest, influence of, 205
foreign conspiracy, social unrest protest attributed to, 195–96, 197–98
foreign-invested enterprises and labor disputes: FDI (foreign direct investment), effects of liberalization of, 67, 166; mediation/arbitration rates, 68–69, 71, 72; ownership type, disputes by, 59, 64

Galanter, Marc, 15, 21
Geertz, Clifford, 15
Gu Linfang, 196
guanxi, see connections
Guthrie, Doug, 17

hegemony of market, labor disputes and worker acceptance of, 80n30
historical approach, 4–5; legal culture and legal consciousness, 14–16; role of law in Chinese culture, 162–63
Huang, Philip, 4
humanity/inhumanity, letters and visits offices complaints emphasizing, 101–2
Hungary, pension reform in, 111
Huntingdon, Samuel P., 202–3
Hurst, William, 65, 108

identity transformation via legal engagement, 13–14
India, 10
injustice, expressions of, *see* expressions of injustice in arbitration committees and letters and visits offices
inspection and licensing powers used to enforce pension compliance, 117
intellectual property disputes, foreign actors in, 161–92

—administrative enforcement, 162–65; bureaucracies involved in, 167–70; Chinese firms, strategies used by, 170–71; foreign actors' role in shaping, 171–72; outcomes, 176–77
—AIC (Administration for Industry and Commerce), 167–70; criminal prosecutions, reluctance to pursue, 183–85; division of labor with QTSB, 176; enforcement outcomes, 176–77; participant observation in AIC enforcement action, 172–74; rivalry with QTSB, 169, 173; subsidization of enforcement activities, 172
—CACC (China Anti-Counterfeiting Coalition), 171, 180–82, 190–91n62
—Chinese firms, strategies used by, 170–71
—Civil Trademark Law, 162
—Criminal Law, use of, 162, 170, 177–80, 183–85
—deterrence, 179–80, 185–86
—growing importance of foreign actors, 165–67
—legal culture and legal consciousness, 16
—legislation and predictability, 17
—legislative vagueness, problems with, 185
—litigation, 162, 164, 170–71
—local protectionism (*difang baohuzhuyi*), 162, 175–76
—police and public security bureaus, involvement of, 183–85
—QBPC (Quality Brands Protection Committee), 181–83, 191n70
—QTSB (Quality Technical Supervision Bureau), 167–69; criminal prosecutions, reluctance to pursue, 183–85; division of labor with AIC, 176; enforcement outcomes, 176–77; local protectionism (*difang baohuzhuyi*) case study, 175–76; rivalry with AIC, 169, 173; subsidization of enforcement activities, 172
—subsidization of enforcement activities, 171–72
—TSB (Technical Supervision Bureau), 168–69
intellectuals, attitudes of, 16
interdisciplinary approach, 4–6
IPR (intellectual property rights), *see* intellectual property disputes, foreign actors in

Japan, 142
Jiang Chunze, 109
Jiang Zemin, 206
Jianguo Xu, 109
judicial review, *see* litigation

Kagan, Robert, 21
Kirchheimer, Otto, 214
Korean War, 138, 140, 141–42, 147, 154n5

Labor Arbitration Committees (LACs), 58, 62, 65, 71, 80n36, 86–87. *See also* expressions of injustice in arbitration committees and letters and visits offices
labor-contract system (LCS), 60–66
labor disputes (*laodong zhengyi*), 54–83; appeals, 59, 73–74; causes of, 64–65, 77–78n7, 91–92; counter-mobilization by officials, 74; defined under Chinese law, 55–56; "hegemony" of market, worker acceptance of, 80n30; labor-contract system (LCS), 60–66; legal culture and legal consciousness, 16, 17, 74–77; legislation, 17, 56–59, 75, 86–87, 104n11; litigated cases, 59, 72–74; mediation, 58, 67–71, 86; methods and processes for resolving, 58–59, 67–74, 85–86; moral grievances, delegitimization of, 55, 60–61, 63, 65–66; "mutual empowerment," concept of, 76; "other means," resolution by, 70, 72, 73; ownership type, disputes by, 56, 59, 63, 64; rates of, 54–56; rights and rights consciousness, 74; social contract system, replacement of, 60–61, 63; *xiagang*, 62. *See also* arbitration of labor disputes; expressions of injustice in arbitration committees and letters and visits offices; National Labor Law (1995); migrant workers; state-owned enterprises (SOEs), labor disputes in
—foreign-invested enterprises: FDI (foreign direct investment), effects of liberalization of, 67, 166; mediation/arbitration rates, 68–69, 71, 72; ownership type, disputes by, 59, 64
—mobilization processes, 12; arbitration committees and letters and visits offices compared, 95–102
labor inspection campaigns (*laodong jiancha*), 88, 105n23
Labor Law, *see* National Labor Law (1995)
labor reeducation camps, *see* reeducation through labor camps
labor reform camps, *see* reform through labor camps (*laogai* or *laodong gaizao*)
laid-off workers, 62, 65–66, 123–24
laodong jiancha (labor inspection campaigns), 88, 105n23
laodong zhengyi, *see* labor disputes
laogai or *laodong gaizao*, *see* reform through labor camps
laojiao or *laodong jiaoyang*, *see* reeducation through labor camps
law and society, 3–27; destruction and reconstruction of legal system, 163; growth of legal apparatus, 17–18; interdisciplinary approach, 4–6; legal culture and legal consciousness, 14–17, 21; legislation and predictability, 17; mobilization processes, 6–14, 21; perspective on state, 6–7, 17–20. *See also specific entries*
law enforcement, *see* police and public security bureaus
Law on Assemblies, Marches, and Demonstrations (1989), 196, 200–201
lawful rights and interests (*hefa quanyi*), 4, 17
LB Laojiao Institution, *see* reeducation through labor camps
LCS (labor-contract system), 60–66
Lee, Peter, 109
legal culture and legal consciousness, 14–17, 21; ALL suits, 33–36, 42–43, 44
labor disputes, 74–77
legal institutions' weakness as explanation for social unrest and protest, 199–200, 202–4
legal norms, 11–12
legalization (*fazhihua*), 3, 6, 17–18
legislation: Bankruptcy Law of 1988, 123; Civil Trademark Law, 162; criminal law use in intellectual property disputes, 162, 170, 177–80, 183–85; growth of legal apparatus, 17–18; labor disputes (*laodong zhengyi*), 17, 56–59, 75, 86–87, 104n11; Law on Assemblies, Marches, and Demonstrations (1989), 196, 200–201; Marriage Law (1950), 16, 17, 132, 153; predictability and, 17; Prison Law (1994), 216; social unrest and protest, analysis of, 196, 200–201, veterans, lack of legislation protecting, 132, 135, 153–54. *See also* Administrative Litigation Law (ALL); National Labor Law (1995)
—pensions, local legislation (*difang lifa*), 118; national legislation, need for, 110–12,

Index   237

114–15, 117, 124, 127n24; predictability, providing, 17
letters and visits offices, *see* expressions of injustice in arbitration committees and letters and visits offices
Liang Qichao, 6
licenses and inspections powers used to enforce pension compliance, 117
Lieberthal, Kenneth, 114, 166–67
litigation: intellectual property disputes, 162, 164, 170–71; labor disputes, 59, 72–74; pension cases, reluctance to use judicial means in, 118–19, 121–24, 125; repeat vs. "one-shot" litigants, 27n63. *See also* Administrative Litigation Law (ALL)
litigation masters (*songgun*), 4
Liu Huaqiu, 182
Liu Shaoqi, 149
local administrative suits, *see* Administrative Litigation Law
Locke, John, 14

Ma Xiuhong, 182
Macauley, Melissa, 4
Mao, veterans' letters to, 138, 150
Maoist period and Maoist ideology: AIC's secondary role under Mao, 168; destruction of previous legal infrastructure by, 163; labor disputes, 81n45, 82n40, 84, 93, 103, 107n40; legal culture and legal consciousness, 15, 16; mobilization processes, 8, 10; neo-Maoism, 196, 206; veterans, 133–34
marital problems of veterans and soldiers, 147, 154n5
Marxist ideology, 101, 103
McCann, Michael, 5, 13, 15, 193
media, *see* press and media support outlets
mediation used to settle labor disputes, 58, 67–71, 86
Merry, Sally Engle, 5, 15, 16
Michelson, Ethan, 11
Migdal, Joel, 5, 19, 166
migrant workers (*dagongzai*): basic human rights and dignity, appeals to, 101, 103; legal culture and legal consciousness, 16; letters and visits offices, complaints registered with, 90–91; limited resources and rights of, 78n8, 91; percentages facing labor problems, 85; unpaid wages as main reason for complaints by, 92

Mill, John Stuart, 14
Ming dynasty: Confucian discourse during, 15; historical research into role of law during, 4
Ministry of Foreign Trade and Economic Cooperation (MOFTEC), now Ministry of Commerce (MOFCOM), 181–82
Ministry of Public Security (MPS), 194, 195, 196, 197
mobilization processes, 6–14, 21. *See also* press and media support outlets; support structures and advocacy groups
— labor disputes, 12; arbitration committees and letters and visits offices compared, 95–102; SOEs and labor-contract system, 59–66
moral and ethical norms, 8, 11–12; delegitimization of moral grievances in labor disputes, 55, 60–61, 63, 65–66; letters and visits offices complaints emphasizing, 101–2, 103
"mutual empowerment" in labor disputes, concept of, 76
Myles, John, 108

Nader, Laura, 5, 8
National Labor Law (1995), 57; different experiences and backgrounds affecting perception of, 17; mobilization processes for arbitration committees and letters and visits offices compared, 16, 95–102; pension entitlements, 114; range of options available under, 67; status and characterization, 86
National People's Congress, 3
neo-Maoism, 196, 206

Oksenberg, Michel, 166–67
ownership type, labor disputes in firms by, 56, 59, 63, 64

Pensions: central control and standardization, 111, 114; constitutional provisions, 114–15; deficit problem, 109–10, 115; delinquent payments, collection methods for, 116–19; enterprise-based pensions, transition from, 110–11, 112, 115–16; enterprise perspective on local regulations, 119–21; incremental reform, tendency towards, 111–12, 114–16; individually funded account system, reform aiming for, 110–11; labor disputes caused by, 64–65; legal culture and legal consciousness, 17, 121; licenses and inspections powers used

238   Index

to enforce compliance, 117; litigation, reluctance to use, 118–19, 121–24, 125; localized administrative "social pool" (*shehui tongchou*) system, 109–10, 112–14, 116–21; mobilization processes, 12; pensions, 108–30; press and media, local administration's use of, 117–18; social contract, effect of reforms on, 108–9, 124–25
—legislation: local legislation (*difang lifa*), 118; national legislation, need for, 110–12, 114–15, 117, 124, 127n24; predictability, providing, 17
People's Armed Police (PAP), *see* police and public security bureaus
people's congresses intervening in ALL litigation, 39–40
Perry, Elizabeth J., 19, 139
Pierson, Paul, 108
Poland, pension reform in, 111
police and public security bureaus: ALL suits, interference in, 33–34, 36–38; "Brazilianization" of, 206–7; inaction, requirement to pay compensation for consequences of, 43; intellectual property disputes, 183–85. *See also* social unrest and protest, analysis of
political entrepreneurs, 9
preferential rights for veterans, 133–35, 138, 149–50, 153, 154–55n12. *See also* veterans
press and media support outlets, 10–11; ALL suits, 39; pension collection efforts, 117–18
prison, *see* reeducation through labor camps; reform through labor camps
Prison Law (1994), 216
protests, police handling of, *see* social unrest and protest, analysis of

Qiao Shi, 195
Qing dynasty: Confucian discourse during, 15; historical research into role of law during, 4, 163; letters and visits offices compared to appeal of capital cases during, 88; rights consciousness during, 14–15
Quality Brands Protection Committee (QPBC), 181–83, 191n70
Quality Technical Supervision Bureau (QTSB), *see* intellectual property disputes, foreign actors in

Rankin, Mary, 16
rational-choice analysis, 207–8n4

Reed, Bradly, 4
reeducation through labor camps (*laojiao* or *laodong jiaoyang*), 213–29; analysis of penal economy and financial crisis, 214–16; dominance of productivity goals over rehabilitative purposes, 221–22; funding problems, 215–16, 217–18; number of, 216; organizational structure and role of cadre police, 216–17, 222–24; production items and income, 218–20; rehabilitative purposes and processes, 214, 220–22, 226; responsibility system contracting, 218–22; rights and living standards of inmates, effect of productivity requirements on, 222–25; short-term vs. long-term economic planning, 220, 226, 228n22; spending allocations for inmates, 224–25, 229n39
reform through labor camps (*laogai* or *laodong gaizao*), 213; penal economy and financial crisis, 214–16; rights and living standards of inmates, effect of productivity requirements on, 222–23
repeat vs. "one-shot" litigants, 27n63
Republican China: historical research into role of law during, 4; rights consciousness during, 14–15
responsibility system contracting and reeducation through labor camps, 218–22
retaliation against ALL plaintiffs, 41–42
rights and rights consciousness, 4, 6, 13–14; ALL suits, 42–43, 44; labor disputes, 74, 101–2; letters and visits offices complaints emphasizing, 101–2, 103; preferential rights for veterans, 133–35, 138, 149–50, 153, 154–55n12; reeducation through labor camp inmates, rights of, 222–25; Western vs. Chinese concepts, 13–14. *See also* legal culture and legal consciousness
Rosenberg, Gerald N., 5, 134
Rusche, George, 214
Russia, 142

Scott, James, 152
Selznick, Philip, 21
settlement or withdrawal of ALL cases, 36–37, 48–49n33
severance pay protests, 123–24
shehui tongchou (social pools), pension administration under control of, 109–10, 112–14
Silbey, Susan, 4, 5, 9

Index 239

Sklar, Judith, 152
social contract: labor disputes, 60–61, 63; pension reforms, effect of, 108–9, 124–25; veterans, 109, 132–35, 140, 151–54
social pools (*shehui tongchou*), pension administration under control of, 109–10, 112–14
social unrest and protest, analysis of in public security apparatus, 18, 193–212; 1980's, rethinking process and return to conspiratorial view in, 194–96; 1990's to present, reconceptualization of protest during, 196–201, 205; "Brazilianization" of police force, 206–7; common "recruitment pool" for officers and protestors, 205; explaining changing police attitudes, 204–6; foreign conspiracy, protest attributed to, 195–96, 197–98; foreign/Western concepts, influence of, 205; increase in protests, 1993–1996, 196–97; legal institutions, weakness of, 199–200, 202–4; legislation, 196, 200–201; moderate strategies, problems arising from, 201–2; self-restrained protests, 205; socio-economic explanations, 198–99; Tiananmen protestors, 18, 165, 194–96, 197, 204
SOEs, *see* state-owned enterprises (SOEs), labor disputes in
Sommer, Matthew, 4
South Korea, 193
Soviet Union, 142
state-owned enterprises (SOEs), labor disputes in: arbitrated cases, 72; firm or enterprise-level mediation, decline in, 67–68, 69, 71; labor-contract system, 59–66; moral grievances, delegitimization of, 55, 60–61, 63, 65–66; percentage of workers in SOEs, 78–79n18, 79n21; rates of, 56, 59–60; temporary and contract vs. permanent workers, 78–79n19
Steinfeld, Edward, 17
"Strike Hard" campaigns, 18
suicides of veterans, 147–48
support structures and advocacy groups, 8–11; ALL suits, 38–41; veterans, 131, 133, 137–39, 145, 148–51, 154

Technical Supervision Bureau (TSB) and administrative enforcement of intellectual property disputes, 168–69
tests of justice (*épreuves de justice*), 84–85. *See also* expressions of injustice in arbitration committees and letters and visits offices
"Three Represents" strategy, 206
Tiananmen protests, 18, 165, 194–96, 197, 204
Tibetan protests (1989), 197
TSB (Technical Supervision Bureau) and administrative enforcement of intellectual property disputes, 168–69
Tyler, Tom, 16

unions: All-China Federation of Trade Unions (ACFTU), 57, 121; mediation rates for labor disputes, 69–70; veterans prevented from joining, 144
United Kingdom, 156n57
United States: Chinese attitudes towards, 142; intellectual property disputes and CACC, 180–81, 190–91n62; veterans, 142, 156–57n60, 158n93, 158n96
U.S.S.R., 142

Veteran Resettlement Division of Interior Ministry, 149
veterans, 131–58; behavioral problems of, 146–48; the Center, appeals to, 135, 149–51, 154; complicated histories of, 145–46, 149; counter-mobilization by officials, 135, 144–46; demobilization and resettlement problems, 136–41; disaggregated perspective, need to use, 134–35; economic backwardness and employment problems of, 135, 137, 139–40, 146–47, 149–50; legal culture and legal consciousness, 16, 17, 152–53; legislation, lack of, 132, 135, 153–54; mobilization processes, 8, 9, 11, 12, 13, 40; national veterans' association, 131, 133, 149; patriotic sentiment regarding, 133–35, 140, 142–44, 146, 150, 152–53; political status, 141–48; preferential rights, 133–35, 138, 149–50, 153, 154–55n12; public opinion, attempts to mobilize, 137–38; salary levels, complaints about, 131, 139, 153; social contract, sense of betrayal of, 109, 132–35, 140, 151–54; support structures and advocacy groups, 131, 133, 137–39, 145, 148–51, 154; widows of, 132

Walder, Andrew, 63
Wang Guangying, 182
Weber, Max, 17

withdrawal or settlement of ALL cases, 36–37, 48–49n33
Women's Federation, 147
Wong, Linda, 109
World Bank, 124
World Trade Organization (WTO), Chinese membership in, 161, 199
Wu Bangguo, 182

xiagang, 62

Yaohu Zhao, 109
Yu Lei, 195
Yuebin Xu, 109

Zhang Shengqian, 202–3
Zhou Enlai, 149, 150, 151
Zhou Yehe, 203
Zhu De, 138, 150
Zhu Rongji, 182, 191n70

The authorized representative in the EU for product safety and compliance is:
Mare Nostrum Group
B.V Doelen 72
4831 GR Breda
The Netherlands

www.ingramcontent.com/pod-product-compliance
Lightning Source LLC
Chambersburg PA
CBHW020647230426
43665CB00008B/341